T0330110

The Political Economy of Population Ageing

To my parents

The Political Economy of Population Ageing

William A. Jackson

Lecturer in Economics, University of York, UK

Edward Elgar
Cheltenham, UK • Northampton, MA, USA

© William A. Jackson, 1998

All rights reserved. No part of this publication may be reproduced, stored in a
retrieval system or transmitted in any form or by any means, electronic,
mechanical or photocopying, recording, or otherwise without the prior
permission of the publisher.

Published by
Edward Elgar Publishing Limited
8 Lansdown Place
Cheltenham
Glos GL50 2HU
UK

Edward Elgar Publishing, Inc.
6 Market Street
Northampton
Massachusetts 01060
USA

A catalogue record for this book
is available from the British Library

Library of Congress Cataloguing in Publication Data
Jackson, William A., 1959–
    The political economy of population ageing / William A. Jackson.
    Includes bibliographical references.
    1. Aged—Government policy. 2. Ageing—Economic aspects.
    3. Ageing—Social aspects. 4. Age distribution (Demography)–
    –Economic aspects. I. Title.
    HQ1061.J28 1998
    362.6—dc21

                                                                97-39375
                                                                CIP

ISBN 1 85278 692 2

Printed and bound in Great Britain by Bookcraft (Bath) Ltd.

Contents

List of tables and figures   vi
Preface   vii

1 Introduction   1
2 Ageing and dependency   18
3 Population ageing and neoclassical economics   44
4 Alternative views of population ageing   69
5 Productivity and employment   95
6 Pensions and retirement   121
7 Health care and social services   148
8 Informal economic activity   173
9 Conclusion   198

Bibliography   207
Index   235

Tables and figures

TABLES

1.1   Population ageing in Great Britain, 1851–2051   3
1.2   Population ageing in OECD countries, 1980–2040   5
1.3   Dependency ratios in OECD countries, 1980–2040   7

FIGURES

1.1   The demographic transition   12
2.1   The transfer possibilities line   31
3.1   Life-cycle saving behaviour   53
4.1   Ageing and ideology   90
5.1   Flattening out the age–wage profile   105
6.1   Alternative modes of retirement   140
7.1   The rectangularization of the survival curve   151
7.2   The compression of morbidity   152
7.3   Ageing and health care   154
7.4   Dependency and the costs of care   161
8.1   Four sectors of the economy   177

Preface

Population ageing and its attendant problems have been discussed extensively in recent years. Politicians, social commentators and academics have all pointed out the difficult policy adjustments that may be required to accommodate unprecedented numbers of old people. Much of the discussion has had an alarmist tone and has sought to convince the reader that, without evasive policy action, a demographic crisis is imminent. Any such crisis is not yet upon us, however, and its eventual appearance and nature remain open to doubt. This book takes a critical view of the policy debates over population ageing. The aim is not to accentuate and reinforce the concerns about a demographic crisis, but to give a more realistic account of the economic effects of population ageing.

The book deals with general principles rather than empirical details and sets population ageing within the context of long-run structural changes. It concentrates on ageing among the older age groups (the 'elderly' or 'old people'), because this is where the severest problems of population ageing are expected to arise and constitutes the main focus of the academic and policy literature. Population ageing is treated as an exogenous event, coming from outside the economy, to which policy makers have to react. In reality, demographic change and economic growth are intertwined, so that causality is highly complex and economic development is a key causal factor behind population ageing. Causality goes in both directions: the economy influences ageing and ageing influences the economy. Treating population ageing as an exogenous event may be somewhat unrealistic, but it avoids the intractability of a fully integrated economic/demographic approach and reflects the standard mode of policy analysis.

Much economic discussion of ageing has emphasized a few key issues such as pensions and social security and, when theory has been used, adhered strictly to mainstream, neoclassical economics. The present book considers a larger set of issues than most discussions of ageing, for instance, by looking at informal economic activities and the ways in which they can be allowed for when evaluating demographic change. It also draws on a wider range of academic literatures than usual, by including arguments from non-neoclassical economics, social gerontology and sociology. This broader view suggests that population ageing is too complex a phenomenon to be characterized as a simple tightening of demographic constraints. The social construction of old age, the prevalence of unemployment, and the importance of informal economic activities imply that conventional economic discussion can be misleading and overstate the effects of population ageing on the economy. A wider perspective on ageing gives a more optimistic outlook that recognizes the need for some adjustments but does not interpret ageing as a crisis.

My initial interest in the subject matter of this book was prompted by my appointment to a New Blood lectureship in the economics of population ageing at the University of York. I should like to express my thanks to Edward Elgar, who encouraged me to write the book and has been patient in awaiting its completion.

William A. Jackson

1. Introduction

Population ageing on a large scale was unknown before the twentieth century. During most of the history of the human species, people have aged whereas populations have not. Individuals have passed through the typical human life cycle whereas societies have changed little in their age composition. The ageing of the individual is an involuntary process undergone by human beings at all times and places; nobody has ever been able to youthen or maintain a constant age. A population, on the other hand, can either age or youthen if its age composition shifts towards older or younger age groups. The possibilities for population ageing or youthening have always existed but have seldom been realized. Until the twentieth century most human populations had a roughly constant age composition, with a small but stable proportion of the population in the older age groups. Fertility and mortality rates were high and almost equal, so that populations remained in a long-run steady state. Temporary, localized demographic crises could bring a short-run disruption of the steady state and a brief interlude of population ageing or youthening, but the long-run trend was to move back to the normal steady-state population structure for pre-industrial societies. Only within the last 100 years has there been a consistent trend towards ageing populations in virtually all industrialized countries. A few decades of population ageing, confined mainly to the developed world, have come after thousands of years in which human populations had a more or less constant age composition.

The unprecedented character of population ageing creates uncertainty. A new policy question has arisen: how should we adjust economic and social arrangements to allow for a rising and permanently higher proportion of old people? This question has never been posed or answered before, and its very novelty may provoke alarm. Population ageing in itself should be little cause for concern. People generally wish to live as long as possible, and an ageing population is usually (though not inevitably) a sign of greater longevity. Few are aware of or interested in the age composition of the population for its own sake, and concern over population ageing is overwhelmingly based on its expected consequences, not its inherent properties. Most of its expected adverse consequences are economic. A growing number of old people will, other things being

1

equal, raise the proportion of the population who are economically inactive. The proportionally declining active population have to meet the consumption demands of the inactive, and so there will be fewer economically active people to support each inactive person. Unless productivity rises fast enough, some difficult choices will have to be made and current arrangements for supporting the elderly population may be in danger of collapsing under the mounting strains of demographic changes. The economic problems seem clear, although (as later chapters will argue) they are less obvious than they appear.

THE NATURE OF POPULATION AGEING

A population is said to be ageing if it satisfies either or both of two conditions. The first is that its average (mean or median) age is increasing. If the age of the average person rises, then the population mimics individual ageing, and the idea of population ageing has an intuitive appeal. All the individuals belonging to a population must, of course, be ageing at the same rate, but the population as a whole can have a rising, falling or constant average age. Changes in a population's average age derive from the ageing of existing cohorts, a qualitative change in the living population, and the addition and subtraction of cohorts through births and deaths, a quantitative change in the size and composition of the population. The interplay of these effects ensures that population ageing is a more complex process than individual ageing.

The second condition defining an ageing population is an increase in the proportion of the population above a certain threshold age. By far the most common threshold is the statutory retirement age that divides those expected to be economically inactive from those expected to be active. An increase in the retired elderly population as a proportion of the total denotes an ageing population. Other threshold ages with economic significance are the statutory school-leaving age, which gives the normal date of entry into the working population, and the age of 75, which distinguishes the older sections of the retired population (the 'old old') who are the most prone to severe disabilities. The choice of threshold depends on the section of the population under scrutiny: the higher the threshold age, the greater the concentration on ageing among the older age groups. Any age would, nevertheless, suffice to be a threshold by which one could identify population ageing. As with the average-age criterion, populations can maintain a steady state with a constant proportion of people above the threshold age, or youthen if large birth cohorts lead to a rising proportion below the threshold. The average-age and threshold criteria usually agree with each other, but one criterion could conceivably be satisfied without the other. Such cases are largely hypothetical. Most countries with ageing populations satisfy both conditions, and whether a country is really experiencing population ageing is hardly ever a cause of controversy.

Population ageing in developed countries can be illustrated by taking Great Britain as an initial example. Table 1.1 gives data on the population of Great Britain over a 200 year period from 1851 to 2051 (Northern Ireland is excluded because of the political changes affecting the geographical composition of the UK during this period). Figures for 1991 and earlier are based on census information; figures for future years are based on official projections. As always with projections, the figures are more speculative the further they are in the future.

Table 1.1 Population ageing in Great Britain, 1851–2051

Year	Total population (m)	Population over 65 (m)	Population over 75 (m)	% of population aged:			
				0–14	15–64	65+	75+
1851	20.9	1.0	0.3	35.4	60.0	4.6	1.4
1861	23.1	1.1	0.3	35.7	59.6	4.7	1.4
1871	26.1	1.2	0.4	36.2	59.0	4.8	1.4
1881	29.7	1.4	0.4	35.5	58.9	4.6	1.3
1891	33.0	1.6	0.4	35.1	60.1	4.8	1.3
1901	37.0	1.7	0.5	32.5	62.8	4.7	1.4
1911	40.8	2.1	0.6	30.8	63.9	5.2	1.4
1921	42.8	2.6	0.7	27.9	66.0	6.0	1.7
1931	44.8	3.3	0.9	24.2	68.4	7.4	2.1
1951	48.9	5.3	1.7	22.4	66.7	10.9	3.5
1961	51.3	6.0	2.2	23.2	65.0	11.8	4.2
1971	54.0	7.1	2.5	24.0	62.8	13.2	4.7
1981	54.8	8.3	3.1	22.1	62.8	15.1	5.6
1991	56.1	8.9	3.9	19.1	65.1	15.8	7.0
2001	57.8	9.0	4.3	18.9	65.5	15.6	7.4
2011	58.8	9.7	4.4	17.1	66.5	16.4	7.5
2021	59.4	11.5	5.1	16.5	64.2	19.3	8.5
2031	59.0	13.8	6.3	16.1	60.6	23.3	10.6
2041	57.3	14.5	7.6	15.4	59.3	25.3	13.3
2051	55.0	13.8	7.7	15.5	59.2	25.3	13.9

Source: UK Census information and national population projections, 1994–based.

The total population column in Table 1.1 shows that population growth was rapid during the nineteenth century, gradually slowed down during the twentieth century and is expected to come to a halt early in the twenty-first century. The next two columns give the population over the ages of 65 and 75. A threshold age of 65 is chosen as the statutory male retirement age. The numbers over 65 have grown at a much higher rate than the total population: between 1851 and 1991 the total population almost trebled, while the population over 65 grew more than eightfold. This age group will carry on growing until the mid-twenty-first century, though the future increases are no greater than those that have already taken place during the twentieth century. A threshold age of 75 divides the elderly population into the 'old old' over 75, who are the people most likely to be suffering severe disabilities, and the 'young old' between 65 and 75. The over-75 population has increased thirteenfold between 1851 and 1991, a higher growth rate than that of the over-65 population and much higher than that of the total population. Again the future increases are in line with twentieth-century experience and expected to continue until the mid-twenty-first century. The last four columns in Table 1.1 show the proportions of the population in the age groups 0–14, 15–64, 65+ and 75+, corresponding roughly to children, the working population, the retired, and the 'old old'. The proportions of the population aged over 65 and 75 have been steadily rising, with the fastest growth in the over-75 group. Both these groups are proportionally far more conspicuous than ever before. The proportion of the population aged below 15 has been declining, and in the early years of the twenty-first century the proportion of over-65s will for the first time exceed the proportion of under-15s. The proportion of the population aged between 15 and 65 shows no consistent trends because the declining proportion of children offsets the rising proportion of old people. In the mid-twenty-first century the proportion of the population aged between 15 and 65 will probably fall to just under 60 per cent, a fairly modest change and not unprecedented: a similar proportion was observed in the mid-nineteenth century. The general pattern of Table 1.1 is an ageing trend that starts in the late nineteenth century, at first accelerates and then from the mid-twentieth century starts to decelerate until the population returns to a new steady-state age composition in the middle of the twenty-first century.

Demographic changes in the UK resemble those in other developed countries, as Table 1.2 illustrates. The countries listed in Table 1.2 are experiencing a common trend towards population ageing. The UK is by no means an extreme case, and several countries (such as Japan and Germany) have populations ageing at a faster rate. The USA displays an ageing trend closely resembling those of Western Europe. Virtually all

Table 1.2 *Population ageing in OECD countries, 1980–2040*

| | 1980 | | | Year 2010 | | | 2040 | | |
Percentage of population aged:	<15	15–64	≥65	<15	15–64	≥65	<15	15–64	≥65
Australia	25	65	10	20	67	13	19	61	20
Austria	21	64	15	17	66	17	17	59	24
Belgium	20	66	14	17	67	16	17	61	22
Canada	23	67	10	17	68	15	18	59	23
Denmark	21	65	14	15	68	17	16	59	25
Finland	20	68	12	16	67	17	17	60	23
France	22	64	14	18	66	16	18	59	23
Germany	18	66	16	13	67	20	15	57	28
Greece	23	64	13	18	65	17	17	62	21
Iceland	27	63	10	19	70	11	19	61	20
Ireland	30	59	11	21	68	11	21	62	17
Italy	22	65	13	16	67	17	17	59	24
Japan	24	67	9	18	63	19	17	60	23
Luxembourg	19	68	13	16	66	18	17	61	22
Netherlands	22	66	12	16	69	15	16	59	25
New Zealand	27	63	10	19	69	12	17	61	22
Norway	22	63	15	17	68	15	17	60	23
Portugal	27	63	10	20	66	14	18	62	20
Spain	26	63	11	17	68	15	18	59	23
Sweden	20	64	16	17	66	17	17	60	23
Switzerland	20	66	14	15	65	20	15	57	28
Turkey	39	56	5	27	67	6	26	64	10
UK	21	64	15	20	65	15	18	62	20
USA	23	66	11	19	68	13	19	61	20

Source: OECD, 1988a.

developed countries are facing a similar pattern of demographic change, and they all have to decide how best to accommodate this.

By contrast with the developed countries, most Third World countries have yet to experience significant population ageing. The predominant demographic trend has been a fall in mortality without an equivalent fall in fertility. The net result is rapid population growth accompanied by a fairly stable age composition biased in favour of the younger age groups. Future prospects rest on whether, as Third World countries undergo economic development, their fertility declines in the same way that it has declined in the developed countries. If so, then Third World countries will have decreasing population growth rates and ageing populations until they attain a new steady state with a higher proportion of old people. A few Third World countries have begun to face population ageing, and eventually this may be true of most if not all of the Third World. Given the low productivity levels of these countries, the economic difficulties could be worse than those encountered in the developed world. At present, however, population ageing is concentrated heavily in the developed countries. Discussion of population ageing, now almost wholly directed at the developed world, may well become pertinent to the future experiences of the Third World.

Besides a rising average age and a rising proportion of old people, the other main way to characterize an ageing population is through dependency or support ratios. A dependency ratio expresses the dependent elderly population as a proportion of the total population of working age. Normally the dependent elderly are defined as people over the statutory retirement age; likewise, the working population is defined as people between the statutory school-leaving and retirement ages. The stress is on people expected to be economically active or inactive because of their age, rather than on people who actually are active or inactive. Total dependency ratios include children below the school-leaving age among the dependants and express both young and old dependants as a proportion of the working population. Alternatively, old-age or pensioner dependency ratios are based on the dependent elderly population alone. An ageing population means that the proportion of the population over the statutory retirement age, and with it the old-age dependency ratio, will almost certainly be rising. When children are added to give the total dependency ratio, the outlook becomes ambiguous: ageing causes a declining proportion of children that can offset the rising proportion of old people. Population ageing can be consistent with a falling total dependency ratio.

Dependency ratios aim to show the average number of dependent people supported by each economically active person. Another method of showing this is through support ratios, the reciprocals of the corresponding dependency ratios. A pensioner support ratio is defined as the population of working age divided by the population above the statutory retirement age; it gives the average number of economically active people available to support each retired elderly person. Falling support ratios imply rising dependency ratios and a growing burden of dependency. Table 1.3 sets out estimated dependency ratios in OECD countries. The dominant trends in Table 1.3 confirm the general incidence of population

Table 1.3 Dependency ratios in OECD countries, 1980–2040

	1980		2010		2040	
	ODR	TDR	ODR	TDR	ODR	TDR
Australia	0.147	0.535	0.187	0.482	0.321	0.630
Austria	0.242	0.563	0.266	0.525	0.408	0.701
Belgium	0.220	0.525	0.235	0.479	0.359	0.643
Canada	0.141	0.482	0.214	0.466	0.378	0.684
Denmark	0.223	0.545	0.245	0.458	0.420	0.701
Finland	0.176	0.475	0.249	0.483	0.388	0.677
France	0.219	0.568	0.245	0.508	0.384	0.685
Germany	0.234	0.508	0.306	0.505	0.482	0.748
Greece	0.206	0.561	0.256	0.532	0.339	0.618
Iceland	0.143	0.571	0.150	0.400	0.333	0.667
Ireland	0.185	0.705	0.165	0.477	0.271	0.603
Italy	0.208	0.549	0.257	0.486	0.410	0.699
Japan	0.135	0.484	0.295	0.586	0.378	0.668
Luxembourg	0.200	0.480	0.280	0.520	0.348	0.609
Netherlands	0.174	0.512	0.221	0.460	0.420	0.695
New Zealand	0.155	0.580	0.175	0.459	0.360	0.640
Norway	0.233	0.585	0.225	0.481	0.383	0.676
Portugal	0.162	0.587	0.214	0.512	0.331	0.623
Spain	0.172	0.581	0.229	0.478	0.382	0.685
Sweden	0.253	0.559	0.266	0.524	0.375	0.665
Switzerland	0.210	0.507	0.316	0.546	0.497	0.764
Turkey	0.084	0.781	0.082	0.490	0.159	0.567
UK	0.232	0.562	0.223	0.527	0.331	0.621
USA	0.171	0.511	0.188	0.472	0.323	0.604

Notes: Old-age dependency ratio (ODR) = (Popn ≥65) / (Popn 15–64)
Total dependency ratio (TDR) = (Popn <15 and ≥65) / (Popn 15–64)

Source: OECD, 1988a.

ageing throughout the OECD countries. Virtually all countries are facing a chronic rise in the old-age dependency ratio and a fall in the equivalent old-age support ratio. For some countries the old-age dependency ratio is expected to double between 1980 and 2040. Movements in total dependency or support ratios are less clear cut. Often the declining number of children is of a similar magnitude to the rising number of old people, and when both are added into a total dependency ratio they cancel each other out. The total dependency ratio for some countries has recently been falling because the large postwar 'baby-boom' birth cohorts have been entering the working population. When these cohorts retire towards the mid-twenty-first century, the total dependency ratio will begin to rise again. Table 1.3 shows a general but variable upward trend in total dependency ratios, far less obvious than the upward trend in old-age dependency ratios.

The age distribution of a country's total population can conceal disparities between regions. In the UK, for example, the overall proportion of people aged over 65 at the 1991 census was 15.8 per cent, but the proportion in particular local authority areas varied between a maximum of around 35 per cent and a minimum of around 9 per cent. The places with the highest concentrations of old people are the favoured retirement areas located mainly on the south coast of England and several other coasts (Law and Warnes, 1976; Warnes and Law, 1984). Similar retirement areas have emerged in other countries: in the USA, for instance, old people have congregated in parts of Florida and Arizona, and in Europe along sections of the Mediterranean coast. The key influence on regional age distributions has been differences in age-specific migration and, above all, the growth of migration upon retirement (Warnes, 1983). As real incomes have risen and formal retirement has become the norm, increasing numbers of old people have large pension entitlements or savings and no employment ties to their current locality. Their prosperity and mobility permits them to move to a preferred retirement area which, if it proves popular with many such pensioners, will acquire a more aged population than other regions. Most migration by old people has been away from large cities or industrial areas to regions with warmer climates and a more scenic (generally coastal) environment. This is in the opposite direction to the typical migrations of younger people, who move away from rural and agricultural areas to urban and industrial areas where employment is more readily available. When combined, the migration patterns of young and old can create large differences in regional dependency ratios that are self-perpetuating once established. The problems of ageing have a regional aspect, as some regions have much larger elderly populations than others and greater needs for social and medical care. Regions cannot be separated from the aggregate picture, however, because many social and medical services are publicly financed. When public policies operate according to common national standards, the levels of provision are decided nationally and taxpayers subsidize the regions with the greatest needs. Retirement communities often have high unearned incomes to compensate their higher needs: it does not follow inevitably that regional differences in age distribution will create localized 'crises' of ageing. Most academic literature on ageing has centred on the national issue of the financial and real costs of supporting the total elderly population. The national age distribution has received more emphasis than regional age distributions. Although the regional allocation of resources is important, the crucial decisions concerning population ageing are taken at the aggregate, national level. The present discussion will follow standard academic practice and concentrate on the age composition of national populations.

THE CAUSES OF POPULATION AGEING

For an individual, ageing is merely the elapsing of time, with its various social and biological consequences. A person's chances of reaching old age depend wholly on mortality and are independent of fertility. For a population, ageing depends on all three sources of demographic change: fertility, mortality and migration. Mortality is the most obvious cause of population ageing, as it forms a clear parallel with the ageing of the individual. If mortality falls and people live longer, then the average age of the population will rise and population ageing will begin. Other sources of population ageing may also be relevant. The size of each birth cohort has an effect on relative generation sizes. A declining fertility rate creates smaller birth cohorts and a fall in the size of younger generations relative to older ones; the population ages even if there is no increase in the life expectancy of individuals. The birth of new generations and the survival of existing generations influence a population's age composition. Fertility is just as important an influence as mortality, and population ageing could be induced by falling fertility combined with stable (or even rising) mortality. The third source of demographic change is migration. This can act in the same way as fertility, when inward migration adds new members of the population, or in the same way as mortality, when outward migration removes current members of the population. The effects on the age composition are more ambiguous than those of fertility and mortality: the population gained through migration is not inevitably young as with fertility, and the population lost through migration will frequently be younger than that lost through mortality. Migration is also partial and usually voluntary. All individuals are born and die, but only some will choose to migrate. In most cases, migration has a limited influence on population ageing, as international migration flows are far smaller than national populations. Long-run changes in the age structures of the developed countries are due almost entirely to changes in fertility and mortality, not migration.

Under normal circumstances, fertility has greater importance for population ageing than mortality. Mathematical modelling of populations suggests that, unless mortality is exceptionally high, fertility will be the prime influence on the age distribution (Lotka, 1907). The intuitive reason is that fertility determines the initial size of each generation, and its effects persist throughout the generation's full life cycle: a relatively small or large generation affects the age distribution for 70 or more years. Mortality can influence generation size only by removing people from an existing generation. Changes in infant mortality alter the size of a generation over its full life cycle and have a similar effect to changes in fertility. But mortality occurs chiefly among the older age groups and affects the age distribution only for the rest of the generation's life cycle, a period of, say, ten to 15 years in comparison with the 70 or 80 years of life expectancy at birth in a developed country. Fertility changes add or subtract people of age zero who have a full life cycle ahead of them, whereas mortality largely removes people who have completed all or most of a typical life cycle. A changing age composition driven by fertility varies from the youngest age groups upwards. Reduced fertility shows up immediately as fewer children, and when the new smaller birth cohorts grow older the trend towards smaller generation sizes becomes visible among the whole population. Reduced mortality causes ageing at the opposite end of the age distribution: old people live longer, the older birth cohorts gain improved survival rates, and ageing appears first among the elderly.

To explain the onset of population ageing, one has to look at long-term movements in fertility and mortality. Any such movements almost certainly result from changes in economic conditions and themselves have economic implications. The underlying causality is complex, and the unreliability of past demographic data compounds the difficulties of interpretation. Demographers have, nonetheless, pieced together some stylized facts about the world's population history and given a tentative economic interpretation to the main developments.

The best-known account is that of Cipolla (1978), who emphasizes changes in energy sources and divides world population history into three stages separated by the agricultural and industrial revolutions. Homo sapiens as a distinct species has existed for less than 200 000 years, a tiny fraction of the age of the Earth. During most of this time, human beings have lived as hunters and gatherers, more advanced than animal species but with the same basic form of economic organization. Hunting/gathering populations do not have systematic access to energy and rely instead on random access to organic energy sources through hunting animals or gathering plant material. There is no agriculture, no domestication of animals, no accumulated capital, and no exploitation of inanimate energy sources such as fossil fuels. Around 8000 BC occurred the agricultural revolution or neolithic demographic transition, which marked the beginnings of systematic access to organic energy sources: crops were planted, agricultural surpluses were stored and traded, and livestock were domesticated and exploited for food. Surpluses led to the accumulation of capital and the development of an economy in the modern sense. Demographically, the new economic system as it became firmly established brought a small but sustained increase in the rate of world population growth. The mechanism of the neolithic demographic transition is unclear, and a lack of reliable evidence makes it difficult to decide between the competing interpretations (Livi-Bacci, 1992, Chapter 2). What is clear is that the transition did not cause any great divergence between fertility and mortality. The effects on world population were significant, but the growth rate remained low by current standards and the age composition remained stable.

Population ageing is associated with the second revolution in world population growth, the industrial revolution or modern demographic transition. This dates from the upsurge of manufacturing industry, which for Britain started in the late eighteenth century but for many countries only in the late nineteenth and early twentieth centuries. The demographic transition model, popularized by Frank Notestein in the 1940s, refers to a generalized description of demographic events with no theories or causal mechanisms attached. The model indicates the prominence of economic development, but does not specify the precise relation between population and the economy. While the basic facts of the demographic transition are uncontroversial, their economic interpretation and future implications leave room for conflicting views. Figure 1.1 illustrates the demographic transition model. Four stages can be identified. Initially fertility and mortality are roughly equal and at the high levels observed in pre-industrial societies. Mortality is, if anything, slightly below fertility, permitting slow population growth, and more variable because of periodic famines and epidemics. On the whole, however, there is no marked disparity between fertility and mortality. In the second stage, the population moves out of its initial steady state, thanks to a fall in mortality unmatched by any fall in fertility. Since fertility is now higher than mortality and the gap between them is increasing, the population grows at an accelerating rate. Lower mortality causes population ageing, though its effects will be small and concentrated among the older age groups. In the third stage, fertility also begins to fall. The decline in mortality peters out, and the gap between fertility and mortality ceases to widen and starts to narrow. Total population is still growing but at a decelerating rate. A fall in fertility, compared with an equivalent fall in mortality, produces a more thoroughgoing ageing of the population from the youngest age groups upwards. The fourth and final stage sees the fall in fertility

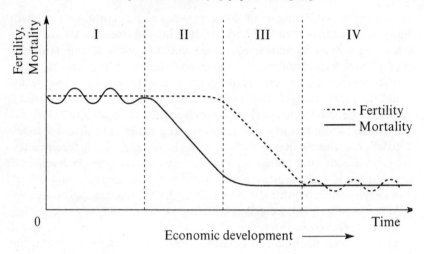

Stage I: Initial steady state
            Stable age distribution
Stage II: Accelerating population growth
            Start of population ageing
Stage III: Decelerating population growth
            Main period of population ageing
Stage IV: New steady state
            Convergence on stable age distribution with a higher proportion of
            old people

Figure 1.1 The demographic transition

slowing down until fertility and mortality are once again roughly equal.
Fertility now varies cyclically with economic conditions as people exercise
discretion over family size; mortality remains relatively stable. A new
steady state is attained in which the total population has increased, the
average age is higher and a larger proportion of the population belongs
to the older age groups. Most developed countries are in the third or
fourth stages of the transition and well on the way to a new, more aged
steady-state population. Many less developed countries appear to be in
the second stage of the transition: they have had a fall in mortality as yet
unmatched by a fall in fertility and are facing very high population
growth rates.

Population growth is known to be related to economic growth, but the
causal mechanisms behind the relationship are uncertain. Lower mortality betokens better health and higher living standards. The experience of
countries such as the UK suggests the value of improved nutrition and

sanitation in combating infectious diseases. Falling mortality during the nineteenth century seems to have resulted largely from the greater prosperity generated by industrialization and not immediately from the associated technical and medical advances (McKeown and Record, 1962). Falling fertility too has been an outcome of rising living standards, rather than technical changes: improved birth control methods have made it easier for people to curtail their family size, yet on its own this does not guarantee falling fertility. The incentive to have smaller families comes from socioeconomic development, especially the growth of female education and labour force participation. The negative relation between income and fertility is well established empirically in the developed countries and has lately been explained through economic theories of fertility (see, for example, Willis, 1973; Leibenstein, 1974; Cochrane, 1975; Becker, 1991, Chapter 5; Easterlin, 1980; Donaldson, 1991). These theories are controversial in some respects (notably the use of rational-choice methods), though the negative influence of rising real incomes on fertility is generally agreed. Population ageing, founded chiefly on falling fertility, has been a side-effect of the economic growth enjoyed by the developed countries over the last century.

The causal relation between economic growth and population growth is a perennial topic of debate. Economic conditions influence demographic change, and demographic change influences the economy. As with any such simultaneous causality, a simple theoretical account of the relation between population and the economy has proved elusive. Academic debate over the part played by population in economic growth has produced conflicting attitudes (Jackson, 1995). The original Malthusian stance of classical economics, which rested on diminishing returns to labour, portrayed population growth as detrimental to economic growth: if economic growth occurred it was in spite of, not because of, population growth. A similar pessimistic view has persisted into the modern neoclassical era, for example, in the Coale–Hoover model of economic development (Coale and Hoover, 1958). The pessimistic outlook has not gone unchallenged. Some economists have singled out population growth as the motivating factor behind the introduction of markets, the discovery of new resources and the adoption of new technology (Boserup, 1965; Simon, 1977; Hayek, 1989). The cornucopian optimism of Simon (1981) contrasts starkly with the Malthusian pessimism that has characterized much economic discussion. Between the negative and positive extremes stand the more cautious views of Kuznets (1974), who argues that population growth is neither necessary for economic development nor on its own sufficient to cause economic growth. Economists are still as far as ever from reaching a consensus on the interaction between population growth and economic growth (for summaries of the literature, see Birdsall, 1988, and Kelley, 1988). The inconclusiveness of the theoretical and empirical debates testifies to the complexities involved.

Discussing population ageing does not require a complete theory of long-run economic and demographic development. Attention can be concentrated on one particular matter, the effect of an ageing population on the economy. This abstracts from other important matters, but the simplification is acceptable as long as one remembers the wider demographic background. The protagonists in the debates on population growth agree that population ageing in the developed world is part of a larger process of economic development. The productivity gains and higher real incomes that have gone with economic growth counterbalance any adverse consequences associated with population ageing. To this extent an ageing population is an emblem of economic success as well as a source of economic difficulties.

POPULATION AGEING AS AN ECONOMIC PROBLEM

Before the twentieth century population ageing had never happened on an appreciable scale, so economists had little reason to consider its hypothetical economic consequences. When widespread population ageing first emerged in the early twentieth century, economists and other academic commentators scarcely noticed it. The first substantial discussions of population ageing date from the 1930s and 1940s, and the bulk of the literature on ageing has been produced since the Second World War, several decades after population ageing first appeared (Clark and Spengler, 1980). The delayed discussion of ageing demonstrates its moderate influence. When populations started to age, the social implications were barely perceptible and created no instant crisis. Population ageing, compared with other events and trends of the twentieth century, has only limited significance. This is not to deny its real economic consequences or the difficulties that may ensue from it, but merely to put it in perspective. Recent discussions of demographic change have used dramatic language: there is talk of demographic 'crises', 'revolutions' and 'time-bombs' (Shegog, 1981; World Bank, 1994; McLoughlin, 1991; National Economic Development Office, 1989). The dramatization seems somewhat misplaced. A development that went unremarked for several decades must have been less than overwhelming in its impact on the economies concerned.

Another reason for the initial neglect of population ageing by economists was their switch away from demographic questions during the nineteenth century. The classical economics of Ricardo and J.S. Mill had the Malthusian population principle as one of its core components and placed population at the heart of economic theorizing. It held sway until the late-nineteenth century, when neoclassical economics superseded it as the economic mainstream. The neoclassical approach retains certain elements of classical economics, such as diminishing returns to labour, but gives much less prominence to population and often treats it as being fixed and separable from the economy. The emphasis on static resource allocation with a constant population diverts neoclassical theory away from broad macroeconomic issues to a microeconomic method centred on rational individual behaviour. A strict application of neoclassical principles goes against the grain of the long-run, aggregative, non-steady-state matters invoked by demographic change. At the time when population ageing emerged, economists were committing themselves to a theoretical model ill equipped to cope with it.

Academic discussion of population ageing has been in two periods, explicable partly by the pattern of demographic changes and partly by economic conditions. The first period started during the interwar years and lasted until the early 1950s (Thane, 1990). Anxiety about the chronic depression and high unemployment of the 1930s prompted interest in ageing and declining populations. Slower population growth might, it was feared, cause dwindling demand and an even deeper depression. Disquiet over the effects on economic activity stimulated theoretical work on the budgetary and other consequences of an ageing population. The early concerns about ageing were allied to the new, iconoclastic Keynesian economics; neoclassical orthodoxy, by contrast, would have welcomed a declining population as raising the marginal returns to labour and having a positive effect on productivity. The postwar years saw several articles and official reports on the problems of a declining population and ways of resolving them (Sauvy, 1948; Royal Commission on Population, 1949; Phillips Commitee, 1954). Interest in population ageing slackened during the late 1950s, largely in response to demographic conditions: the postwar 'baby boom' from the late 1940s to the mid 1960s meant that the populations of developed countries were no longer ageing as quickly as had hitherto been expected. Along with the rise in population growth came a rise in economic growth rates to unprecedented levels. The fears of permanent depression now seemed too pessimistic, and the pressures on public budgets were relaxed. Ageing did not disappear from policy discussion, but it was only a peripheral topic during the 1960s and 1970s.

Within the last twenty years or so, the economic and demographic trends have reversed themselves. The 'baby boom' is over, and fertility has resumed its long-run downward trend; as a result, population ageing should continue until well into the twenty-first century. The postwar economic boom drew to a close during the late 1960s, at roughly the same time as the 'baby boom'. Since then, unemployment has proliferated in most developed countries and, despite cyclical fluctuations, seems set to remain at much higher levels than in the 1950s and 1960s. The demographic and economic position is now broadly similar to that of the 1930s and, as before, economists and other academics have discussed population ageing extensively. This second period of policy discussion is no longer Keynesian in hue, reflecting changes within the economics profession, but the unease about the effects of population ageing on public budgets and the economy's productive potential resembles that voiced in the 1940s. After two spates of academic interest, albeit with a thirty-year interlude, the principal themes and issues raised by population ageing are now quite familiar. The following chapters take a critical view of them.

OUTLINE OF THE BOOK

Chapters 2–4 consider general theoretical approaches to population ageing. Chapter 2 examines the relation between population ageing and a rising dependency burden, an idea that underpins much popular discussion of the 'ageing crisis'. Dependency is found to be a vague concept only weakly connected with population ageing. Commentators on ageing have often regarded rising dependency as a problem not because of its intrinsic properties but because of its ultimate consequences for resource transfers, disincentives and intergenerational conflict. A terminology of dependency may thus be redundant. Chapter 3 discusses the application to population ageing of neoclassical economic theory based on rational individual behaviour and market-clearing equilibria. Most analyses of ageing in the mainstream economic literature adopt a life-cycle approach, either at the individual level or integrated into general-equilibrium or public-choice models. This approach, Chapter 3 argues, can produce only a partial, distorted view of demographic change. Chapter 4 looks at the theoretical alternatives to neoclassical economics, which permit a less individualistic stance and contribute to a broader perspective on population ageing. The chief alternatives hail from the structural ideas found in sociology, social policy and social gerontology and the disequilibrium ideas found in non-neoclassical economics. A sufficiently elaborate, non-reductionist theoretical framework can bring structural and disequilibrium ideas together in the analysis of ageing.

Chapters 5–8 consider the main policy matters associated with population ageing. Chapter 5 discusses the productivity and employment of old people. There is little evidence to suggest that the work performance of the old is inferior to that of the young, and an ageing population need not therefore have a detrimental effect on productivity. Old people have the potential to stay employed and retrain to cope with new technology, but may be denied the opportunity if institutional pressures and age discrimination stand in the way. Chapter 6 addresses pensions and retirement. The traditional argument is that population ageing will cause severe adjustment problems for public, pay-as-you-go pension schemes, although one can query whether these problems are as severe as some commentators have claimed. Pension reform impinges on retirement behaviour, so any pension adjustments elicited by demographic change should take into account the future character of retirement and the social status of old people. Chapter 7 deals with health care and social services under population ageing. The relation between age and health remains an area about which relatively little is known, despite its obvious importance. An ageing population will raise per capita spending on health care and social services, but the influence of age is flexible and may be less significant than many other influences on spending. Measures to improve the efficiency of services and reduce the incapacity of old people can help to curtail the demands placed on social services. Chapter 8 assesses the consequences of population ageing for informal economic activity. Relatives and neighbours provide much informal care of the elderly, an activity that makes a real contribution to the economy but goes unrecorded in the national accounts. As the population ages, governments may cut public spending on the elderly by treating informal care as a free good and shifting care from the formal to the informal sector. A proper economic appraisal of care should recognize the real costs and benefits of informal economic activities and put them on the same footing as formal activities. Likewise, the planning of social care has to bear in mind the interrelationship of the formal and informal economies.

Chapter 9 draws together the major themes and offers some concluding comments. The drift of the argument throughout the book is that population ageing raises issues broader and more complex but less intense and dramatic than those highlighted in popular and academic discussion.

2. Ageing and dependency

Population ageing is often thought to create economic difficulties through the growth of dependency. A greater proportion of dependent old people is seen as detrimental to both older and younger age groups. The old may suffer wholesale dependency on others, paired with low incomes and living standards; the young may face reduced productivity and unwelcome sacrifices in their consumption. An ageing population appears to enlarge the burden of inactive people that each individual worker has to bear. Population ageing can be characterized as causing a crisis of age-induced dependency that may threaten the well-being of all age groups. Dependency, given its prominence in the discussion of ageing, deserves closer scrutiny. The present chapter considers the meaning of the term dependency, the relation between dependency and ageing, and the consequences of rising dependency for the economy.

DEFINING DEPENDENCY

The term 'dependency' has no accepted definition, even though it occurs widely in academic discourse, and writers on economics and social policy have adopted different and sometimes conflicting definitions. Walker (1982a) lists five ways in which the elderly have been characterized as dependent: life-cycle dependency, physical or mental dependency, political dependency, economic dependency, and structural dependency. The first four of these are considered below; the last of the five, structural dependency, will be discussed in Chapter 4.

Life-cycle dependency pertains to the typical human life cycle that starts with childhood, proceeds through a period of economic activity during adulthood, and ends with inactivity and dependency during old age. An age threshold acts as the yardstick of dependency, so that anyone over a certain age is regarded as dependent. The prime examples of this approach are demographic dependency ratios, which use the customary retirement age to divide the population into dependent and independent groups. The grounds for such a division are commonly left implicit, but rest on a combination of biological and institutional considerations. Biological ageing must eventually bring physical decline and disability. The ageing process is smooth and continuous, however, and does not warrant a strict division of the population at a single age threshold. A fuller account of biological ageing would disaggregate the population into smaller age groups and use information on physical incapacity by age. This has never been the standard way of calculating dependency ratios, but it would raise the informational content and capture the smoothness of the relation between age and physical dependency. The other main justification for life-cycle dependency is institutional. Most developed countries have a statutory retirement age that determines the typical retirement period. Age is not perfectly correlated with economic inactivity, despite the statutory framework, since some people above the retirement age are economically active and some below it are economically inactive. The relevance of the retirement age as a threshold turns on how many people adhere to it. Again, a more disaggregated approach would represent more accurately the relation between age and economic activity. Age-related definitions of dependency are always indirect: age serves as a proxy for dependency in other dimensions. A person's age is merely a number. It indicates other forms of dependency, but is not itself the object of interest. If old people were as physically healthy and economically active as the young, there would be no age-based dependency ratios.

Physical or mental dependency arises when a person loses the capacity to function independently in society. A dependent person cannot undertake the usual round of everyday activities and needs assistance from others. The severer the dependency, the greater the assistance needed, ranging from casual, informal help with household tasks to intensive medical care in hospitals. The standard method of identifying and measuring physical dependency is to obtain information on people's ability to perform various household tasks and assign dependent status accordingly (Harris, 1971; Wright, Cairns and Snell, 1981). This involves far more elaborate procedures than using age as a proxy for physical dependency and should give a better indication of people's true physical capabilities. A physical definition of dependency would normally be applied to practical activities such as the provision of medical services and social care. Physical dependency is not solely biological in origin and is contingent on a person's socioeconomic background; it is not unique to old people, and old age is neither a necessary nor a sufficient condition for being physically dependent. Most physical dependency measures are at least partly based on self-assessment, so they can easily be swayed by subjective, socially implanted attitudes (Wenger, 1986). The apparent objectivity and generality of physical dependency measures may well be spurious. When adopting a physical definition of dependency, one has to bear in mind the complex connections between age, incapacity and social conditions.

Political dependency derives from an imbalance of power between the individual and the state or other social institutions. In developed countries, all citizens are inevitably subject to legally imposed constraints and obligations and usually to paternalistic welfare measures. The key question with political dependency is its extent, rather than its presence or absence. From a libertarian viewpoint, a market economy minimizes political dependency and enhances the power of the individual relative to the state. Libertarians see the apparently benevolent activities of the welfare state as undermining self-reliance and fostering an unwelcome 'culture of dependency'. Taken to an extreme, concerns about political dependency can provoke calls for the dismantling of the welfare state and the withdrawal of the government from economic activity. Such arguments rely on the concept of negative freedom, the absence of constraint; they give little credence to positive freedom, an individual's capacity to act, which can potentially be expanded through paternalistic state intervention (Berlin, 1969). Less extreme views limit their criticisms to the centralization of the welfare state: as social services become formalized, the caring professions may create an institutionalized dependency that subordinates the recipients of care to the providers. The appropriate response may be to reorganize but not dismantle the welfare state, with the aim of avoiding excessive centralization and keeping paternalism to the unavoidable minimum. Attitudes to political dependency bear the stamp of more general attitudes to the state and its relation with the individual.

Economic dependency, like political dependency, is inevitable in developed countries. Development is founded on specialization and interdependence among the members of a society: no one is self-sufficient and everyone depends on others for the production of goods and services. Most people obtain their incomes, and thus their access to goods and services, from employment. By finding employment and securing economic 'independence', an employee becomes dependent on a particular employer, whether a private firm or the state. Such 'independence' is fragile and may be lost during a recession when the employer no longer requires the employee's services. Contrasting the 'dependent' with the 'independent' is a somewhat artificial exercise, yet writers on population ageing commonly portray the retired elderly as an economically dependent group. Economic dependency can be defined in two related but distinct ways. On a financial definition, the receipt of transfer payments or benefits in kind distinguishes dependency. The retired elderly are financially dependent if they receive a state pension, but financially independent if they can subsist from their own occupational pensions or other private income sources. On a real definition, economic inactivity or unemployment distinguishes dependency. Collectively, the employed are independent, since they produce the goods and services consumed by the whole population, even though as individuals they depend on others for the goods and services they consume. The retired elderly, the unemployed and the economically inactive are dependent, even though they informally produce goods and services consumed by the independent population. Many people are economically dependent according to both the real and financial definitions; retirement or the loss of a job brings simultaneous withdrawal from employment and receipt of transfer payments. But it remains possible to have financial without real dependency (when an employed person receives transfer payments) or real without financial dependency (when a retired person lives on a private income). Economists have adopted both definitions: financial dependency predominates in discussions of pension finance, real dependency in discussions of employment and aggregate dependency ratios.

The types of dependency outlined above cover the main senses of the term 'dependency' as it is used in the academic literature on ageing. When referring to dependency, one should ideally point out the type of dependency so as to avoid ambiguity. A proper account of dependency should specify the dimension in which it occurs, the form that it takes, and the individuals or social groups involved. The tendency, however, is to use the unqualified term 'dependency', leaving the reader to deduce what type of dependency is being considered.

THE SIGNIFICANCE OF DEPENDENCY

Interdependence among individuals and social groups is a defining characteristic of advanced societies. Everyone depends on others in some respects. Dividing the population into dependent and independent groups on the basis of a single indicator of dependency can be a narrow and misleading approach to social analysis (Munnichs, 1976; Johnson, 1993). The negative connotations of dependency are often accepted without demur, but it is by no means obvious why dependency always has to be harmful. If some people are economically, politically or physically dependent on others but have all their basic needs fulfilled and have a good standard of living, then why should this be perceived as a problem? Societies cannot exist without interdependency of one type or another, and some types of interdependency may be a benign outcome of altruism or social solidarity (Johnson, 1995). Dependency is a relational concept that refers to the relations among individuals and social groups rather than the properties of individuals and social groups in themselves. For dependency to underlie policy discussion suggests a direct interest in the dependency relation or its immediate consequences. People's dependency on others, not their disability or pain, is what motivates concern about physical dependency. The same goes for economic and political dependency; the individual's status relative to other individuals or social groups is what matters. A dependency-based approach implies a special concern about the imbalances and asymmetries among the members of a society. The concern arises either because dependency is intrinsically unpalatable, or because its consequences are unpalatable. Both attitudes play a part in the negative perception of dependency.

Dependency can be intrinsically unpalatable because it spells the loss of independence, which may be a valued characteristic. For all people to be wholly independent (on any definition of dependency) is a virtual impossibility, and if it ever were attained it would result in society being replaced by an aggregation of self-sufficient individuals. Acknowledging that dependency is inevitable may be merely acknowledging the essential frailty of humanity (Mendus, 1991). This does not stop libertarian thinkers from presenting a conglomeration of independent individuals as their theoretical ideal. Libertarians value independence as negative freedom giving individuals control of their own destiny and also on instrumental grounds as furthering the rational individualistic decision making that in a market economy is supposed to generate efficiency. The case for independence may thus be seen as an argument for individualism, diversity and decentralization and against structure, monism and paternalism. Another reason for disliking dependency has a very different political tone. Dependency is often the result of inequalities among individuals and social groups. Thoroughgoing interdependence of equals might be deemed acceptable and even welcomed as creating common interests and social solidarity; it is not necessarily interdependence that is objectionable, but the placing of one individual or group in a subservient position to others. Unlike the libertarian arguments, this may yield a case for interventionist social policies and the drawing together of equals into a common culture so as to avoid the fragmentation of society (Tawney, 1964). Aversion to dependency has been a feature of contrasting political views, from extreme libertarianism to support for extensive social planning.

Alternatively, dependency may be undesirable not in itself but in its consequences. A consequentialist stance animates most discussions of dependency by economists. Neoclassical economists evaluate actions or social states through their implications for individual utilities:

dependency is undesirable because it lowers individual utilities or social welfare defined as a function of individual utilities. From this perspective, one has to trace the unwelcome consequences of dependency and thereby explain why it causes a loss of utility. Many adverse consequences of rising dependency have been identified, such as the growing financial burdens on the working population, the threat to tax revenues and productivity from disincentive effects, the potential for intergenerational conflict, and so forth. Later chapters consider these consequences in more detail. At present it suffices to note that dependency is being treated as a link in a chain that extends from an initial extraneous change – population ageing – to a final set of consequences that decide whether welfare has increased or decreased.

Attitudes to dependency influence policy discussion. Where dependency itself is seen as undesirable, the crucial relation is between age and dependency: policy discussion asks whether population ageing can occur without creating dependency. Where dependency is seen as undesirable because of its consequences, analysis becomes more complicated: a further relation is introduced, between dependency and some ultimate definition of welfare. The possibility arises of weakening the relation between dependency and its adverse consequences, so that population ageing could still, in principle, create dependency and yet have fewer or no adverse consequences for welfare. An additional possibility would be to bypass the terminology of dependency altogether and go directly from ageing to its eventual consequences. The following discussion considers both relations, first, that between age and dependency, and second, that between dependency and its economic consequences.

THE RELATION BETWEEN AGE AND DEPENDENCY

Dependency ratios presuppose a close relation between age and dependency. They dichotomize the population into dependent and independent groups on the basis of a single age threshold, usually the statutory retirement age, and use no information other than age to assign people to a dependent status. Dependency takes a life-cycle form, and the source of policy concern remains vague: it might be physical, economic or some other type of dependency that motivates the discussion. All the dependent population are given the same weighting, and aggregate dependency is gauged simply by the total number of dependent people. The dependency ratio – the number of retired elderly divided by the working population – represents the burden on each person of working age. As this is calculated from demographic data alone, demographic changes are assumed to be the sole cause of changes in dependency, an approach that has been described as 'demographic determinism' (Johnson and Falkingham, 1992, Chapter 2). In practice, the relation between age and dependency is far more complex than a solely demographic approach would suggest, and many other social and biological considerations are relevant.

Notwithstanding the impression of demographic determinism, a person's age is linked only indirectly with dependency. Between age and dependency comes the biological ageing process, which erodes people's physical capacity as they grow older and renders them increasingly dependent on others. The upshot is a shift from immediate age-related dependency to a two-stage link passing through physical incapacity, as below:

Age → Physical incapacity → Physical dependency

That ageing originates in human biology is an uncontroversial assumption; in all past and present societies, human beings have experienced physical decline with age, albeit at different rates and to different degrees. Were it not for biological ageing, a person's age would have scant significance. Beneath the institutional structures of different societies lies a common biological ageing process that varies little over time and place. The relation between age and physical capacity is, nevertheless, flexible. One cannot observe biological ageing in a pure form unadulterated by social conditions. Individuals, social groups and societies vary greatly in the rapidity of the ageing process, and health, physical capacity and life expectancy at any given age are strongly correlated with income and social class. Under contrasting social conditions, the same human biology can yield diverse patterns of health and longevity. If it so happens that in one society most people have either died or become physically incapable before the age of sixty, the same is not necessarily true of other, more prosperous societies. Biological ageing can be perceived only through the medium of its social context.

Variability extends to the link between physical incapacity and dependency. Physically incapable people become physically dependent on others only when provided with care, but care is a function of social conditions such as the availability of formal services, the number of able-bodied relatives for each old person, and the willingness of relatives and neighbours to act as carers. Only if care is always provided for those who need it will physical incapacity be synonymous with physical dependency. Under the heading of physical dependency fall numerous alternative social arrangements. Some of them, the ones involving formal professional care, may entail political dependency on the state or the social policy profession. Other, more informal arrangements would be counted as physical dependency but not as political dependency. The apparently deterministic relation between age and physical dependency is in fact quite malleable and contingent on social circumstances.

The connection between age and economic dependency is even more tenuous (Jackson, 1991a). Old age may create economic dependency when physical incapacity forces the elderly to become economically inactive and lose their employment incomes. This gives rise to another two links in the age–dependency relation, as below:

Age → Physical → Economic → Receipt of transfer payments/ → Economic dependency
      incapacity   inactivity   Loss of employment

The relevance of physical incapacity is open to question. Most old people become economically inactive because they have reached the statutory retirement age, not because they have become physically incapable of work. If physical criteria were paramount, retirement could be based on physical grounds alone, and people would then retire at different ages when they became incapable of work. The very existence of statutory retirement ages means that economic inactivity cannot be due merely to the physical incapacity of old people and that it adheres to social conventions. An amalgam of institutional pressures and voluntary decision making determines the retirement date of most people in developed countries, with the physical ageing process playing only a minor role.

Economic activity under standard definitions refers only to formal, paid work recorded by the national accounts. An economically inactive person could well be undertaking informal work without payment and thereby contributing to the economy's aggregate production. The elderly, for example, are important providers as well as recipients of informal care. Likewise, many economically inactive people in the younger age groups are important producers of economic services (such as the housework performed by women). These people, involved in material but unpaid production, should not necessarily be regarded as economically dependent. To exclude them from the productive population when calculating dependency measures gives their activities a zero weighting and clouds the supposedly clear relationship between economic inactivity and economic dependency.

Another complicating factor is unemployment. Many people of working age are currently unemployed; their 'economic activity' has not enabled them to avoid economic dependency. The number of unemployed bears comparison with the number of retired elderly, so dependency through unemployment is far from negligible and the retired elderly are not the only major dependent group. Unemployment hits mainly the low-paid, who have few private savings and rely heavily on state pensions and transfer payments to finance their retirement. Many retired people, by contrast, were well paid during their employment and have unearned incomes sufficient to survive comfortably with little or no state pension; they have much greater financial independence than the typical unemployed person. Equating economic dependency with economic inactivity underestimates the independence of the elderly and overestimates that of the working population.

A response to the complexities of the age–dependency relation is to recalculate dependency ratios using additional information (Falkingham, 1989). By disaggregating the population into more than two age groups, one can dispense with the assumption that the economic activity rate jumps from a hundred per cent to zero at the statutory retirement age. Data on age-specific activity rates can allow for a gradual change in economic activity with age. Other forms of disaggregation are also relevant. Disaggregation by gender can affect aggregate dependency measures, given that there are systematic differences in the levels and rates of change of male and female activity rates. If an economy has large variations in regional activity rates, further disaggregation of the population by region may be appropriate. Along with disaggregation, information on employment rates (as opposed to economic activity rates) and informal economic activity can enhance the accuracy of dependency measures. The unemployed in each age group are economically dependent and should be included in the dependent population to obtain a better assessment of total dependency. A more difficult adjustment is to account for informal economic activity, which goes unrecorded in the official statistics. Exactly how many economically inactive people undertake informal economic activity and to what extent remains unclear. Instead of ignoring informal economic activity and giving it a zero weighting, it may be preferable to attach an approximate weighting between zero and unity to every economically inactive group. Falkingham (1989), for example, makes an educated guess at 50 per cent as the suitable weighting for the domestic production of economically inactive women in the normal working age groups. Any such adjustments are crude, but arguably no more so than ignoring informal economic activity altogether. Additional information reduces the element of demographic determinism in the dependency ratio and demonstrates that population ageing is not the only cause of changes in aggregate dependency.

All dependency ratios, even ones modified by additional information, have some disadvantages. In the first place, they rest on a unidimensional notion of economic dependency that overlooks the other, non-economic types of dependency; a fuller picture would require a range of summary statistics, rather than a single dependency ratio. Second, they do not allow for the intensity and distribution of dependency. A person is either dependent or independent, with nothing between the two extremes. Introducing weightings that register the intensities of dependency would give a more accurate measure of total dependency, although it would greatly increase the information needed to produce summary statistics. If different intensities of dependency lead to qualitative differences in people's experiences or in the appropriate policy responses, then it may be preferable to adopt a less unified approach. A single dependency measure also neglects distribution; dependency could be concentrated among certain social groups or spread evenly among the population. Summary statistics showing the distribution of dependency would have to be more disaggregated than the standard dependency ratio. Third, dependency ratios can only hint at the causality behind observed trends. Disaggregated dependency ratios can divide changes in total dependency into components due to, say, a changing age distribution and changing employment rates. The results suggest possible reasons for changes in dependency, but do not provide a proper theoretical account. Additional information built into summary statistics will not on its own explain changes in dependency, and some explanatory theory is needed. Several theorists have developed models of dependency, notably the structured dependency approach discussed in Chapter 4.

Avoiding dependency is often an implicit objective of economic and social policy. Most welfare assessments are based on some other yardstick, such as utilities or needs. Unless policy rests directly on dependency, it is a moot point whether a terminology of dependency is necessary when there are major problems in defining and measuring dependency. Most economic discussions of ageing adopt an economic definition of dependency and then consider the adverse consequences of such dependency. The consequences could be discussed without recourse to the intermediate step of dependency, and any gains from having a general dependency concept have to be set against the difficulties that ensue from a term with so many overtones and implications. Even if one retains the term 'dependency', within a consequentialist framework one still has to identify and evaluate its consequences.

THE CONSEQUENCES OF INCREASING DEPENDENCY

Economic dependency is founded on the contrast between the economically active and inactive. A rise in dependency, in other words, a rise in the number or proportion of economically inactive people is believed to have several undesirable consequences: it increases demands on scarce resources and threatens the general standard of living; it requires greater transfers of resources from producers to non-producers, with producers having to relinquish a larger fraction of their incomes; it creates disincentives for producers that may diminish aggregate productivity; and it causes conflict between generations, endangering the implicit intergenerational contract that underlies public pensions and social services. The following discussion looks at these consequences in turn.

Resources Problems

A resources problem arises if the extra resources demanded by the growing inactive population cannot be met without encroaching on the existing uses of the national product (Paish and Peacock, 1954; Williams, 1985). Consider, as an example, a population composed of A active people and I inactive people, so that the total population is $A + I$. Suppose that the A active people are the sole producers of a real homogeneous output. The average productivity of an active person is p, and the total output available to be distributed among the population is pA. Let M and B denote the average consumption per period by an active and an inactive person. If all output is consumed, the economy faces the resource constraint $pA = MA + BI$. Dividing by A gives $p = M + BD$, where $D = I/A$ is the dependency ratio. An exogenous rise in D through population ageing, with M and B held constant, will create a resources problem if $BdD>dp$, that is to say, if the rise in resources demanded per head of the active population exceeds the rise in productivity. Under these conditions, a higher dependency ratio must result in cuts in the resources per head devoted to the inactive population or the active population or both. The economy is subject to a tightening resource constraint.

While it may capture some aspects of population ageing, the idea of a resources problem has drawbacks. It assumes a binding, real, cross-sectional resource constraint that governs the availability of resources at all times. A rising dependency ratio tightens the constraint, but productivity growth slackens it: a resources problem derives from the former effect outweighing the latter. For an actual economy, however, an aggregate resource constraint is difficult to identify. Economies operating with chronic unemployment and excess capacity are never producing at their full potential and, although output must have a hypothetical upper limit, this limit is unattained and awkward to pin down. As in any real, aggregative approach, the meaning of a homogeneous 'output' or 'resources' remains unclear, and to model an economy as if it were bounded by a fixed stock of real resources is questionable. Labour cannot be a scarce resource if economies retain a permanent pool of underutilized workers. Chronic unemployment and excess capacity might perhaps be thought to reduce the available resources and increase the significance of the resources problem; in a sense this is true, but it also means that current output is determined endogenously and not by exogenous demographic constraints.

The resources problem has the further drawback of being based exclusively on formal economic activity. People not undertaking paid employment have to be classified as economically inactive, irrespective of whether they undertake informal, unpaid activities. Services supplied outside the formal economy receive no credit in standard accounting procedures: a prominent example is the informal care of old people, which is missing from the national accounts but makes a real contribution to the economy. Much the same applies to housework, whose informal character conceals a wide array of productive activities. Implicitly, the national accounts treat informal production as a free good, so that a transfer of economic activities from formal to informal sectors appears as a saving of resources. The resources problem is defined arbitrarily according to incomplete accounting procedures that omit much of importance. Informal services are overlooked, and their providers are often classified not as workers but as inactive dependants. To avoid such an outcome, Williams (1985) suggests obtaining a more accurate view of the system's productive capacity by redefining the resources problem to embrace informal, non-marketed production. This would improve conceptually on the narrower interpretation, but raises the difficult issue of how to deal with informal economic activity, an issue considered more fully in Chapter 8.

The definition of the resources problem assumes that any additional output can be devoted to newly occurring needs: the economy faces a resources problem only if the whole of output growth is insufficient to meet the needs of the growing inactive population. In practice, the whole of any additional output would not be devoted exclusively to the needs of old people. The resources problem is too optimistic in its assumptions about resource allocation: new resources will probably be allocated between the active and inactive populations in roughly the same proportions as existing resources. It follows that, as well as considering the aggregate availability of resources, one has to consider distribution.

Transfer Problems

A transfer problem arises if the extra resources demanded by the growing inactive population cannot be met without reducing the share of total output going to the active population (Paish and Peacock, 1954;

Williams, 1985). In the previous model, suppose that the total output pA is divided such that apA goes to the active population and $(1-a)pA$ to the inactive $(0<a<1)$. If output is equally divided within the active and inactive groups, then each active person receives ap and each inactive person $(1-a)p/D$. Policy makers aiming to uphold the living standards of the inactive can adopt either an absolute or relative approach: they can set either a minimum guaranteed real income for the inactive or a fixed proportional relation between the real incomes of the active and inactive. The former case corresponds to an income maintenance safety net, the latter to the avoidance of poverty defined relative to average incomes. Assume initially that the aim is to preserve a minimum consumption per period of B for each member of the inactive population. The aggregate resource constraint is $pA = apA + BI$. Dividing by A and rearranging gives $(1-a)p = BD$. An exogenous rise in D, with a and B held constant, will create a transfer problem if $BdD > (1-a)dp$, that is, if the additional resources required by the inactive exceed the resources available to them from productivity growth. Substituting from the resource constraint, one can rewrite the inequality as $dD/D > dp/p$, and so a transfer problem occurs if the proportional growth rate of the dependency ratio exceeds that of productivity. Under these conditions, B can be maintained only by reducing a and thus the active population's share of total output. Assuming that all incomes originally accrue to the active population, the proportion of incomes transferred to the inactive is equal to $1-a$ and increases as a falls. Producers must make a growing proportional sacrifice of real income, even though their net real incomes may still be rising.

The likelihood of a transfer problem increases when the aim is to maintain the relative consumption levels of the inactive population. Let b denote the ratio between the incomes of the inactive and active, so that $b = (1-a)/aD$. As D rises, the only way for b to stay constant is for a to fall, regardless of what is happening to p. The need to raise the consumption of the inactive in proportion to that of the active nullifies any productivity increases. When p is rising, the active population may well be enjoying rising living standards, but if D is also rising and b is constant, they must be sacrificing a higher proportion of their incomes in transfers to the inactive population. The conclusion from this simple model is that for constant absolute living standards of the inactive a transfer problem arises only if D increases proportionally faster than p, but for constant relative living standards it arises in all cases where D increases.

Policy responses can be illustrated diagrammatically using a transfer possibilities line (Preston, 1988). If the average contribution to the inactive by each active person is expressed as C, such that $C = (1-a)p$, then the budget constraint can be written as $C = DB$. With C plotted on the vertical axis and *B* on the horizontal axis, the budget constraint gives a linear relation between *C* and *B*, of slope *D*. This is the transfer possibilities line, which shows the contributions by the active population required to sustain any given consumption level for the inactive. Under population ageing, the dependency ratio *D* rises and the transfer possibilities line rotates upwards from T_1 to T_2, as in Figure 2.1.

Policy makers have to decide the best adjustment path in response to population ageing from a starting point *A* on T_1 to a final point on T_2. There are four main possibilities. Path α holds contributions fixed, on the assumption that the members of the active population may only be willing to contribute a fixed total sum. It favours younger over older generations and the active over the inactive, because the living standards of the inactive are certain to fall in both absolute and relative terms, whereas the active may be contributing a smaller proportion of rising real incomes. Path β maintains the relative living standards of the inactive population, so that *B* is a constant proportion *b* of the incomes of the active. Consequently, $B = bap$ and $C = p - B/b$. Assuming that productivity *p* stays constant, path β must follow a northeasterly direction along a straight line of slope $-1/b$. The desire to preserve equity ensures that adjustment costs are shared, with both active and inactive groups facing a fall in their living standards. Path γ holds *B* fixed and thus protects the living standards of the inactive. It favours older over younger generations, because contributions by the active rise and, for constant productivity, their incomes fall relative to those of the inactive. If productivity is

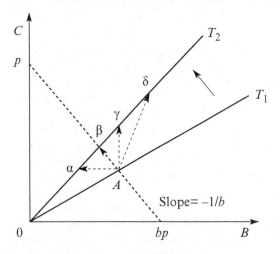

Figure 2.1 The transfer possibilities line

increasing, however, the higher contributions of the active need not imply a falling relative income: a productivity rise may well mean that the incomes of the inactive can stay constant and at a constant proportion b of the incomes of the inactive. Path δ combines higher incomes for the inactive with higher contributions from the active and is the one that Preston (1988) observed in his empirical data for the USA. He interpreted this as being exceptionally generous to older generations, since it offers them higher real incomes during a period of population ageing and magnifies the rise in contributions by the active population. Productivity rises could lessen the apparent inequity and, if sufficiently large, could still result in the living standards of the active remaining constant or rising relative to those of the inactive. Policies that preserve constant relative living standards must, nevertheless, create a transfer problem as they require the active to contribute a higher proportion of their incomes.

The idea of the transfer problem, like the resources problem, has drawbacks. It shares with the resources problem the implicit assumption of full employment; an economy operating below full employment can alleviate any transfer problem by increasing economic activity and providing work for the unemployed. The transfer problem is also defined in real terms and depicts transfers as if they convey real, physical output from active producers to inactive non-producers. In reality there is no transfer of a clump of homogeneous physical output, and transfers are effected through monetary rather than real measures. The government implements the most visible transfers through the tax system, compelling the active to forgo some of their purchasing power in order to finance the public pensions and welfare benefits of the inactive. Even here it may be difficult to know what transfer has been made: nobody records a separate old-age budget that relates the contributions of the currently active population to expenditures on the dependent elderly. Tax payments are by no means perfectly correlated with economic activity. Many payments come from unearned incomes unassociated with employment or with any participation or interest in business. Beneficiaries of large unearned incomes are frequently outside the labour force (perhaps elderly themselves) and therefore non-producers according to employment-based criteria. They are net recipients of real goods and services but net contributors to tax revenues. The contradictions between real and monetary measures can cause confusion over what is meant by a transfer of resources.

Transfer problems, as commonly defined, have omitted informal economic activity. Ever since Paish and Peacock (1954), policy commentators have emphasized transfers through the tax system and neglected resource transfers carried out informally and unrecorded in the national accounts. They have underestimated the full extent of resource transfers and directed their attention exclusively at formal economic activities. By such criteria, switching an activity from the formal to the informal sector must reduce recorded costs and relieve the transfer problem (and any resources problem), even if real costs have increased. The remedy for the neglect of informal activities would be to embody them in the definition of the transfer problem. There is no obvious informal counterpart to tax rates. If population ageing brings about higher taxes, then this is visible and known to all: the budgetary transfers and greater burdens on taxpayers are readily quantifiable. Informal activities are far less visible and adjust only through complex, piecemeal changes with no monetary yardstick and a much less uniform impact on the population as a whole. Williams (1985) suggests recasting the transfer problem to encompass all economic activity, including the informal economy. The transfer problem would then properly account for the real costs borne by the informal economy and concern itself with the total welfare losses from rising dependency, not just the greater burdens on taxpayers. This augmented transfer problem offers a superior analytical framework to the narrower version, but its huge informational requirements hinder its practical application.

In defence of the traditional emphasis on monetary variables, one can argue that they are important because they directly influence behaviour. The transfer problem is significant because it shows up the effects of ageing on individuals and social groups. It is not intended to raise fundamental questions about the ultimate consequences of ageing and is only an intermediate step in a longer argument passing from demographic changes via the transfer problem to further individual and group responses. The implications of population ageing for economic welfare hinge on these further responses. Because individuals and groups in general respond only to what is observable, there may be a case for limiting the transfer problem to its more manageable, monetary form, the form perceived by economic agents. A more comprehensive assessment of welfare effects allowing for informal economic activity could then be made separately from the transfer problem at a later stage, without being incorporated in the definition of the transfer problem itself. The main behavioural responses to the transfer problem are the disincentive effects of higher taxes and the intergenerational conflicts over attempts to introduce higher taxes. These responses are interrelated, though they are often seen as being distinct and unrelated to any transfer problem.

Economic Disincentives

A disincentive occurs when people relax their efforts in response to a reduced reward to their activities. Higher income tax rates causing lower net returns to employment are a classic source of disincentives; other forms of taxation can have similar effects. A generalized definition of a disincentive includes any change in individual behaviour engendered by changes in government policy. Whenever individual motives differ from those of the government, the behavioural responses of individuals will be detrimental to the government's objectives; they result in an outcome inferior to what would have ensued if individual behaviour had remained unchanged. Public policies almost always call forth such responses, unless private and public interests are in perfect harmony. Government and individuals have an incentive compatibility problem, and individual behaviour will at least partially offset the government's policy activities. According to this general formulation, a disincentive may not be a reduction of efforts following a reduction of rewards; any individual response to government policy will constitute a disincentive. To attain their objectives, governments must anticipate and accommodate disincentive effects when designing their policy.

Population ageing creates disincentives chiefly through the need to raise taxes in order to finance public pensions and social services. The individualistic approach of neoclassical economics revolves around the responses of individuals to changes in their tax rates. The main concerns are whether higher taxes have adverse effects on labour supply, work effort, savings, and investment. A fall in labour supply or work effort would reduce the productivity of the working population and damage its capacity to support the growing numbers of dependent elderly. It might still be desirable to raise taxes as the population ages, but severe disincentives would encourage the government to consider alternative approaches, such as cuts in public pensions and social services or measures to raise the capabilities of old people. A fall in savings or investment might slow down capital accumulation and decrease the capital available per worker, thereby holding back productivity growth. As with labour supply disincentives, strong saving or investment disincentives should prompt governments to think more carefully about the alternatives to higher taxation. Strictly speaking, the expected direction of most disincentive effects is ambiguous because economic theory does not generate definite predictions. One might, for instance, expect that higher taxes would curtail the rewards to labour and reduce labour supply, but in theory they could also under certain conditions raise labour supply. Given the theoretical ambiguity, the onus falls on empirical work to establish the existence, direction and magnitude of tax disincentives. A large empirical literature on disincentives has accrued, which is general in scope and says little specifically about population ageing. Few clear-cut results have been obtained, and the whole topic of disincentives remains contentious. Chapter 3 discusses some of the relevant findings.

The best way to cope with disincentives, assuming that they exist and enough is known about them, is to build them into the policy calculus. A policy maker should design policies that are alert to the behavioural changes they bring about. In neoclassical terminology, this is referred to as a 'second-best' outcome, as it must satisfy behavioural constraints and responses missing from the ideal, 'first-best' case (Ng, 1983, Chapter 9). A second-best outcome is inferior to the first-best but nevertheless a constrained policy optimum attaining efficiency within its own constraints. Where policy makers are unaware of disincentives and omit them from their calculations, they will not reach a policy optimum and the disincentives will cause inefficiency. Adding complex behavioural constraints to economic modelling rapidly makes it analytically intractable. Most theoretical discussion in economics has to be limited to first-best cases or, at most, piecemeal second-best cases derived under highly restrictive simplifying assumptions. A rigorous theoretical resolution of the difficulties posed by particular disincentives or other constraints is normally out of reach. Theoretical work falls back on arbitrary and often implicit simplifying assumptions, which create further doubts about the significance of disincentives. Under these circumstances, it is unsurprising (and excusable) that discussion of disincentives has proved inconclusive.

Individualistic disincentives can be criticized as neglecting the institutional setting of individual behaviour. Models of tax disincentives juxtapose a government raising tax revenue with a population of individual taxpayers responding to government policy. Firms, or any other social institutions apart from the government, are usually absent, and attention is confined to interactions between individuals and the government. This is a restrictive framework, as much public policy affects individuals only through their employers or other intermediate institutions. With labour supply disincentives, for instance, individuals can rarely make a smooth, flexible choice of working hours; employers typically offer work in an all-or-nothing package of a given number of hours per week. Many people have little discretion over their working hours or conditions, which remain constant in the short term and leave scant leeway for disincentive effects. Fixed working hours reduce the magnitude of disincentives, especially over a short time horizon. In the longer term, people can influence their working hours by changing jobs or taking part-time work, but the range of possibilities still depends on their institutional surroundings. Changes in working time emerge from a complex institutional process that may not be responsive to marginal changes in tax rates. With saving disincentives, too, individual behaviour is institutionalized: most people save through a formal saving or pension scheme that sets aside a fixed proportion of their income each period. The scope for marginal

changes in saving behaviour is limited, and many people do not make conscious saving decisions on a day-to-day basis; marginal tax changes can
have an effect only in the longer term. Another complication is the weak
link between saving and investment. From a Keynesian perspective, investment decisions rely chiefly on the expectations of businessmen about
future market sizes and are largely independent of saving behaviour.
Population ageing might influence investment through anticipated changes
in market size, but not through the individualistic mechanisms envisaged
by the neoclassical economic literature. Disincentives depend on the institutional context of individual behaviour, and models of individual agents
reacting to government policy are too narrow to allow for this.

Intergenerational Conflict

A possible consequence of population ageing and rising dependency
ratios is a growing awareness of intergenerational equity. Social policy
measures have not sought to preserve uniform treatment among generations, and some generations may well have fared better than others. This
has recently come to the fore in policy discussion, notably in the USA
where commentators such as Preston (1984) have remarked on the differ-
ing treatment of the young and old within the welfare system. The
inconsistencies may not have arisen by design, but they may still be a
cause for concern and a reason for welfare reform. Discussion of intergenerational equity in the USA has brought forth a new 'politics of
ageing', with each generation supposedly having its own interests and its
own pressure groups to promote them (Longman, 1987). Old people are
represented by groups like the Gray Panthers, which campaign for more
generous pensions and social services, and the younger generations by
groups like Americans for Generational Equity, which campaign for cuts
in pension and welfare payments. Future population ageing will, it
seems, occur in an environment where intergenerational equity is a more
sensitive matter than it has been previously. As the elderly population
expands, the shares of national income and total public spending going
to older age groups will rise, and the tax payments of younger generations will have to finance this. Such distributional changes may cause
tensions between age groups as the younger generations become aware of
the burdens they must bear. Pensions and social services rest on an
implicit intergenerational contract whereby the young meet the needs of
the current elderly generation on condition that, when they in turn are
elderly, the next generation will meet their needs. If population ageing
aggravates intergenerational conflict, then younger generations might
breach the intergenerational contract and refuse to finance the public

pensions and social services of the elderly. The desire to avoid tax increases might give rise to a political disincentive alongside the economic disincentives based on labour supply or work effort.

Some recent commentary on population ageing has suggested that intergenerational equity is one of the most important issues in government policy and that a new intergenerational conflict paradigm should be established (Johnson, Conrad and Thomson, 1989; Thomson, 1991, 1992; Kessler, 1996). The belief is that people are becoming more age-conscious and beginning to act as generational interest groups; age now stands alongside the other characteristics, such as class, race and gender, that create social divisions, and so the old intergenerational contract is in danger. The idea of an intergenerational contract draws an analogy with the family, in which the adults of working age support children and the elderly. Support provided within the family may sometimes have been founded on notions of reciprocity or duty as opposed to the purest altruism, but it does at least acknowledge a mutual dependence between generations. The ties with the previous and next generations are ties with the past and future that encourage a longer term outlook in public and private decision making. Once generations are perceived as interest groups, these ties are weakened and may be severed. A conflict perspective gives little credence to the obligations on which families and the welfare state have traditionally relied and foresees greater uncertainties about future social provision. It also means that appeals to intergenerational equity are unlikely to be based on the ethical assessments of a disinterested outside observer and depend instead on the subjective attitudes of the various age groups in society, who may be acting largely from self-interest with little concern for altruism or equity. Older generations will fight to preserve their welfare entitlements, while younger generations, goaded by self-interest or perceived intergenerational unfairness, could try to break the implicit intergenerational contract underlying the welfare state.

Many developed countries have, it is claimed, created inequity among age groups by favouring a particular cohort that reached adulthood in the twenty or so years after the Second World War (Thomson, 1989, 1991). This age group, dubbed the 'welfare generation', benefited as children and parents from the early years of the welfare state and the generous post-war welfare provision for the young. They entered work during a period of high employment and rapid economic growth, experienced high and rising living standards and, largely because of increased female labour force participation, chose to have smaller families than previous generations. Now that they are approaching retirement, they expect to receive generous support from a welfare state financed by smaller generations at a time of chronic recession and unemployment. Despite its benevolent facade, the welfare state has ignored intergenerational equity and favoured one generation above all others. The conflicting interests of generations are reputedly becoming widely recognized and acted upon. Younger generations are tempted to disband public support for old people, return to private provision, and so put an end to the implicit intergenerational contract. As a result the welfare state could become a single-generation phenomenon, captured and exploited by the 'welfare generation' and then abandoned, perhaps for good, by the next. Recent welfare cutbacks in many developed countries can be seen in this light. The faltering political will to sustain the welfare state may be the start of a backlash against the relative prosperity of some old people. Belief in a welfare state that implements intergenerational redistribution may wither away to be replaced by a more individualistic approach holding people responsible for their own incomes in old age. The haphazard, unplanned demise of the welfare state can be prevented, so the argument goes, only if we reappraise and renegotiate intergenerational equity in a planned fashion. What is needed is a constructive rather than destructive awareness of intergenerational redistribution; generational effects, in this view, should be the hub of social policy.

To facilitate assessments of intergenerational equity, some authors have proposed that generational accounting should replace the conventional deficit accounting approach to constructing public budgets (Auerbach, Gokhale and Kotlikoff, 1991, 1994; Kotlikoff, 1992). Generational accounts provide a present-value estimate of the net taxes paid by a typical member of each generation now and in the future. The aim is to take a long-run view of fiscal planning, so that the financial implications of current policy decisions are fully appreciated. This could permit more even treatment of young and old, as it clarifies whether public pension, health care and social security arrangements are imposing heavy fiscal burdens on younger people. Calculations by Auerbach, Gokhale and Kotlikoff (1994) for the USA do indeed suggest that old people have a surplus on their generational account and younger people have a deficit. A government rectifying the apparent inequity between generations would have to cut public spending on the elderly. In practice, generational accounts may be too partial and unreliable to be a satisfactory basis for equity assessments. They concentrate only on present and future taxes and transfers, ignoring past contributions (unless specifically recalculated to include them); they restrict themselves chiefly to monetary payments and benefits, obscuring any real, non-monetary benefits; they are highly sensitive to the choice of discount rate when calculating present values and to dubious assumptions about future events and budgetary procedures; they dwell only on the immediate financial effects of policy changes without allowing for behavioural responses to policy; and, like other forms of accounting, they are based on particular definitions and conventions, so it is unclear why they should be granted a unique significance over and above any other procedures (Haveman, 1994). The difficulties with generational accounts are substantial, and claims that all accounts should be presented in this way have to be viewed with scepticism. Generational accounting is one approach among others; it may be relevant when generational matters are the focus of attention but not necessarily otherwise.

There is room for doubt about the whole concept of intergenerational equity. A key problem is how to define a generation. As Daniels (1989) observes, the word 'generation' can describe either an age group living at a particular time in a particular place or a birth cohort living through its full life cycle. Equity among age groups is ethically distinct from equity among birth cohorts, but they must be addressed simultaneously and continuously. In most of the literature on intergenerational conflict, the main concern is with equity among birth cohorts, assessed by estimating the net lifetime welfare benefits to typical members of each cohort. An alternative approach would give priority to equity among age groups by determining from the outset what is considered to be an equitable distribution of resources over the life cycle (Daniels, 1988, 1989). Most people now live through all the major stages of the life cycle, and any differences between age groups will not produce large differences of individual experience: gains at one stage of the life cycle will offset losses at another. Policy makers can concentrate on finding the best allocation of resources over the life cycle and, correspondingly, among age groups alive at any given time. Equity among birth cohorts is secondary, although it might be desirable to maintain a roughly constant benefit–cost ratio for each cohort so as to forestall any perceived inequalities among cohorts. Intergenerational transfers, in this view, should be a means of ensuring a stable solution of the age-group equity problem and not an equity issue in their own right.

Critics of the intergenerational conflict (or equity) approach have argued that it is politically motivated and fulfils an ideological function (Minkler, 1986; Binney and Estes, 1988; Quadagno, 1989; Minkler and Robertson, 1991; Walker, 1990, 1996; Marmor, Smeeding and Green, 1994; Vincent, 1996). Discussion of intergenerational conflict pays special heed to pensions and social security. The desire for reduced public expenditure often eclipses any concerns over intergenerational matters, and the literature effectively becomes part of a wider argument about the economic role of the state. A growing 'burden' created by population ageing presents a dramatic, highly visible and apparently obvious reason to reduce the generosity of public pension and social security arrangements. The political case for privatizing welfare can be concealed behind the seemingly objective need to curtail public support for old people as the dependency ratio rises. Free-market doctrine can be toned down, because a movement towards laissez-faire can be justified as a 'common-sense' response to the changing age distribution. The 'crisis' of intergenerational conflict may be only a new rhetorical device in the long-standing debate on public intervention in the economy. Inflated concerns about intergenerational equity may be nothing more than a spin-off of the resurgence of libertarianism, with its laissez-faire outlook and suspicion of collectivist ideals.

If the state retreats from providing services for old people, then more weight falls on the private intergenerational relationships within families (Walker, 1996). Assistance for the old is transferred from public sources based on tax-financed pensions and social services to private sources based on unpaid informal care. Those who claim that population ageing will destroy the public version of the intergenerational contract often seem willing to assume that the private version will stay intact and that families will step in to replace the missing public services. It remains unexplained why intergenerational tensions will affect the public sector so badly and yet have much less effect on the private relationships within families. A more consistent position would be to argue either that intergenerational conflict will undermine both public and private relations between age groups, in which case a switch from public to private activities would not resolve the problem, or that it will have a minimal effect on both public and private relations, in which case a switch from public to private activities would be irrelevant. Critics of the intergenerational conflict approach have accused it of exaggerating tensions between age groups over public expenditure while ignoring the private, informal activities vital for old people. This one-sided view is another instance of economists' habitual neglect of informal economic activity. It can also be construed as an ideologically motivated ploy to overstate the difficulties in the public sector and promote privatized 'solutions'.

The intergenerational conflict approach can be presented in a different light, as helping to protect the welfare state and guarantee its long-run future (Thomson, 1989). According to this argument, intergenerational conflict will intensify spontaneously as the population ages, and policy makers should anticipate it and make appropriate adjustments to welfare measures. Otherwise conflict might increase until the whole public welfare system is threatened with collapse. Awareness of intergenerational conflict could offer a way to shore up the welfare state, even if social policies might have to be scaled down to manageable proportions. The worries over intergenerational conflict can therefore be portrayed as a defence of the welfare state, rather than a case for wholesale privatization. It is a matter of interpretation whether the defence of a diminished welfare state is really a defence at all and whether partial and total dismantling of public services are essentially distinct from each other. Such a 'defence' of the welfare state regards intergenerational conflict as having arisen of its own accord; this overlooks the ideological functions of the policy discussion in widening the divisions between age groups and hence contributing to the difficulties it is said to be resolving. Whatever the motives (hidden or open) of commentators on population ageing, one has to be conscious that policy responses to ageing do have ideological implications and that the discussion of intergenerational conflict is set within a broader context of economic, political and social debate.

Empirical studies of intergenerational transfers have not produced unanimous results, and the size of any transfers from young to old remains uncertain. Defined comprehensively, intergenerational transfers can be private as well as public. Transfers can be made publicly through retirement pensions and social services or privately through borrowing and lending, saving and dissaving, and any gifts or bequests within families. The typical life cycle starts with welfare benefits and net borrowing during childhood and early adulthood, which permit current consumption to exceed income and imply a transfer from older to younger generations, and ends with pensions and dissaving during retirement, which imply a transfer in the opposite direction from younger to older generations. Transfers occur in both directions and the net outcome is uncertain, though population ageing should swing the balance towards transfers to the retired elderly. Empirical studies have attempted to identify the net direction of total (public and private) intergenerational transfers: the general conclusion is that total transfers are from young to old and that the average age of consumption is greater than the average age of production (Lee and Lapkoff, 1988; Ermisch, 1989). The total transfer is lower if non-market activities such as household services and education are included in the assessment. When discussing intergenerational conflict, the visible public transfers through the welfare state may be more relevant than private ones, as they are the immediate source of political tensions over tax rates. Public transfers, like private ones, can go in either direction: the young are net gainers from educational expenditures, while the old are net gainers from public retirement pensions and health care. Empirical studies of public intergenerational transfers have been less conclusive than might have been expected from the intergenerational conflict literature. Hills (1992, 1995), for example, finds that the direction of transfers for most generations born in the UK during the twentieth century is unclear, and any net gains are insignificant. The only exception is the generation born between 1901 and 1921, who were net gainers from the welfare measures introduced during the 1940s. This is not the cohort most commonly singled out as a 'welfare generation', and later cohorts experiencing the benefits of a mature welfare state have only tended to break even in their contributions and receipts. Preconceptions about large-scale intergenerational transfers of public resources are questionable on empirical grounds.

Further problems stem from the assumption that generations can cohere as collective entities. Within any one birth cohort there are large differences in income and status, often greater than the differences between cohorts. An example is the contrast between those old people with an occupational pension, lifetime savings and inherited wealth, whose standard of living compares favourably with that of the employed, and those with a past history of unemployment and low-paid work, who are dependent on social security benefits and fall at or near the poverty line. Neither group is easily envisaged as belonging to a closely knit cohort of elderly beneficiaries of an overgenerous welfare state. The variations in experience among old people cast doubt on whether the birth cohort should be the chosen unit of social analysis (Easterlin, 1987; Binney and Estes, 1988; Walker, 1990; Phillipson, 1991, 1996). Many variations within cohorts are related to a person's socio-economic background, and divisions by social class may be more meaningful than divisions by age or birth cohort. The age-based organizations that do exist may be merely reacting to structured inequalities rooted in the wider social context (Ginn, 1993). Cohorts can be safely treated as collective entities only if people are conscious of age as a determinant of life chances.

Despite efforts to encourage age-consciousness and promote generational accounting, it is speculative and implausible to regard birth cohorts as cohesive interest groups. An ageing electorate will gradually enhance the political influence of old people, but this will not necessarily be exerted through age-based pressure groups (Wilson, 1993). Societies can be subdivided in a myriad of ways, and to accord birth cohorts pride of place seems arbitrary. Age distinctions have existed in every society, so the belief that they are becoming more important requires some justification. Changing attitudes to age, a cultural matter, cannot be isolated from their social context. If generations are to become a major component of social scientific explanations, an account of their social formation is needed. As yet, the birth cohort has not been generally accepted as a relevant unit of social analysis, and the intergenerational conflict paradigm remains controversial.

The disparate views of dependency considered here do not amount to a single, unified dependency approach. They have little in common apart from a vision of a population dichotomized into dependent and independent groups that change in relative size as the population ages. The best argument for an 'economics of dependency' is if some formally defined concept of dependency is held to be intrinsically undesirable: dependency then has its own direct role in evaluating the effects of population ageing. Dependency is rarely given such fundamental significance. When neoclassical economists make general welfare assessments, they usually base them on individual utilities or a social welfare function; a separate concept of dependency is redundant. If dependency is undesirable because of its adverse consequences, and not because of its intrinsic properties, then there is scope for dropping the term 'dependency', together with dependency and support ratios. The pejorative overtones of dependency ensure that it can never be a wholly neutral term and will always be emotive and controversial. For some purposes, such as dramatizing population ageing as a crisis, this emotive quality may be helpful; for others, such as explaining and understanding the effects of population ageing, it is unhelpful.

3. Population ageing and neoclassical economics

Mainstream economics abides by the neoclassical tradition that dates from the late nineteenth century. The economic literature and the number of economists have expanded enormously since then, but the predominant theoretical method still grounds itself squarely on neoclassical principles. The recent growth of the discipline has involved greater use of mathematics and statistics, rather than greater diversity of theory. As a result, economics is sometimes identified with a particular approach founded on rational individual behaviour and market-clearing equilibrium; other approaches are regarded as alien and non-economic. Some authors avow that the 'economic approach to human behaviour' has true generality and can be applied successfully in areas well outside the usual remit of economics (Becker, 1976, 1993; Hirshleifer, 1985). An approach with such universal validity would be expected to shed light on the issues raised by population ageing. To say that there is a well-defined neoclassical 'economics of population ageing' would be an overstatement, but certain sections of neoclassical economics are widely believed to be relevant to population ageing and a valuable aid to evaluating policy. The present chapter considers this literature and discusses it critically; the next chapter considers alternatives to neoclassical economics.

CHARACTERISTICS OF THE NEOCLASSICAL APPROACH

The defining characteristics of neoclassical economics are individualism, rational behaviour, and market-clearing equilibrium. Individualism sets out the fundamental vision of society and determines the nature of the theory. Theorizing starts at the bottom with individual behaviour and then seeks to explain social outcomes as emanating from interactions between individuals. The individual thus becomes the building block of theorizing. Explanations that do not reduce things to the individual level are regarded as unsatisfactory and 'ad hoc': they breach the principle that human behaviour and institutions originate in the actions of individuals.

Economists rarely make an explicit case for individualism and usually presuppose it without further discussion. The implicit case, however, is that it represents a liberal standpoint and guarantees against collectivist and authoritarian extremes; only individuals have preferences and there is no such thing as a 'social will' distinct from the wishes of individuals. This approach has the disadvantages of separating the individual from society and neglecting the role of culture and social conditioning in fashioning individual attitudes (Jackson, 1993). Anxious to avoid a collectivist extreme, it goes to the opposite extreme – an individualistic reductionism – and bypasses the middle ground between the extremes. It has been less influential in other social sciences (notably sociology) than in economics and is by no means generally accepted as essential for social-scientific explanation (Hodgson, 1986). Social theorists (if not economists) have endlessly debated individualism, and their inability to reach a consensus around individualistic or collective explanations might be taken to imply that both can have explanatory power.

The second characteristic, rationality, is a property of individual behaviour. Individuals are portrayed as maximizing an objective function: the standard objective is to attain the highest possible utility, which is a general-purpose goal for all individual behaviour. Rationality takes an instrumental form such that individual actions are a means to the end of producing utility. The chief argument for instrumental rationality is that it can summarize the particular behaviour found in economic transactions. Its adoption as an axiom of economic theory permits elaborate economic models to be constructed from simple and elegant behavioural postulates. Against this, instrumental rationality (like individualism) can be seen as an excessively narrow basis for economic or social theory, giving an impoverished account of human agency. Individuals are assumed to respond mechanically to external events, in a manner perfectly predictable once their objective function has been specified. This may not be a proper account of individual agency, if agency denotes the possession of free will or the ability to do otherwise (Loasby, 1976; de Uriarte, 1990). Instrumental rationality also ignores the limitations on the individual's ability to act efficiently or independently. People may lack the information and computational skills required to behave as if they are continuously maximizing an objective function; instead, it may be more plausible to depict behaviour as 'satisficing' (Simon, 1957). Habits, rules of thumb and social norms may develop, and individual behaviour may have a more socialized character than models of instrumental rationality would acknowledge. Normalized behaviour can be viewed as conforming to an alternative, rule-bound, procedural rationality, which differs from the instrumental rationality presupposed in neoclassical economics

(Hargreaves Heap, 1989). As with individualism, instrumental rationality is an assumption widespread among economists, though there is no consensus among social scientists on its value.

The third characteristic of neoclassical economics is market-clearing equilibrium. A market is defined as a place where rational, self-interested individuals come together to transact to their mutual advantage. Once they have exploited all the opportunities for transactions, the result will be a stable equilibrium with desirable efficiency properties. As long as laissez-faire prevails and individuals are free to make their own transactions, the market will produce the best possible results. Intervention in markets will impede the attainment of efficiency, and attempts to replace markets with planning will founder on informational and computational obstacles; the market offers the only effective, decentralized method of allocating resources among millions of people. Market-clearing equilibrium brings together individualism and rational behaviour to create a complete theoretical system that serves as a benchmark for economic theorizing. A perfectly competitive equilibrium may not be a plausible policy goal, but it provides the universal reference point in neoclassical economics. Elaborations of the competitive model are relegated to the status of special cases, mere deviations from the ideal, while perfect competition has about it an aura of sanctified theoretical generality.

Neoclassical economists use the competitive equilibrium model in contrasting ways, according to the stress they place on market imperfections and divergences from equilibrium. Adherents of the 'economic approach to human behaviour' argue that neoclassical theory has relevance throughout the social sciences and that models displaying the three characteristics of individualism, rational behaviour and market-clearing equilibrium are applicable to all human behaviour, at all times and places, with minimal need for adjustments (Becker, 1976, 1993; Hirshleifer, 1985). Economics, they claim, has little to learn from the other social sciences and should, if anything, be exporting its methods beyond the traditional boundaries of the discipline. Other mainstream economists are less ebullient about neoclassical theory and use it only in a qualified, circumscribed form. Any of the three main characteristics of neoclassical economics can be modified or (temporarily) set aside. Individualism can be set aside if modelling requires a division of the population into homogeneous groups (say, the young and the old when discussing ageing), but rationality and market-clearing assumptions may be retained. Rational behaviour can be relaxed owing to informational problems, especially when long-run decisions are being made. Market-clearing equilibrium can have diminished importance in models where imperfections cause temporary divergences from efficient equilibria, so that special cases take priority over the benchmark case of competitive equilibrium. Between the 'perfectionist' and 'imperfectionist' versions of neoclassicism comes a continuum of shades of opinion about the neoclassical model. The variations on the neoclassical theme are innumerable, and yet a common language of individualism, rationality and market-clearing equilibrium unites this mainstream work.

Neoclassical economics has been fertile in spawning specialisms and sub-disciplines. The list of them is constantly growing: labour economics, international economics, development economics, industrial economics, monetary economics, public economics, environmental economics, health economics, transport economics, urban economics, defence economics, and so on. Most economic specialisms adhere to the same neoclassical approach that dominates economic theory in general. The versatility of neoclassicism discourages customized, 'ad hoc' theorizing; a specialist in an economic sub-discipline is someone who applies neoclassical theory to a specialized subject matter, not someone who produces specialized (potentially non-neoclassical) theory tailored to a particular area. Most economic specialists stay with the mainstream and confine their activities to elaborating neoclassical theory or attempting to apply it empirically. This preserves academic respectability and avoids the risks of espousing non-mainstream theory or formulating new theories and models. Now that the economics discipline has set up an extensive apparatus of specialisms, it can expand its numbers through ever-increasing specialization and at the same time uphold a narrow, unchanging set of core principles that goes largely unchallenged and gives economics its unity and identity. Economists become preoccupied with their own specialism and have little need or incentive to raise more fundamental questions about the discipline as a whole.

Until recently, population economics did not appear in the list of economic specialisms. From Malthus onwards, many economists have discussed population, but their work has been disparate and has not coalesced into a distinct sub-discipline called population economics. Within the last ten years or so, attempts have been made to rectify this omission: there is now, for instance, a European Society for Population Economics (founded in 1987) and a *Journal of Population Economics* (first published in 1988). Population economics seems to be following the familiar pattern of becoming another variant on the neoclassical theme; its interests and methods are those of the economic mainstream (van Praag, 1988). Indeed, much work in population economics (notably on fertility) has been informed by Becker's 'economic approach to human behaviour' and takes a stringently neoclassical line that obscures social and cultural ('non-economic') considerations. The growth of population economics has been a mixed blessing, in that it has stimulated interest in demographic matters but sanctioned a particular, narrow mode of analysis. The upshot may, unfortunately, be the creation of a neoclassical orthodoxy within population economics, which makes it harder for non-neoclassical approaches to gain acceptance.

Mainstream population economics faces the difficulty that neoclassical methods were never intended to cope with demographic change. Population problems are, by their nature, at an aggregative, macroeconomic level and occur in a long-run, historical setting; neoclassical economics operates at a disaggregated, microeconomic level and frequently adopts static, timeless models. Certain demographic topics, such as fertility, lend themselves quite well to neoclassical treatment, hence the prominence of economic theories of fertility within population economics. Other topics, population ageing among them, are less amenable to the neat application of neoclassical methods. As economic specialization proceeds, the economics of ageing ought to become a subset of the sub-discipline of population economics. So far, however, there is no definitive mainstream account of individual and population ageing. Neoclassical economics has to overcome or evade several problems before it can analyse ageing. In dealing with individual ageing, for example, the neoclassical abstraction from biological ageing is counterproductive and leaves unclear the relation between age and individual preferences. In dealing with population ageing, a timeless, individualistic approach rules out demographic change and therefore has little value. These problems have hindered the development of a neoclassical account of population ageing and its economic effects. Discussion is fenced into a few areas where neoclassical modelling impinges on individual and population ageing. A common theme to most of the discussion is rational decision making over the individual life cycle, although what would ideally be a complete lifetime plan is subdivided into separate aspects such as saving, labour supply and voting behaviour. The rest of this chapter considers the life-cycle model and its applications to ageing.

LIFE-CYCLE MODELLING

The neoclassical model of individual ('consumer') behaviour, as set out in microeconomics textbooks, represents individual preferences by an undated, single-period utility function, with utility dependent on the consumption of goods. The individual allocates income among goods in each period so as to maximize utility. Because the model is timeless, it cannot depict individual or population ageing, and an extended life-cycle model is required. Interpreted literally, a life-cycle model stretches the time horizon from a single date to the individual's entire lifetime. The desirability of long-term decision making is evident, as nothing can be gained by shortening the time horizon and neglecting long-term considerations. The feasibility of life-cycle planning may, nevertheless, be doubtful. For individuals to maximize their future utility, they must know their future preferences, consumption opportunities, income, employment prospects, health, returns to education, and anything else affecting their utility. Some deficiencies in knowledge about the future are permissible, provided that they take the form of risk, such that a probability can be attached to each possible outcome. Fundamental uncertainty, where probabilities cannot be assessed, is enough to prevent optimizing behaviour. The framework of life-cycle planning presupposes a well-defined lifetime objective and at least probabilistic information on the various constraints and events that may influence utility. These conditions granted, the individual can plan over the full life cycle.

Timeless, single-period models are confined to the spending of a money income on consumption goods. Life-cycle models include a wider range of activities: the individual may sacrifice present consumption in favour of saving or undergo education or training as a means of raising productivity and future earnings. Such decisions have a closer resemblance to investment planning than to daily consumption activities. Early versions of the life-cycle model sought to explain long-run aggregate consumption behaviour (Modigliani and Brumberg, 1954; Ando and Modigliani, 1963; Modigliani, 1975). Since the early 1960s, life-cycle modelling has been linked with the human capital research programme, which makes the analogy with investment explicit (Schultz, 1961). Human capital can be defined as an individual's skills and knowledge, accumulated through education, formal training and informal learning by doing. Investment in human capital need not be undertaken on an individual basis and can be organized centrally by the government, but the neoclassical literature concentrates on rational individual decision making. Becker (1964) is the most commonly cited source for human capital theory and, as the chief advocate of the 'economic approach to human behaviour', he gives the human capital analogy an individualistic slant. The 'human capital research programme' and the 'economic approach to human behaviour' are sometimes treated as synonymous, although the idea of human capital does not in itself dictate an individualistic method. Human capital theory has proved influential and evoked a vast theoretical and empirical literature applying it to various topics.

How well suited is life-cycle modelling to the analysis of ageing? Ageing and life-cycle modelling do share a time horizon covering a person's full life span, but neoclassical theory, whether in its timeless or intertemporal guise, provides no account of the ageing process. Individual utility functions are black boxes, given from the outset, that generate an output of utility from inputs of goods in a known, predictable manner. The relation between utility functions and biological ageing or social structure goes undiscussed, and theorizing about individuals abstracts from their biological and social context. Biological ageing might, for instance, be an external, physical constraint on people's true psychic desires as represented by their utility functions; preferences might be invariant over time but, other things being equal, people's behaviour would still change in response to the tightening physical restrictions that ageing imposes upon them. On the other hand, utility could be interpreted more generally, so that it embodies biological ageing; preferences themselves would change as the person ages, and behaviour would change accordingly. Economic theory avoids these matters and takes a given intertemporal utility function as its starting point without delving into the connection between utility and human biology or social conditions (Jackson, 1991b). The theory is so empty of detail that it is difficult to set out precise points for or against it, unless one objects to its emptiness as a lack of explanatory power.

What intertemporal decision making does entail is people's ability to reach decisions in one period that govern their activities many periods in the future. They formulate a perfect life-cycle plan at the start of their life cycle, which reduces their life to the playing out of a preordained scheme. Individual decision making implodes into a single instant, yielding an abstract notion of ageing in which time is merely a logical progression that can be readily coped with through earlier plans and decisions. Plans may have to be revised or implemented only in probabilistic form, but the efficacy of individual planning nevertheless requires the ability to act now to make reliable arrangements for the future. This places a heavy weight on people's knowledge of the future and the stability of their preferences and identity. Neoclassical economists defend the life-cycle model on the grounds that probabilistic methods can model all types of uncertainty (ruling out the fundamental uncertainty that dispenses with probabilities) and that it is not the task of economics to address the biological or social processes of ageing. As a last resort, they can defend the model on instrumentalist lines, by presenting it as an instrument for generating predictions, rather than an explanatory theory in its own right (Friedman, 1953). Such views are commonplace, though most mainstream economists would probably claim that their theories have an explanatory function. Whatever its aims, the life-cycle model implies a strong faith in individuals being able to plan over a long future time horizon.

Suppose that a population is composed entirely of rational, utility maximizing life-cycle planners who make rational decisions covering their full life span. What are the consequences of this for government policy? As one might expect, government policy is severely restricted in scope. Individuals can look after their own saving decisions and have no need for the state to organize them centrally. Leaving people to their own devices will be efficient, and public intervention will merely distort private decisions and incur unnecessary administrative and transaction costs. Under market-clearing assumptions, prices adjust smoothly to accommodate demographic changes and ensure continuous economic efficiency. The age distribution is of little interest, and there is no reason to regard population ageing as a cause of economic problems requiring corrective policies. Specific public responses to population ageing are superfluous, and fears about a demographic crisis are misguided. Concern for equity might stimulate redistributive policies, which might be influenced by changing cohort sizes and thus appear to be a response to population ageing, but even here the efficient mode of intervention would redistribute lifetime incomes through lump-sum transfers (so as to permit the efficient functioning of markets) and would be independent of a person's age. Any disincentive problems from the redistributive measures would be caused by the obstacles to redistribution, not the population's age composition. Changing cohort sizes may give grounds for wanting to redistribute income, but they are not responsible for the difficulties in implementing redistribution. An idealized neoclassical model endorses laissez-faire policies, and adding an ageing population does nothing to change the laissez-faire rule.

A more robust case for state intervention can result only from relaxing the assumptions that underpin the basic life-cycle planning approach (Diamond, 1977; Kessler, 1989). If individuals are at least partially myopic or ill-informed about future economic conditions and unable or reluctant to plan, then it may be advantageous for a paternalistic government to take over the planning role. Even if individuals are rational and well-informed, they may still find it difficult to plan their life-cycle consumption and saving efficiently because of imperfections in the labour and capital markets. Restricted access to employment or capital may hamper life-cycle planning and justify government intervention to offset the imperfections. People in developed countries are bound by external constraints on their life-cycle planning; formal full-time education and retirement mean that the basic structure of their lifetime activity has already been determined from without. Life-cycle modelling can reflect the institutional setting of individual behaviour by taking an imperfectionist form in which people are subject to external constraints such as formal pension schemes, statutory retirement ages and fixed working hours. This has the advantage of portraying individual decisions more accurately, but is silent about why the formal pension and retirement schemes were introduced in the first place. Most applications of the life-cycle model deal with only one particular aspect of lifetime planning, usually either individual saving or labour supply.

INDIVIDUAL SAVING

In a single-period model, rational consumers spend all their current income and save nothing; in a many-period life-cycle model, they can save or borrow to redistribute consumption over time. The choice of an opti-mal lifetime consumption and saving profile depends partly on intertemporal preferences and partly on income and other constraints. A person whose preferences are stable over the life cycle and who receives a constant income per period has little need for large-scale borrowing or saving. Most people do not have constant incomes and experience signifi-cant earnings variations during their lifetimes. In the early phase of the life cycle, when a person is undergoing education and training, earnings are low but on a rising path as skills and knowledge accumulate. Earnings normally rise or stay constant during employment, but manual workers dependent on physical strength may suffer a fall in earnings as their human capital depreciates with age. On retirement, earnings from employment decline to zero, and people have to finance their consump-tion from savings or pension receipts. The typical life-cycle income pattern is hump-shaped, with rising incomes reaching a peak at or near to retirement and then falling back in the retirement phase.

Spending may display a similar hump-shaped pattern. Certain expen-ditures, such as those associated with education, arise in the early phase of the life cycle; others, such as those associated with raising a family, arise in the middle of the life cycle. Spending on education and household formation will generally precede the earnings maximum attained towards the end of a person's working life. Figure 3.1 depicts the expected life-cycle patterns of income, expenditure and saving. The typical person should start with a period of dissaving (income lower than expenditure), then move into a period of saving in the middle of the life cycle (expendi-ture lower than income), and finish in retirement with another period of dissaving. This means that consumption varies less than income over the life cycle, so that saving and borrowing cause a smoothening or flattening of the life-cycle consumption path. As people grow older, they should increase their net saving to reach a peak in late working life and then

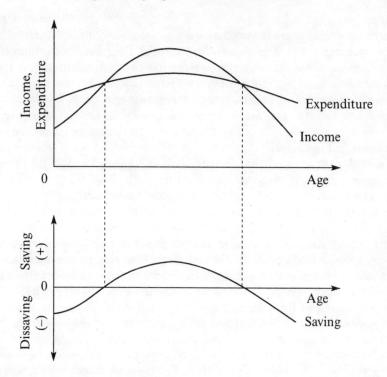

Figure 3.1 Life-cycle saving behaviour

reduce it as they approach and enter retirement. The age-saving profile, like the age-earnings profile, is hump-shaped. Unless they want to leave a bequest, rational individuals with perfect foresight of their date of death will reduce their assets to zero at the end of their life cycle.

Discussion of individual life-cycle behaviour makes no reference to population ageing. If everyone behaves similarly, then it requires only an aggregation of typical individuals to move from individual saving to total saving for the whole economy. With no major changes in individual behaviour or economic conditions, aggregate savings should vary system-atically with the age composition of the population. At the individual level, increasing age will probably raise and then reduce the rate of saving. A changing age distribution for a population of such individuals will have an ambiguous effect on total savings. In an ageing population, total saving could rise if the largest birth cohorts are passing through the middle, saving phase of the life cycle, or fall if they are entering the later, dissaving phase. Strictly speaking, the life-cycle model makes no clear-cut theoretical predictions on the relation between population ageing and aggregate saving: in any particular case, the nature of the relation depends on preferences, incomes and the age distribution. Nevertheless, the presumption is often that the influence of the retired age groups will predominate and that aggregate saving will fall as the population ages. According to neoclassical theory, a fall in saving will, via the capital market, bring higher interest rates, lower investment and a slowing down of economic growth. An ageing population could raise average needs, while simultaneously putting a brake on the economy's productivity growth and threatening its ability to meet these needs. Such an argument assumes that ageing depresses individual and aggregate saving, and that aggregate saving is linked with investment.

The relation between age and individual saving comes prior to that between the population's age composition and aggregate saving. If old people show little inclination to dissave, then fears about a fall in aggregate saving are misplaced. Whether old people are reluctant to save can only be discerned empirically. An extensive literature on life-cycle saving behaviour has accumulated, without producing a consensus on the age-saving relationship. The initial work on the life-cycle hypothesis by Ando, Modigliani and Brumberg in the 1950s claimed to be empirically well supported, but recent empirical work has been more equivocal. A life-cycle model can be tested using either cross-section data comparing individuals of different ages at the same time, or time-series data comparing the same individuals over time. Cross-section data, more readily available and easier to collect, are less well suited to testing the life-cycle model because there is no control for systematic cohort differences within the cross-section sample. Time-series data, by contrast, can follow a single cohort through its life cycle and thus correspond more closely to the life-cycle model.

Several cross-section studies have contradicted the life-cycle model by showing that the old save as high a proportion of their income as the young and, if anything, are likely to save more (Lydall, 1955; Mirer, 1979; King and Dicks-Mireaux, 1982; Danziger et al., 1982; Blinder, Gordon and Wise, 1983; Menchik and David, 1983; Wiseman, 1989; Börsch-Supan, 1992). These results may be attributed to cohort differences, as opposed to a failure of the life-cycle model, but they suffice at the very least to cast doubt on the reliability of the standard life-cycle assumptions. Empirical work based on time-series data should in principle be more amenable to supporting the life-cycle model. Studies of saving behaviour in the US using time-series data have generally shown that the elderly do dissave, as the theory predicts (Mirer, 1980; Diamond and Hausman, 1984; Bernheim, 1987). Even here, however, certain studies have not supported the life-cycle model (Venti and Wise, 1989).

Hurd (1990), in his review of the empirical literature, puts greater weight on the time-series studies and concludes that on balance the life-cycle view of saving can claim empirical backing: the studies that confirm the model outnumber those that contradict it. The backing is far from unanimous, though, and weaker than one might expect from the prominence of the life-cycle approach.

Empirical, cross-national studies of the macroeconomic relation between aggregate saving and the age distribution have in general found a negative correlation between age and saving: the older the population, the lower the aggregate rate of saving (Weil, 1994; Disney, 1996). This contrasts with the weak relationship observed in individual behaviour and suggests that additional factors may be operating at the macroeconomic level. One possibility is that the old save in order to make bequests to the young, and that when the young anticipate receiving bequests they reduce their saving (Weil, 1994). An ageing population would then increase intergenerational transfers and promote dissaving by the young, not by the old as seems intuitive. When considering aggregate saving rates it may be necessary to look at intergenerational transfers, as well as private consumption, as a motive for individual saving.

In a standard life-cycle model the elderly are assumed not to make bequests; rational self-interested behaviour implies that they should dissave in old age and, if possible, run down their assets to zero at the end of the life cycle. An augmented version of the life-cycle model introduces altruism towards future generations and a bequest motive for saving. This can lead to significant changes in saving behaviour, to the extent that some economists classify the bequest model of saving as being distinct from the life-cycle model (Aaron, 1982). Both models rest on lifetime utility maximization, and they are variants of a common neoclassical approach. The bequest model implies that public retirement pensions need not displace private savings: the elderly might instead wish to increase their bequests and therefore actually increase their saving (Barro, 1974). Appending bequests to the life-cycle model extends the range of behaviour it can embrace and reduces the number of predictions it makes. The empirical doubts about the standard life-cycle model could be seen as indirectly confirming the more complex bequest model. Efforts to test the bequest model directly have proved inconclusive. At face value, the persistence of saving behaviour among the elderly is more consistent with the bequest model than with the standard life-cycle model, and some formal empirical studies have suggested this (Bernheim, 1987, 1991; Kotlikoff, 1988; Gale and Scholz, 1994). Other empirical studies have queried whether bequests can explain saving in old age (Hurd, 1987, 1989; Börsch-Supan and Stahl, 1991). It often transpires, for example, that the elderly with the most children have the least wealth and little scope for leaving substantial bequests. Hence, while there is evidence that people save during old age, this may not be due to a rational bequest motive. The doubts about the bequest motive heighten the general uncertainty about life-cycle planning.

At the aggregate level, public pension schemes are often argued to magnify the depressing effect of ageing on savings. In a life-cycle model the availability of public pensions discourages private saving. If the government finances the public pension scheme from general tax revenues, then the economy's aggregate saving rate will, it is argued, be reduced and so will the rates of investment and economic growth (Feldstein, 1974). Several studies have claimed to demonstrate this empirically (Feldstein, 1976, 1977; Munnell, 1974), while others have been more sceptical (Rosen, 1977; Esposito, 1978; Hemming, 1978; Leimer and Lesnoy, 1982). The argument sounds intuitive, but is not strictly valid. In a steady-state economy with a stable age distribution and zero income growth, saving by the working population (whether voluntary or through funded pension arrangements) exactly balances dissaving by the retired and the young. Aggregate net saving is zero, as with unfunded public pensions, and there is no difference between the public pension scheme and private saving. Because individuals adhere roughly to a life-cycle budget constraint, saving at one point in the life cycle generally means equivalent dissaving at some other point; in a steady-state population the dissavers counterbalance the savers. A funded pension scheme raises aggregate saving when it is still maturing, with more savers than dissavers, but this is first a transitory phenomenon that ceases when the pension scheme reaches maturity. Aggregate saving should be lowest in economies with low economic growth rates (which push down the incomes of working-age savers), ageing populations (which reduce the proportion of working-age savers and raise the proportion of elderly dissavers), and unfunded public pension schemes (which forgo the temporary boost to aggregate saving that would ensue from a maturing system of private, funded pensions). The last of these characteristics – unfunded public pensions – is less general than the others and rests on an arbitrary comparison with partially implemented funded pension schemes.

For developing countries, some economists have claimed that population youthening (not ageing) reduces aggregate saving and curtails investment and economic growth: the preceding argument is turned on its head. This is the view expressed in the Coale–Hoover model of economic development (Coale and Hoover, 1958), which is based on neoclassical life-cycle saving behaviour but, unlike the arguments applied in developed countries, emphasizes the additional dissaving by younger age groups in a youthening population. The model's empirical status has been contentious, because it is difficult to carry out reliable empirical tests in developing countries and the few tests that have been carried out have produced conflicting results (Kelley, 1988). Conceivably, both the Coale–Hoover model and the conventional life-cycle approach could be accurate: in developing countries population ageing could reduce the burden of children and increase aggregate savings, whereas in developed countries it could increase the burden of the elderly and reduce aggregate savings. The contrast between the views should, however, serve as a warning about the dangers of assuming simple unidirectional relationships between population ageing and aggregate saving. Prediction at the aggregate level depends on the validity of the life-cycle model at the individual level, and the empirical doubts about individual behaviour remain relevant.

The second assumption in the argument that population ageing slows down productivity growth is the link between aggregate saving and investment. In neoclassical economics a fall in saving is regarded as a fall in the supply of capital within an equilibrating capital market. Other things being equal, the capital market will attain a new equilibrium with a higher interest rate and lower quantity of capital supplied and demanded each period. Investment will be reduced, and the smaller capital stock (or growth rate of capital) will ensure lower productivity per head. This argument, long queried by Keynesian economists (Keynes, 1936, Chapters 13–15), was a cornerstone of pre-Keynesian, neoclassical macroeconomics, which assumed that a market economy attains full employment without government intervention. A more Keynesian view of the economy has no equilibrating capital market, and divorces investment behaviour from saving. As investment is volatile and independent of other economic considerations, Keynesian modelling treats it as exogenous; what matters is the willingness to invest, as distinct from the availability of capital. Economies typically operate below full capacity, and investors can find the resources and capital they need without capital constraints or interest rates hampering them too much. Population ageing might discourage investment, but if so this would be a direct effect, arising through investors' reduced expectations of market size, not through reduced aggregate savings. Changes in savings rates induced by population ageing are no longer crucial.

The assumption that investment raises productivity also becomes questionable when one moves beyond neoclassical economics. Neoclassical theory presupposes technically efficient production functions that relate inputs of labour and capital per period to outputs of a good. As with the individual utility model, production functions lack internal details and subsume the organization of production in a black-box functional relationship. More capital per unit of labour must, according to the neoclassical view, raise the productivity of labour, resulting in a positive relation between investment and productivity. Outside neoclassical economics, the social aspects of production take on a greater importance: matters such as work intensity, working conditions, hours of work, and employer–worker conflicts come to the fore (Hodgson, 1982). These variable factors, which represent the specific social context of work, weaken the supposedly deterministic relation between investment and productivity. Consequently, all the links in the neoclassical chain between population ageing and productivity – individual life-cycle saving decisions, the aggregation of these saving decisions, the link between aggregate saving and investment, and the link between investment and productivity – are somewhat fragile. Since each link is fragile, the same goes for the chain as a whole.

LABOUR SUPPLY

The life-cycle or human capital approach aims to cover every decision influencing the long-term welfare of a rational individual. Alongside consumption and saving, the model should embrace labour supply, education and training, household formation, fertility, attitudes to health, and any other long-run aspect of the individual's behaviour. A single life-cycle planning decision should bring together all relevant considerations and simultaneously determine education, labour supply, family formation, consumption, and saving; treating the various issues separately would neglect their interrelationships and yield suboptimal behaviour. For reasons of analytical tractability, life-cycle modelling usually addresses only one decision at a time and keeps saving and consumption apart from labour supply and investment in education. Labour supply has become a subject in its own right with an extensive literature, the bulk of which is only peripherally concerned with demographic matters and must be adapted or extended before it can be applied to population ageing.

Behind most labour supply decisions in neoclassical economics is the trade-off between wage earnings and leisure. Under normal assumptions, time spent in work has no intrinsic value but is the main income source for most people. The residual time not spent working appears in the utility function as leisure, and has the status of a good that contributes to utility. Unlike saving decisions, which have to be intertemporal, labour supply decisions are conventionally represented by single-period models of an income/leisure trade-off. This assumes that labour supply decisions are separable between periods. A longer-term approach, better suited to the time scales involved in population ageing, would allow for the intertemporal dimensions of labour supply. Integrating labour supply decisions into a life-cycle saving model gives what is termed 'dynamic labour supply', whereby a person is free to choose labour supply in each period as well as consumption and saving (Weiss, 1972; Ghez and Becker, 1975). An optimal life-cycle plan under these assumptions will have a continuously variable time path of labour supply, unconstrained by fixed working hours or a statutory retirement age.

The optimum lifetime work profile in a dynamic labour supply model depends on preferences, wages, and the availability of unearned income. A person with standard preferences will probably have a pattern of labour supply in which working hours start high and decline smoothly as the future time horizon draws closer. At some point working hours may decrease to zero, and the person can then be said to have retired from work. Retirement in this model is a gradual, continuous process, rather than a discrete jump from work to no work, and bears little resemblance to the abrupt cessation of work that most people experience. Mandatory retirement at a fixed age discords with neoclassical theory, since constraints on rational people's behaviour must make them worse off. A few authors have tried to explain mandatory retirement on neoclassical principles as the outcome of mutually beneficial interactions between individuals and firms (Lazear, 1979; Lapp, 1985; Ippolito, 1991). Alternative views prefer a less individualistic approach and interpret state retirement policies as a means of regulating labour supply (see Chapter 4). Explaining retirement practices goes somewhat beyond the scope of the current discussion, but it is worth noting the contrast between the smooth, gradual retirement observed in dynamic labour supply models, which count as the perfectly flexible neoclassical ideal, and the constrained retirement decisions observed in reality.

When the government and employers enforce a statutory retirement age, some people may have no discretion over their labour supply. If they do have a choice of retirement age, their decision may be confined to a discrete choice between working a fixed number of hours and not working at all. Attention is then diverted away from decisions about working hours to decisions about labour force participation. The design of pension schemes may further constrain rational choice: a common feature is a retirement condition insisting that a person must be retired and not merely above a certain age before the pension is paid. People have to decide whether to continue in work and retire later with a slightly higher pension, or retire now with a lower pension. External constraints such as a statutory retirement age and a retirement condition can be introduced into life-cycle modelling, but they inevitably reduce the role of individual preferences in determining retirement. A binding statutory retirement age artificially raises the significance of a particular age far above what it would have been under unrestricted individual choice. The distribution of the population around this age has serious policy implications, albeit for reasons unconnected with individual labour supply decisions or the bio-logical ageing process.

Where people have some discretion over their retirement date, the neo-classical literature emphasizes the disincentive question: how do pension and social security measures affect individual retirement decisions? In a pure life-cycle model, individuals assess their total social security wealth and include this in the full lifetime wealth used for life-cycle planning. Pensions influence the life-cycle plan to the extent that they alter lifetime wealth, and it is long-term, life-cycle considerations that prevail. Higher public pensions raise social security wealth and thus lifetime wealth, giving individuals an opportunity to combine the same consumption levels with increased leisure time. The labour supply decision will depend on individual preferences, but in most cases higher pensions should encourage earlier retirement and a fall in labour supply. As with models of life-cycle saving, the theory can be tested empirically using cross-section or time-series data, with time-series data again being the better option. The literature is extensive and diverse enough for commentators to have summarized it differently. Boskin (1977) and Campbell and Campbell (1976) identify a conflict between studies giving social security benefits little or no importance in explaining retirement and studies giving them a paramount importance. Mitchell and Fields (1982, 1984) draw no overall conclusions about the results of the empirical literature. Clark and Spengler (1980) and Hurd (1990) argue that the weight of empirical evidence supports an inverse relation between social security payments and labour supply. Many empirical studies based on US data have found the effect of social security and pensions on earlier retirement to be positive but variable in strength (Gordon and Blinder, 1980; Fuchs, 1982; Hurd and Boskin, 1984; Burtless and Moffitt, 1984, 1985; Hausman and Wise, 1985). There does seem to be a relation between higher incomes in old age and early retirement, but its meaning is debat-able and the causality behind it is capable of alternative interpretations. A positive correlation between social security payments and early retirement may simply reflect the secular trends towards rising living standards, higher real pensions, shorter working hours and earlier retirement. Social and cultural factors that go beyond individual choice may be essential to a full explanation of these trends.

GENERAL EQUILIBRIUM APPROACHES

The theory considered above has rested on the first two characteristics of neoclassical economics, namely individualism and rationality. The third characteristic, market-clearing equilibrium, is omitted from most of the literature on life-cycle behaviour, which concentrates on the individual. A comprehensive neoclassical treatment of population ageing should have a population of rational individuals interacting through markets to give a general equilibrium model. This kind of modelling is theoretically complex even in a timeless situation where neither the population nor any other exogenous variables are changing. When population ageing takes place, the economy cannot be in a steady state, and the usual simplifying assumptions are ruled out. New individuals, with their own unique preferences, are being added to the population and old individuals, equally unique, are being removed. An efficient market economy can supposedly adjust its equilibrium continuously to accommodate these demographic changes. Market adjustments are a daunting theoretical problem in the simplest of circumstances; in an economy undergoing population ageing, mixed with other exogenous changes, it is unclear theoretically how markets would adjust. A further complication is the host of social institutions prominent in reality but excluded from models of perfectly competitive equilibrium. To build institutional details into neoclassical modelling and achieve a more realistic, imperfectionist version of general equilibrium would be to create a 'second-best' framework more complex than the 'first-best'. Casual observation suggests that the real world is a 'second-best' place (as many neoclassical economists would probably concede), yet seeking to adapt neoclassical theory to depict it in all its essentials would be a futile occupation. The usual theoretical abstractions fall short of a full 'second-best' general equilibrium approach, but retain enough detail to hope to shed light on the consequences of population ageing.

The model most frequently adopted to represent demographic change is the overlapping generations model (Samuelson, 1958). This simplifies demographic change by dividing a person's life cycle into a finite number of periods and, correspondingly, splitting the population into the same number of generations. The choice of the periods that define generations is arbitrary. Most overlapping generations models, for pragmatic reasons, take the simplest possible case of a two-period life cycle and two overlapping generations at any one time. Each person has a youth and old age, and the population divides into a young and old generation. The modelling can permit the relative sizes of generations to change, thereby illustrating some characteristics of population ageing. Members of each generation are normally assumed to be identical, so as to bring out the differences between generations and hold the scale of modelling down to manageable proportions. The model treats generations as homogeneous, single-minded decision making units, which implies a relaxation of a strictly individualistic outlook. Under rationality assumptions, each generation chooses its consumption and saving to maximize its intertemporal utility over its expected life span. Models vary in their theoretical details (for example, life span, separability of preferences, discounting of future utility, and presence of bequest motives), although they are all rooted in the same theoretical abstraction. Overlapping generations models can portray many long-run issues involving savings, investment and growth, and the models addressed specifically to population ageing are only a small part of a larger literature.

General equilibrium approaches aim to take account of the interactions between individuals, producers and the government. Models of individual life-cycle behaviour, which might illustrate some specific issues that pertain to ageing, are on too small a scale to handle the general, economy-wide effects of population ageing. An overlapping generations model, while abstracting from many aspects of reality, can aspire to give a more complete view. Several interactions missing from the discussion of individual behaviour can be modelled in a general equilibrium framework. An older population might, for instance, hold a larger stock of accumulated capital (even if the saving rate falls) and thus, in models with a production sector, bring about a higher capital–labour ratio and an enhanced capacity to finance retirement pensions. Similarly, models with a government sector can include the effects on individual behaviour of anticipated changes in pension levels. The result is a model combining rational decision making with the efficient, neoclassical, price-based adjustments that coordinate the various sectors of the economy.

One of the most elaborate attempts at a general equilibrium approach is the model of Auerbach and Kotlikoff (1987), adapted to discuss population ageing by Auerbach et al. (1989). In this model, individuals live for 75 years, which creates 75 overlapping generations with identical individuals in each generation. Individuals are rational intertemporal utility maximizers who have perfect foresight about life span and pension receipts and derive utility from their own consumption, their children's consumption, and bequests to their children; they become adults at age 21, spend 20 years as parents, and retire when their labour supply declines to zero. Along with rational individuals, the model also has a competitive production sector and a government sector. Individuals supply labour under given assumptions about the age-productivity relation and the effects of technical change; they supply capital too through an efficient capital market. The government allocates public expenditures among the age groups and levies payroll taxes on the working population so as to balance the social security budget at all times. A general equilibrium coordinates the three sectors of the economy, ensuring market clearing in all past, present and future periods. Population ageing is represented by choosing values for the demographic variables that correspond as closely as possible to the past age composition of the population and the projected future age composition. Individual preferences are unobservable, but they can be assigned a functional form that, for past years, generates a numerical equilibrium solution close to the actual values of the key endogenous variables. Policy responses to population ageing can be simulated by making alternative assumptions about future benefit levels, tax rates and retirement ages, subject to the constraint that the social security budget remains balanced.

Compared with simple projections of past trends, a general equilibrium approach puts a more optimistic complexion on population ageing. Efficient market pricing steers adjustments in the right direction to alleviate the resources and transfer problems. An older population raises the economy's capital stock, causing capital deepening (more capital per worker) and a rise in the marginal productivity and real wages of the working population. With this type of model, concerns about dissaving among the elderly are unfounded; what matters is the large stock of assets held by old people, not the low rate of addition to the stock. Population ageing brings automatic adjustments that stimulate productivity and help the working population to meet the increased demands placed upon them. The market adjustments suffice only to reduce the effects of population ageing, without removing them entirely. For constant pension and benefit levels, an ageing population necessitates higher tax rates in the general equilibrium model, but not quite as high as the tax rates predicted from simple projections.

If policy changes are built into the model, then a further set of accommodating market adjustments will ensue. Later retirement raises savings, capital per head, real wages and productivity; it acts as a double palliative for population ageing in both loosening the social security budget constraint and enlarging the capacity of the working population to pay taxes. A pension cut has similar effects: lower pensions raise savings and productivity and ease the budgetary tensions that population ageing creates. In both cases, the policy changes are disadvantageous to older generations affected only by the social security cutbacks, but beneficial to younger generations whose tax payments fall. Any decisions to implement the policies would have to address intergenerational equity. Market adjustments reduce the impact of population ageing, but the general equilibrium framework does not overturn the conclusions of simpler modelling. An ageing population still increases the tax burden on the working population, and social security cuts can still reduce it. Social security cuts become an even more effective response to population ageing because of the market adjustments they induce; the cuts needed may be smaller than previously thought, but the case for making them appears more persuasive. The general equilibrium outlook, despite its air of sophistication, adds little to policy discussion. It is not accurate enough to offer reliable quantitative results (as its proponents admit), yet its qualitative policy conclusions replicate the results of much simpler approaches.

Attempts to depict the macroeconomic effects of population ageing have produced varied findings. Some studies have suggested that population ageing will have substantial effects on macroeconomic variables such as aggregate saving, capital formation, productivity and employment (Masson and Tryon, 1990; Fair and Dominguez, 1991). Other studies have played down the macroeconomic effects of population ageing and concluded that there will be no major problems for productivity or social security finance (Cutler et al., 1990). The outcomes of macroeconomic modelling are highly sensitive to the initial assumptions and should be regarded as conjectural. Empirical work on consumption behaviour has found that population ageing makes little difference to the pattern of aggregate consumer demand and has only a small influence on the relative pricing that underpins the general equilibrium approach (Eilenstine and Cunningham, 1972; Espenshade, 1978; Musgrove, 1982). The important demand effects of population ageing are gathered in a few areas like health care, social services and housing. Even here, doubts arise. In discussing housing, for instance, Mankiw and Weil (1989) argue that population ageing in the US will cause a lower rate of household formation by young adults, a lower demand for housing, an excess supply of property, and a resulting fall in house prices. Börsch-Supan (1991), by contrast, claims that population ageing will create excess demand for property and higher prices, because increased life expectancy among the elderly will reduce the amount of property that young adults inherit. Demographic influences on household formation and the supply of property (not to mention the non-demographic influences) are sufficiently complicated to obfuscate the net effect of population ageing on housing markets. General equilibrium modelling, where each economic variable depends on all the others, can easily get bogged down in indeterminacy and cannot on its own distinguish the dominant factors in any policy issue; this will require empirical work together with good judgement by the economist and the policy-maker. The more complex, indirect macroeconomic effects of population ageing have little practical significance. Population ageing has its main significance in the more obvious areas of health care and social services, a fact that could have been recognized without the benefit of general equilibrium modelling.

PUBLIC-CHOICE APPROACHES

Government behaviour is often omitted from models of an idealized competitive economy. With population ageing, however, government activity is pivotal to the matters being discussed, and modelling should be mindful of political issues (Bös and von Weizsäcker, 1989). Arguably, a full neoclassical account of the economy should explain government behaviour, along with everything else, as the outcome of rational self-interest. The government need not be a single agent but an expression of the interactions among individuals or interest groups. Extending rational-choice methods to politics has inspired the 'economics of politics' approach of Downs, Buchanan and Tullock, which has close affinities with neoclassical economics and extends beyond standard neoclassical theory to bring politics within the ambit of economics (Downs, 1957; Buchanan and Tullock, 1962). Political processes as well as efficient market equilibria are assumed to resolve conflicts over scarce resources. When discussing population ageing, the relevant conflict is that between generations: the young versus the old, or workers versus pensioners. The issues are the ones raised by the intergenerational conflict literature discussed in Chapter 2. Formal models of intergenerational conflict, constructed on neoclassical principles with endogenous government behaviour, can supposedly illuminate the economics of population ageing.

The median-voter framework of Downs (1957) assumes that both ordinary citizens and political parties are rational, self-interested agents: individuals maximize their utilities, political parties aim to maximize their share of the vote and so gain power through the electoral process. Under the assumption that individual preferences are single-peaked, with a single, clear preference among the available alternatives, the verdict of an election will coincide with the preference of the median voter. A vote-maximizing political party will try to please the median voter and if it succeeds will win an electoral mandate to enact its policies. Browning (1975) first applied the median-voter approach to public pension decisions, in a model with three overlapping generations, of which the oldest generation is retired and receives a public pension and the two younger generations work to produce consumption goods. In the absence of saving or borrowing, the median voter falls among the older members of the working population, who will gain from higher public pensions but will only pay the corresponding higher tax rate during the second half of their working lives. The model predicts that a democratic government will overprovide public pensions relative to the requirements of the younger members of the working population; an alliance between the retired elderly and the older members of the working population turns out to be the dominant force in the electoral process. Later work, surveyed by Verbon (1993) and Breyer (1994), has considered variations on the Browning model and produced different results. In a model with individual saving but no borrowing, the attitudes to public pensions may differ between generations: those making low contributions when young will raise contributions when they enter the median-voter generation, but the next generation, which makes high contributions when young, may reverse this policy (Boadway and Wildasin, 1989). The result may be a cyclicity that sees successive generations raising and lowering public pensions; it is no longer inevitable that governments overprovide pensions relative to the preferences of the young.

Alternative approaches have taken a longer-term perspective, with an optimum public pension scheme planned over many generations. Instead of separate political decisions in each period and constant readjustment of the pension scheme, there is a single policy optimization determining pension levels into the distant future. The usual policy objective is to maximize a utilitarian social welfare function, subject to an intertemporal resource constraint. Pension models constructed on these principles have produced ambiguous results and shown the difficulties of reaching definite conclusions about pensions and other policies (Boadway, Marchand and Pestieau, 1991; Peters, 1991; Blanchet and Kessler, 1991). A long-term perspective, in an overlapping generations framework, requires that every generation should be precommitted to the pension and contribution rates decided by a single intertemporal planning exercise. Future generations may not find the existing arrangements desirable, but they are assumed to honour previous decisions and refrain from tampering with pensions or contributions (Hansson and Stuart, 1989). The models make no allowance for the practical difficulties of upholding pension arrangements: governments may not regard pensions as immutable, and there is little to prevent later generations changing the pension policies decided previously.

Some public-choice models have introduced strategic interactions between generations, on the assumption that each generation can predict how subsequent generations will behave. With altruistic behaviour, each generation knows that a reduction in current saving will elicit a larger income transfer from future generations prepared to guarantee it a minimum income (Veall, 1986). Public pensions may end up displacing all private saving and effectively becoming a social security payment to people who have no other income source. A problem of strategic arguments is that the same considerations apply to every generation into the infinite future. The decisions made by the current generation should be contingent on the anticipation that similar decisions will be made by all subsequent generations. This perfect foresight assumption somewhat overestimates the planning capabilities of most decision makers, but is normally required in many-period models depicting pension policies as the outcome of rational public choice (Verhoeven and Verbon, 1991; Verbon, 1993; Meijdam and Verbon, 1996). Current decision makers must foresee the behaviour of future generations, as well as future demographic change, and build it into their plans.

Population ageing can be modelled in a public-choice framework either by introducing demographic changes into a full intertemporal planning decision covering all periods or by having separate policy decisions in each period and considering the period-by-period effects of demographic changes. Full intertemporal planning requires perfect foresight or rational expectations assumptions if a policy objective is to be maximized. Under these assumptions, the government decides future policy at the outset and then works through a predetermined plan dependent on population ageing (along with many other things). There can be no ageing 'crisis', as demographic developments have already been allowed for in the policy planning. This bears little resemblance to the practical concerns about population ageing, which come from the absence of optimal planning and the need to move suboptimal states marginally in the right direction. Piecemeal, imperfect policy reform, as distinct from a perfect policy optimum, is the matter at hand. Period-by-period decisions, revised in response to demographic changes, seem closer to actual political decision making. Governments do not have perfect foresight and are continuously adjusting their policies to accommodate the greater numerical importance of the elderly. Public-choice models suggest that in these periodic policy adjustments the voting power of the elderly can offset the political pressures to cut pensions and social services: an example is the model of Drissen and van Winden (1991), which combines public-choice modelling with a simplified general equilibrium approach (omitting private saving) and then considers the effect of exogenous demographic changes.

All the various public-choice models rely on restrictive assumptions about political decision making. Assuming perfect foresight over many future generations is implausible yet crucial to models that invoke intertemporal social welfare maximization or strategic interactions between generations. Such models may be theoretically rigorous, in that they are based on consistent, rational decision making, but the more rigorous they are, the further they diverge from the real world. The ability of professional economists to predict a single generation ahead is severely limited, and the idea that politicians or ordinary citizens have perfect foresight into the infinite future seems far-fetched. Even models defined over single-generation planning horizons make strong assumptions.

Democratic processes are not guaranteed to be an outlet for intergenerational conflicts between cohesive age groups. Many voters will have no independent knowledge of demographic changes, and population ageing will become an active political issue only if existing political parties have taken it up. Under these circumstances, its role is merely to buttress existing political arguments, and this might not suffice to cause major policy changes. Population ageing has a flexible political appeal: it can justify either public-sector retrenchment or higher public expenditure on the elderly. Which argument prevails will depend on many factors other than the small, slow-moving changes in the electorate brought about by population ageing. Formal public-choice models are prone to overstating the influence of generational preferences on public policy.

Neoclassical economics encounters serious obstacles in dealing with individual and population ageing. At the individual level, it ascribes instrumental rationality to human behaviour and takes no account of biological ageing or the relation between individuals and society. When it occasionally sets aside its individualism and adopts group or generational preferences, it cannot explain the origins of this uniform behaviour. It plays down social structure and moves from the micro to the macro level only through the interaction of atomistic individuals or groups. Universal market clearing, vital for general equilibrium theory, is difficult to swallow as a description of reality. Capitalist economies operate with significant unemployment and excess capacity, which preclude a perfectly competitive equilibrium. To model population ageing using general equilibrium approaches requires strong equilibrium assumptions: the economy has to be in a full intertemporal equilibrium and all agents must perfectly anticipate future developments. This is a far cry from the unstable, unpredictable character of much economic behaviour. Alternative approaches would place greater stress on both the structural qualities of capitalist economies and their failure to reach stable, full-employment equilibria. Although structure and disequilibrium are given short shrift in neoclassical economics, they are compatible with the less individualistic, more interdisciplinary theorizing found in non-neoclassical economics and the non-economic social sciences.

4. Alternative views of population ageing

The theoretical alternatives to neoclassicism are separate but related entities that do not cohere into a single, axiomatic theoretical model. Some economists would interpret this as a sign of woolly-mindedness and imprecision compared with the firm axiomatic foundations of neoclassical economics. When discussing a subject as complex as ageing, however, a single theoretical model founded on a few simple axioms may not be the best approach. Neoclassical economics omits many of the social and biological aspects of ageing, and in its simpler versions often omits time itself. A theory cannot be clear or rigorous about the things it omits, and these missing items are indispensable to an understanding of individual and population ageing. To explain the economics of ageing more fully requires a broader and more diverse theoretical approach, akin to the theoretical pluralism that has characterized non-economic research on ageing (Marshall, 1996). Different theoretical abstractions may represent different facets of the same complex reality. The alternatives to neoclassical views have appeared independently of each other, in non-neoclassical economics and the non-economic social sciences, but they share several common features from which one can discern a richer perspective on the economics of ageing, closer to political economy than to economics.

Neoclassical economics is so narrow because it always relies on individualistic, rational-choice behaviour and assumes that economic arrangements can be modelled as market-clearing equilibria. A wider outlook on the economics of ageing should be seeking to remove these restrictions on theorizing. Removing strict individualism allows a more structural form of theory, which lets people's social context and biological make-up have a bearing on their actions and pays attention to the institutional setting of individual and population ageing. One no longer has to construct theory from individualistic first principles. Removing market-clearing equilibrium assumptions allows a disequilibrium form of theory that denies the practical relevance of universal market clearing and full employment; if the economy does tend towards steady-state or equilibrium outcomes, they will not be market-clearing equilibria and there will be no natural state of full employment. The structural and disequilibrium arguments may seem to be unconnected, but they have common properties and can be brought together to give a more unified view (Jackson, 1994). The following discussion looks first at the structural arguments about the economics of ageing, then at the disequilibrium arguments, and finishes by bringing them together.

STRUCTURAL ARGUMENTS

A structural approach proposes that the individual experience of ageing should be placed within a wider social structure so as to recognize the significance of social institutions. Such an approach is commonly associated with sociology, in contrast with the individualistic approach of neoclassical economics. Despite the apparent gulf between the two disciplines, nothing in the subject matter of economics or sociology dictates a strictly individualistic or structural method, and ageing is, in any case, a subject that impinges on both disciplines. Introducing structural ideas can move theory away from an extreme individualistic method to a middle ground where both individual ageing and social structure are important influences on behaviour.

The claim that a more structural approach can benefit the economics of ageing need not amount to an argument for a structuralism reducing all human behaviour to social structure. This would merely be the opposite extreme to the individualistic reductionism championed by neoclassical economists. One of the hardest tasks in social and economic theorizing has been to find a theoretical framework that gives due credit to individual agency and social structure without making one or the other predominant and sliding back into reductionism. The study of ageing multiplies the difficulties, as ageing involves a biological element based on neither voluntary individual choices nor social institutions. Ageing cuts across the domains of many social and natural sciences, and theories of ageing should avoid taking a reductive stance. The virtue of structural arguments is not that they can provide a complete, airtight alternative to neoclassical individualism, but that they point the way to a less reductive stance on the economics of ageing.

The original structural accounts of ageing, dating back to the late 1940s and early 1950s, were inspired by functionalist sociology, which at that time constituted the sociological mainstream. As with all functionalist theory, the emphasis is on the smooth functioning of the social system: arrangements for the elderly are explicable by the functions they perform for society as a whole. This general framework leaves room for alternative interpretations of individual and population ageing. Functionalist views on ageing can be divided into two main strands: 'role' and 'activity' theory and 'disengagement' theory (Fennell, Phillipson and Evers, 1988, Chapter 3). The 'role theory' model of ageing stems from the structural–functionalist sociology of Talcott Parsons and gives prominence to social roles as determinants of individual behaviour. Work, the theory argues, has a special value in most people's lives, as their main source of income and self-esteem; ageing can create severe problems through the loss of the work role upon retirement and the simultaneous decline in social activity. Role theory characterizes old people as a group without a proper social role, at risk of becoming demoralized and isolated from the rest of society. Concern about their fate led to the development of 'activity theory' (Cavan et al., 1949; Havighurst and Albrecht, 1953). According to this approach, the elderly should acquire new social roles after retirement or keep their existing ones as long as possible. Only by maintaining their activity levels can they preserve their well-being and remain integrated in society. 'Role flexibility' takes on great importance: the elderly must adapt easily to new roles if they are to stay active during retirement (Havighurst, 1954). Activity theory suggests that policy makers should increase work opportunities for the elderly and promote new leisure openings. Old people can overcome the difficulties of retirement, but only if they are able and willing to exploit their leisure time. This underlies the notion of a 'Third Age', during which the retired use their leisure time actively in education and cultural pursuits (Laslett, 1989). The attitude is optimistic, provided that the elderly can find new roles.

Activity theory has attracted numerous criticisms. The model was initially stated only in a very general form and was difficult to test empirically. A full statement of the theory emerged only in 1972, twenty years after the approach first appeared (Lemon, Bengtson and Petersen, 1972); by that time, the influence of functionalist sociology was waning. Empirical tests of the formal model have proved inconclusive and there remains doubt about the significance of activity. The theory assumes that activity is a prerequisite for satisfaction among the old, but this ignores the people whose activity decreases without a loss of morale and who may be content with low levels of social activity throughout their lives. By emphasizing activity alone, the theory overlooks the diversity of human activities and implies that the old could benefit from any substitute activities, regardless of their quality. Another criticism is that activity theory is vague about the causality and social context of activity loss. Low activity may be a symptom of a more general deprivation and poverty among the elderly, which means that causality may be reversed:

low activity may be a consequence of low levels of well-being, not a cause of them. If so, interest is diverted to the social context of ageing and the reasons why both well-being and activity decline in old age. Concentrating on individual activity alone may be too narrow a perspective for the analysis of human ageing. One can also wonder whether the optimism behind activity theory is justified. Many old people, especially those in the oldest age groups, have little prospect of increasing their activity, and other policy objectives would be more relevant. Activity theory, in its desire to reintegrate the elderly with the rest of society, shies away from the physical decline caused by ageing and the possibility that the elderly may have different needs from the rest of the population.

The alternative functionalist approach of 'disengagement theory' is often seen as the opposite of activity theory, since it is less optimistic about old people's ability to stay active and plays up the differences between the old and young. First formulated in the early 1960s, it argues that the social institutions surrounding the old have the function of disengaging them from society as biological ageing reduces their capabilities (Cumming and Henry, 1961; Cumming, 1963). Formal social arrangements offer a more congenial way to withdraw from work and social activities than to continue until physically compelled to stop. It is better that retirement should become institutionalized than that it should proceed haphazardly, governed by the physical and social circumstances of each individual person. The theory portrays social arrangements as being mutually beneficial to the individual and society: individuals gain by being removed with dignity from occupations unsuited to their age group; society gains by having an institutionalized means of replacing inefficient older workers with younger ones. Social institutions match the capabilities of old people with the tasks they are expected to perform. A good match between capabilities and tasks creates a harmonious relation between the individual and society. Disengagement from society when people reach old age is not thought to be harmful or undesirable; on the contrary, it is depicted as an essential adjustment that will allow people to keep their earlier personality and psychic well-being. The general picture is of social institutions designed to offset the adverse impact of biological ageing on the individual and establish a society well equipped to cope with individual and population ageing.

Disengagement theory, like activity theory, has been much criticized. Empirical work using time-series data has shown that people can maintain their normal range of activities deep into their old age, which casts doubt on the empirical basis of disengagement (Shanas et al., 1968 for three industrialized countries; Hunt, 1978, and Abrams, 1978, 1980, for the UK; Thomae, 1976, for Germany; Munnichs et al., 1985, and Busse, 1985, for the USA). Other criticisms are concerned with theoretical issues. Disengagement theory gives primacy to the biological ageing of the individual and allots social structure only a passive role in reacting to it. This is what Townsend (1986) terms 'acquiescent functionalism', a type of functionalism that acquiesces in an individualistic, biologically centred outlook and gives social institutions no role beyond that of easing the effects of biological ageing. A more thoroughgoing structural approach would give social structure a more active influence, so that some aspects of ageing are socially rather than biologically created. Disengagement theory can be viewed as underestimating the abilities of old people and encouraging a division between them and the rest of society. Disengagement is supposed to be in their interests, but a complete separation from society could be harmful. To make disengagement the kernel of social theorizing about old people may exaggerate its importance and fail to recognize that the elderly are still members of, and participants in, society. A further criticism is that disengagement theory is blind to the differences among old people, who vary considerably in the extent of their engagement in work and other activities (as do all age groups). People need not become disengaged in old age, and even those who are disengaged may not become so at quite the same age or in the same manner. Again the theoretical framework may be oversimplified, and an alternative view encompassing greater diversity of individuals and social structures may be required.

Functionalist sociology has declined in popularity since the 1960s and no longer constitutes the sociological mainstream. Other approaches, such as symbolic interactionism and ethnomethodology, have come to the fore, replacing the macro, structural emphasis with a more micro, individualistic method. The 'grand theory' exemplified by functionalism is now unfashionable, and a more interpretative, less theoretical style of academic work has supplanted it. A similar trend has emerged in social gerontology, with the growth of biographical life-history studies concentrating on the lifetime experience of particular individuals (Marshall, 1980, 1986; Rosenmayr, 1981). This biographical approach has not produced a new theoretical framework, but it has demonstrated the complexity and diversity of ageing, along with the importance of social context. No single pattern of ageing is common to all individuals and societies. A possible conclusion from this is that generalizing theories have little value and that the search for them is a wasted effort: gerontologists and other social scientists should devote their energies to empirical work. An alternative conclusion is that new, more subtle and complex theories are required, so as to place ageing within a general theoretical framework but still allow for diversity, social conflict and historical change.

Functionalism is often contrasted with a conflict approach which, while structural in character, is more alert to the tensions within and between social structures (Dahrendorf, 1959; Rex, 1961). Conflict theorists criticize functionalism as giving too consensual and harmonious an impression of society and neglecting the opportunities for social change. Social arrangements may function efficiently in the interests of a particular social group or class, but clash with the interests of other groups or classes. Stability may ensue if the favoured class is dominant enough to maintain its privileges and quell discontent from below; sectional interests and power then become central to social analysis. The mere fact of conflicting interests implies a latent possibility of social change, however remote this may be at any given time. Conflicting interests mean that the whole population will not in general hold a single set of structured ideas and beliefs. Attempts to universalize the beliefs of the dominant group cannot have total success while individuals and social groups possess a genuine human agency and an ability to exercise a critical faculty. Conflict is socially structured, but its practical expression relies on human agency. The implicit account of social behaviour is richer and more complex than that envisaged in much functionalist analysis.

Marxian thought has always been the prime example of a conflict approach, so it is appropriate at this point to consider Marxian attitudes to demographic change. Marx and Engels wrote little about population; the chief occasion on which they discussed demographic matters was in their critique of the Malthusian population principle, which suffices to demonstrate their general views on population (Meek, 1953). The first version of Malthus's essay on population had sought explicitly to confound the utopian socialist faith in the possibility of an ideal world (Malthus, 1970). Marx and Engels too were critical of utopian socialism, but they did believe in the historical inevitability of communism and found themselves at political loggerheads with Malthus. Much of their commentary on Malthus concerned his alleged plagiarism and his apologetic treatment of the ruling classes, but other criticisms have greater relevance to population ageing. Population has a special significance in Malthusian theory because the pressure of population against the means of subsistence determines long-run real wages: the Iron Law of Wages, derived from Malthus's views, became a core element in the classical (Ricardian) economics of the early nineteenth century. Marx took his economics mainly from Ricardo and the classical school, though the Malthusian population principle was one of the things he discarded. Malthus's claim to have revealed a general law of nature, true at all times and places, went against the Marxian tenet that economic arrangements are historically specific. For Marx, the economic effects of demographic change depend on the mode of production, and the discussion of demo-graphic change should pay heed to the economic system in question. Certain consequences of population growth pertain under capitalism; other consequences pertain under other social and economic systems (slavery, feudalism, communism, and so forth). The Malthusian popula-tion principle might conceivably operate under some social conditions, but it is by no means universal and seriously misrepresents the effects of demographic change under capitalism.

Marx never formulated a comprehensive account of the interaction between population and the economy, under either capitalism or any other mode of production. This is a deficiency of the Marxian standpoint and results from the belief that demographic change has a minimal influ-ence on capitalist economies. Marx and Engels argued that surplus population is created systematically by capitalism, not by population growth, and that a capitalist economy will generate a surplus population, visible as chronic unemployment, regardless of the birth or death rate. A rising population might worsen unemployment and its attendant prob-lems, but does not cause them: population pressures are against the means of employment, not against the means of subsistence. In the longer term, technical change means that labour requirements rise more slowly than capital accumulation. Higher labour productivity ensures the permanence of unemployment and counteracts the Malthusian argument that diminishing returns to labour keep wages at subsistence level. Low wages are not uniquely linked with low productivity and are due largely to the impaired bargaining strength of workers beset by chronic unem-ployment. The experiences of workers are contingent on particular economic and social conditions. To suggest otherwise, as Malthus does, is to depict as inevitable something that is capable of change; the conser-vatism inherent in Malthus becomes clear. Neither Marx nor Engels went on to explain what determines fertility under capitalism or how demo-graphic change influences the economy. Given their conclusions about the unimportance of population, this reluctance to go further is under-standable, although it thwarts a comprehensive Marxian view of demographic change. Marx and Engels only said enough about popula-tion to decide that population size and composition are insignificant in capitalist economies and that social structure, evident in the mode of production, is of greater importance.

If social structure with its embedded conflicts has primacy, then the tenor of demographic analysis changes. Instead of asking how the size and age composition of the population affect the economy and society, one asks how social structure affects the perception and institutionaliza-tion of old age. Ageing as an external, asocial process is seen to be a misconception, and old age is recognized as being at least in part socially constructed. Arguing this way reintroduces some functionalist considerations into the interpretation of ageing: arrangements for old age can have a function in preserving the status quo and thus the privileges of the dominant social class. The institutions surrounding old age may not principally accommodate the physical difficulties of ageing, in the manner of 'acquiescent functionalism', but sustain the economic system and the power of the dominant groups within that system. The vision is of conflict, rather than consensus, and the pressures for social change are greater than in most versions of functionalism. Stable social structures signify the dominance of certain class interests, with no implication of harmony or mutual benefit.

In social gerontology, the role of social structure has been proclaimed by modernization theory (Cowgill and Holmes, 1972; Cowgill, 1974; Fischer, 1978). Capitalism and modern industrial societies have, the theory argues, brought a decline in the status of the elderly. Pre-capitalist societies had a hierarchical social structure in which the elderly were a group small in number but held in high esteem and valued for their wisdom and experience. They were a symbol of continuity in societies that were keen to preserve order; long-standing social institutions enshrined their fortunate position. Capitalism weakened the hierarchical structure by bringing a shift to a more dynamic society in which change became more important than stability and new knowledge more important than old. The elderly represented outmoded social and economic practices, and their knowledge was seen not as a receptacle of ancient wisdom but as a barrier to progress. Younger age groups, with their energy, malleability and physical vigour, had the characteristics that capitalism most valued. Old people found that their privileged position was crumbling, and their status diminished accordingly. Market relations replaced earlier age-based hierarchies.

If the old were unable to compete with the young in providing the qualities demanded on the labour market, then they would end up worse off than the young, a reversal of their former social standings. Eventually, with the development of mass production and the welfare state, the lowly standing of old people became institutionalized. Populations became categorized by age, most dramatically through formal retirement at a single date (Graebner, 1980; Myles, 1989, Chapter 1). The loss of employment income on retirement, combined with low pension levels, reduced many old people to living standards well below those of their younger fellow citizens. Socially structured disadvantages for the elderly superseded their socially structured privileges. It became materially and socially more desirable to be young and in work than old and retired.

Modernization approaches are less prominent in the social sciences than they once were, and evolutionary arguments are no longer so frequently put forward. In the study of ageing, the stress has been transferred from modernization to the social structuring of old age. This may be compatible with modernization theories if current arrangements are the culmination of a well-defined historical trend, but the social construction of old age is logically distinct from modernization. Since the early 1980s, various authors in social policy, sociology and social gerontology have produced a 'political economy of old age' that uses structural arguments (Townsend, 1981; Walker, 1980, 1981; Phillipson, 1982; Estes, Swan and Gerard, 1982; Hendricks and McAllister, 1983). The analysis is essentially Marxian in nature, but explicit references to Marx are few and there are no direct precedents in Marx's work for these particular arguments. According to Townsend (1981), the experience of old age in modern, developed economies is socially constructed and only obliquely connected with biological ageing. Old people are subject to a structured dependency that leaves them financially and physically dependent on others, often at an age when they could work and look after themselves. Townsend (1986) identifies four sources of structured dependency: formal retirement policies; low state benefit levels and the associated poverty; institutionalization of old people; and centralized provision of community care.

Formal retirement is the clearest example of socially constructed ageing. The statutory retirement age defines the elderly as a social group and absolves them from the requirement to work, yet it has virtually no physical justification when longevity is increasing and many retired people are capable of working. Formal retirement policies may have other purposes, such as regulating labour supply. Attitudes to retirement have varied with economic activity. In the UK, the economic expansion and labour shortages of the late 1940s and early 1950s aroused calls for later retirement as a means of increasing labour supply (Hopkin, 1953; Paish and Peacock, 1954). An extended working life was also the intention behind the retirement condition on pensions recommended by the Beveridge Report (Beveridge, 1942). When the long postwar boom had ended and recession reappeared during the 1970s and 1980s, discussion of later retirement petered out and gave way to arguments for earlier retirement (Walker, 1986). In times of high unemployment, a trend towards earlier retirement can convert some of the unemployment into retirement and hold down the official unemployment figures. Changes in retirement practices, whether implemented formally through the statutory retirement age or informally through employers, can regulate the supply of labour. The retired elderly stand behind the unemployed as a second reserve pool of workers, who can be cajoled back into employment when economic activity is exceptionally high. With mass unemployment now seemingly permanent, labour supply so much outstrips demand that arguments for later retirement on the grounds of labour supply (as opposed to public finance) are unlikely to recur in the near future. But the potential labour services of the elderly would be tapped if they were needed.

A second source of structured dependency is poverty among old people. Retirement combined with low public pensions and benefits has long been known to cause poverty (for the UK, see Townsend and Wedderburn, 1965; Townsend, 1979). Old people lose their employment incomes upon retirement and, unless they have private means, become financially dependent on the state. Where the level of social security benefits defines the poverty line, many elderly recipients of public pensions or benefits find themselves bordering on poverty (and below some poverty lines defined by other criteria). Low incomes for the elderly create low living standards, a loss of morale and self-esteem, low social status, and a lack of market power. The retirement condition on the public pension denies them the option of working to supplement their incomes; means testing of benefits causes a low take-up rate, which pushes their actual incomes below their entitlements (Townsend, 1979). As a result, formal retirement and social security policies more or less explicitly structure the financial position of the old. Not all old people are poor, however. Those with a history of secure, well-paid employment, who receive an occupational pension, may have a prosperous retirement. Income differences among the old reflect earlier income differences during employment, and the groups least well off are typically the ones without occupational pensions and financially dependent on the state. Social security measures, despite their benevolent image, can be seen as fostering low incomes for old people and sustaining (or even widening) existing inequalities within age groups.

The other two sources of structured dependency arise from the provision of care. Old people living in institutions such as residential homes or hospitals face the highest degree of structured dependency: professional care determines their whole physical and social environment. In many cases this intensive institutional care is unavoidable, owing to the physical disabilities of the people being cared for, but in other cases the need for it is less obvious. A move into an institution is liable to be permanent, and the elderly fear losing their independence. Institutional care may be thought superior to the less intensive alternatives, a view that professional carers will usually uphold, but not necessarily the recipients of care. Over-reliance on specialized institutions formalizes the separation of old people from the rest of society and accentuates their physical disabilities. Public and private resources devoted to institutional care may be switched from less intensive approaches that could improve old people's current living standards and enable them to maintain their independence. Special institutions for the old may at times be counterproductive in strengthening both the imagery and reality of dependency.

Similar considerations are relevant to community care. The outcome of much professional care has been a top-down perspective, in which the caring profession decides what care should be provided and to whom. Paternalistic care may often be justified but is sometimes extended to people for whom it is unnecessary. The elderly can all too easily be treated as passive recipients of care and given little say in the type of care they receive. When offered few opportunities to participate in the organization and provision of care, they appear more dependent on others than they have to be. The social policy profession deals with the elderly as a homogeneous group of inactive dependants, and the same attitude becomes generalized throughout society. The practice of formal social policy, notwithstanding its good intentions, may contribute to the structured dependency of the elderly.

In combination, the various sources of structured dependency give rise to a socially created conception of old age. The retired elderly are partitioned off from younger age groups and regarded as having different capabilities and needs. Social institutions, not biological ageing, delineate old age. A person's whole life course, from childhood to retirement, complies with the prevailing cultural values concerning dependency, the family and economic activity (Hockey and James, 1993). Cultural values receive concrete expression in public policies. According to the structured dependency approach, the state constructs old age systematically to serve capitalist interests, and the modern experience of old age is therefore an artefact of capitalism (Phillipson, 1982). Retirement and social care exhibit the ambiguity highlighted in Marxian theories of the welfare state (O'Connor, 1973; Gough, 1979; Ginsburg, 1979; Mishra, 1981, Chapter 5; Pierson, 1991, Chapter 2). On the one hand, they provide leisure and transfer payments to the elderly and formal care to the ill and disabled: the spirit is altruistic and collectivist. On the other hand, they divide the elderly from the rest of society and give the state a means of regulating their economic activity and living standards. The apparently non-capitalist nature of the welfare state can be misleading, since most of those receiving support are surplus to current economic requirements; welfare measures do not interfere with the employment relations underpinning capitalism. Keeping a surplus population at a low living standard is a tool of social control, as well as an act of humanitarianism. The need for humanitarianism emerges in many cases because the economic system itself has denied incomes to the unemployed and retired. The benevolence of the welfare state and the harshness of unemployment are parts of a single economic order.

From the structured dependency perspective, divisions between young and old, workers and pensioners, active and inactive, serve to lessen the cohesion of the working class and buttress the interests of employers and capital. The classification of people by age under capitalism foments increasing age-consciousness. Tensions between age groups are an artificially created diversion deflecting attention away from the more important conflicts of interest between social classes. If old people can be made to feel resentment against younger generations and not against the economic system, then this will help to perpetuate the system. Conflicts can be confined to wrangling over tax payments and income redistribution, and fundamental questions about the economic system will go unasked. To widen the perspective, therefore, it is salutary to interpret economic arrangements, including those affecting old people, in terms of the conflicting class interests that characterize capitalist economies. Neoclassical economics with its individualistic methods nearly always omits to do so, and the same is true of theories resting on inter-generational conflicts or 'acquiescent functionalism'. The structured dependency approach rectifies such omissions by arguing that ageing is largely a social phenomenon that suits the dominant class interests.

The modernization and structured dependency views of old age have been criticized on several scores. The historical experiences of the elderly do not necessarily entail a fall from high to low status and from the headship of hierarchical family units to state-induced structured dependency. Age groups are anything but homogeneous, and the status of old people has varied among societies in all periods (de Beauvoir, 1977; McPherson, 1983, Chapter 2; Featherstone and Hepworth, 1993). The 'golden age of the family' supposedly brought to an end by nineteenth-century capitalism now seems to have been a myth. Historical records have shown that old people living in extended, intergenerational families were never treated particularly well or given the respect and authority that the 'golden age' account assumes (Laslett, 1971). Empirical studies have also doubted whether informal, family hierarchies were ever the dominant method of accommodating the retired elderly population. Smith (1984) argues that structured forms of dependency, operating at an institutional level much wider than the family, existed long before industrialization. Capitalism therefore arrived after structured dependency and cannot be uniquely responsible for it. Johnson (1985) queries whether the growth of formal retirement in the UK had a close connection with the provision of public pensions and social security benefits. Formal retirement predates the modern welfare state; the history of retirement and public pensions has been more haphazard and decentralized than a literal interpretation of structured dependency theories would suggest. A wider view of structured dependency, in which the behaviour of employers and the state reflects general class interests without adhering to some master plan, is less susceptible to criticisms based on specific historical details. None of the criticisms goes as far as to nullify the value of a structural approach to ageing; some of them imply that structured dependency has a longer history and deeper roots than was initially thought. They do, however, cast doubt on simple theories of modernization and structured dependency that posit a unidirectional shift for the elderly from high to low status and from an unstructured to a more structured environment.

Other criticisms challenge the theoretical stance of the structured dependency approach. The theory can seem to be preoccupied with a particular, narrow definition of dependency at the expense of broader issues. By placing so much emphasis on retirement, it comes close to equating independence with employment and dependency with the lack of employment (Johnson, 1989). One might well conclude from structured dependency considerations that old people should be allowed to work longer if they wish, in order to fend off the poverty that comes from dependency on state benefits. This is a somewhat restrictive view. To give the impression that old people can best realize their potential through continued formal employment appears to endorse the dominance of employment over other activities in deciding a person's participation in society. The elderly who stay economically active might only be exchanging their financial dependency on the state for a dependency on low-paid private employment. The stress on dependency gives the theory a one-dimensional, employment-centred character that detracts from the more general arguments concerning the social construction of old age. As Chapter 2 observed, the term 'dependency' has many conflicting interpretations and might best be avoided. Arguably, the nub of the theory is the social structuring of old age, not a particular employment-based definition of dependency.

A further theoretical criticism is that structural arguments give old people too little credit for behaving on their own initiative as true human agents. They are modelled as a homogeneous group of passive 'cultural dopes', whose whole life is determined by external norms and constraints. This, it is claimed, understates their capabilities and overstates the government's power to influence their behaviour and circumstances (Dant, 1988). A structural approach intended to expose the ways in which the elderly are manipulated may reinforce their negative image by portraying them as open to easy manipulation. The concept of structured dependency may confirm the low perceived status of old people and thus be part of the phenomenon it is attempting to explain. Such criticism applies only to a crude, reductionist version of the structural approach that regards social structure as explaining everything and excludes other influences on human behaviour. The proponents of structured dependency would probably disown this kind of reductionism and aim to use structural arguments without going to a reductionist extreme. Old people may well experience structured forms of dependency while still retaining their physical capabilities and independence of thought. The prospects for a less reductive theoretical framework are discussed later in the chapter.

Also relevant when evaluating the structured dependency approach is the declining importance of the statutory retirement age over the last two decades. More and more workers have made an 'early exit' from employment through redundancy or early retirement before reaching the statutory retirement age (Laczko and Phillipson, 1991). Workers becoming unemployed in the later years of their working life have only a small chance of regaining employment. They are stranded between employment and retirement, as a group of de facto retired who are denied the public pensions and other benefits available to the officially retired elderly. Workers retiring early are frequently doing so at the behest of employers anxious to reduce their labour forces and willing to provide financial incentives encouraging early exit. Added together, the older unemployed and the early retired make up a new segment of the population that defies easy categorization as workers or retired elderly. The key question is whether the growth of early exit constitutes a departure from structured dependency.

Early exit resembles formal retirement in having little or no connection with biological ageing. The economic system creates the plight of the older unemployed, and employers guide even the apparently voluntary decisions of early retirers. A trend towards early exit need not indicate the end of socially structured retirement and old age, but may signal a switch from a centralized dependency governed by the state to a more decentralized dependency governed by employers. This may be associated with a more general change from Fordist to post-Fordist work practices (Laczko and Phillipson, 1991, Chapter 3). Fordism is the economic system that embraces mass production techniques, large national corporations, standardized products, and intensive specialization among the low-skilled labour force. The governmental counterpart of Fordist industry is the postwar settlement of the welfare state, the mixed economy, nationalization of public utilities, and activist macroeconomic policy on Keynesian lines with a commitment to full employment; the centralized government policies mirror the centralized organization of large firms. Post-Fordism brings a more flexible, decentralized approach. Production uses information technology, which permits smaller-scale production units, flexible production techniques that can respond quickly to changes in demand, less standardization of output, and a more adaptable and mobile labour force. The government too follows a more decentralized line, reducing its commitments to the formal welfare state, public ownership of utilities, and interventionist economic policy.

The transition from Fordism to post-Fordism has been happening over the last 20 years or so, in the opinion of some economists and other commentators, notably the Regulation School and the proponents of flexible specialization (Aglietta, 1979; Coriat and Petit, 1991; Lipietz, 1992; Piore and Sabel, 1984; Teague, 1990). The importance of post-Fordism is by no means universally agreed; neoclassical economists have said little about it, and some non-neoclassical authors have argued against it (for example, Costello, Michie and Milne, 1989; Rustin, 1989; Callinicos, 1989, Chapter 5). In a post-Fordist economy, the formal retirement at a single statutory age found in the Fordist welfare state evolves into a more decentralized early exit that fits the new modes of production. As with employment, the age of retirement becomes less standardized among jobs and individuals. The state's weakening commitment to full employment raises the average unemployment rate and shortens the typical working life as people exit early from employment before the statutory retirement age. Early exit is only a minor element in a much wider transformation of technology, industrial organization and government policy.

The growth of early exit should not be interpreted as the end of structured dependency or the social construction of old age. The state's role in retirement has diminished, but the experiences of old people continue to be socially constructed. If one accepts that the state generally acts in the interests of capital, then a change from retirement organized on centralized, statutory principles to a decentralized early exit from employment may be a change only of means rather than ends. Post-Fordist developments have strengthened capital at the expense of labour, so that the half-palliative, half-manipulative function of the centralized welfare state can be dispensed with and employers can be given a 'decentralized' free hand. What seems to be a technologically induced change of production regime can also be seen as a politically induced reversion to purer forms of laissez-faire capitalism. Fordism and post-Fordism may only be variations on the same capitalist theme.

DISEQUILIBRIUM ARGUMENTS

Disequilibrium here denotes the failure to attain a general, market-clearing equilibrium and the absence of forces impelling the economy towards such an equilibrium. From a disequilibrium perspective, capitalist

economies are unstable and do not spontaneously generate full employment: unemployment becomes normal to the functioning of the economy
and should be included in any theoretical or policy discussion. Non-mainstream, post-Keynesian versions of Keynesian economics are the main
source of the idea that capitalist economies are unstable (Eichner, 1979;
Hamouda and Harcourt, 1988; Arestis, 1992, 1996; Davidson, 1994). The
mainstream 'neoclassical synthesis', expounded by most macroeconomics
textbooks, mixes Keynesian arguments with the neoclassical labour
market and depicts unemployment as the product of wage rigidities that
stop labour markets reaching a full-employment equilibrium. The neoclassical synthesis denies that unemployment is normal in capitalist economies
and regards it as an abnormal special case resulting from market imperfections. By implication, removing the imperfections would restore the
neoclassical ideal of perfect competition and full employment. The more
thoroughgoing Keynesian economics of the post-Keynesian school disso-
ciates itself from the neoclassical labour market and eschews an
imperfectionist stance. Following Keynes, it emphasizes uncertainty and
instability. Relative prices, unable to fulfil their neoclassical role as perfect
coordinators of economic behaviour, become less important as short-term
influences on the economy. For post-Keynesians, the chief short-term
influence on the economy is aggregate demand, which determines
economic activity and employment. Aggregate demand depends mainly
on changes in investment, as investment is more volatile than the other
components of demand. Post-Keynesian economists give special attention
to the investment decisions of employers when explaining movements in
economic activity.

By this Keynesian reasoning, demographic changes will affect the
economy through investment, not through changes in labour supply or
aggregate savings. The connection between population and investment
decisions was recognized in the earliest years of Keynesian economics.
Keynes himself, in the year after he published the *General Theory*, warned
that a declining or static population might discourage investment and
depress economic activity (Keynes, 1937). His argument rested on a
couple of observations. The first was that a country's capital stock is
roughly proportional to its population, especially for basic services such
as housing, schools, hospitals and public transport. If the population
declines, fewer of these facilities are needed (unless the government wants
to increase provision per head), and the capital stock can be reduced.
This may have a sizeable impact on investment expenditures which,
because they depend on changes in the capital stock, are more variable in
proportional terms than the capital stock itself. Variations in investment,
working via the Keynesian multiplier, have a magnified effect on national

income and employment. A declining population will curtail investment and therefore aggregate demand and economic activity. Keynes's second observation was that a declining population reduces the scale and expected growth rate of markets, making businessmen more wary of investing. Demographic changes are one of the few things that can be forecast into the medium-term future with reasonable confidence, and knowledge of smaller or stagnating markets may outweigh any speculative hopes about higher consumption per head. A reliable piece of bad news may increase the uncertainty of investors and lead them to cancel or postpone investment projects. Again there is a causal link between a declining population and declining economic activity. Similar, less pronounced effects can be expected with ageing populations that are not actually declining, but static or slowly growing. Keynes drew the contrast between Malthusian pessimism about population growth and the more optimistic view presented by aggregate demand theories. Generally an admirer of Malthus, he was aware that his own theories were at odds with Malthus's concentration on diminishing returns (Keynes, 1933, 1937). He concluded that economies face the twin hazards of suffering a Malthusian crisis if the population grows too quickly or suffering low aggregate demand and prolonged recession if the population grows too slowly. A middle path of slow population growth, passing between these two hazards, would offer the best outlook for the future.

In the late 1930s, other economists took up Keynes's ideas on population and expanded them (Hansen, 1939; Reddaway, 1939; Harrod, 1939). The 1930s were a period of economic depression and also the period when ageing and declining populations first became widely noticed (Clark and Spengler, 1980, Chapter 1). Demographic events might, it seemed, retard economic recovery and render the depression permanent. Hansen (1939) foresaw major problems from the deflationary effect of slow population growth, and for him this amounted to a fundamental change of economic environment that would require a new, Keynesian approach to policy. As decelerating population growth created a shortfall in aggregate demand, governments would have to become more willing to intervene in the economy and adopt expansionary economic policies. Reddaway (1939) provided a broader treatment of the same issues and similarly observed that declining populations may be deflationary. His discussion was less pessimistic in tone than Hansen's: he saw unemployment as primarily a man-made problem and found no cause for alarm as long as governments took a Keynesian stance on macroeconomic policy. The Keynesian literature of the late 1930s drew attention to both the deflationary pressures from declining populations and the need for active policy intervention in response to these pressures.

The early Keynesian interest in declining populations was not sustained into subsequent decades. During the 1940s, wartime production and post-war reconstruction stimulated an economic expansion that brought the interwar recession rapidly to an end. Fears of a permanent, demographi-cally created depression seemed absurdly misplaced, and it became clear that other influences on investment could overcome the influence of popu-lation. Moreover, the 'baby boom' of the late 1940s to the mid-1960s temporarily halted the trend towards declining and ageing populations. Fertility rates increased, populations started to grow again, and for a while it seemed as if steady population growth was more likely in the long run than population decline. Economic and demographic conditions during the immediate postwar period were wholly different from what they had been during the 1930s. Keynesian economists developed their interests along other avenues and no longer saw population as a prime influence on aggre-gate demand. Demographic change became labelled as a long-run issue distinct from the short-run concerns of Keynesian economics, a view that meshed with the neoclassical understanding of population. In recent years there has been no revival of Keynesian interest in demographic change and no distinctively Keynesian version of population economics. When eco-nomic and population growth in the developed countries eventually slowed down, the rejuvenated interest in population ageing did not produce any specifically Keynesian approaches: the topics discussed were traditional neoclassical ones such as tightening resource constraints, increasing dependency burdens, and tax disincentives. This reflects the dwindling popularity of Keynesianism during the postwar period.

The assumption that demographic change is only a minor influence on investment rests primarily on casual observation, and a more rigorous assessment would require formal empirical work. Much research on this matter has come from a kindred but different source, the theory of eco-nomic cycles. Population has long been recognized as a possible cause of cyclicity in economic activity (Lösch, 1937). Cycles of many lengths have been defined theoretically and, in some cases, identified empirically, but three principal cycles stand out: the 'long wave' or Kondratieff cycle, with a length of 45–60 years; the 'long swing' or Kuznets cycle, with a length of 15–30 years; and the business or trade cycle, with a length of 5–10 years. Interest in population as a cause of cycles has focused on the long swing or Kuznets cycle, because its length coincides with the typical time span between generations. A relatively large birth cohort will tend to produce another relatively large cohort about 20 or 30 years later when its members have their own children. Some initial demographic shock can have an echo effect that yields population cycles of similar length to the Kuznets cycle. If investment is related to the size of birth cohorts, then one would expect waves of investment to harmonize with the population cycles and create a cyclicity in economic activity. Housing investment, especially, depends on the population in the age ranges at which most people form households. Demographically driven variations in housing construction may be a prime mover of Kuznets cycles.

To confirm Kuznets cycles empirically would also confirm the early Keynesian views on the relation between population and investment. Kuznets carried out the original empirical work in the late 1920s and 1930s, finding empirical support for the long swing in the US but refusing to tie it exclusively to population-sensitive investments (Kuznets, 1930, 1958). A theme in Kuznets's work on the relation between population growth and the economy was his unwillingness to reduce his empirical findings to simple theoretical relationships. He concluded that population growth is generally consonant with economic growth, but was cautious about specifying a causal link between them (Kuznets, 1974). Other economists have been less cautious, however, and have sometimes explained the Kuznets cycle by the theory of population-sensitive investments, even though there is little in Kuznets's work to justify this. Empirical evidence for the US gives limited backing to a population-based Kuznets cycle, while still leaving some doubts (Easterlin, 1968). In Europe, there have been no clear-cut Kuznets cycles in the twentieth century, and the question of population-induced cycles does not arise (Solomou, 1988). What does seem clear is that any relation between population and investment is far from having an overriding importance in determining economic activity. Investment has always been difficult to model theoretically, and few theories of investment can claim solid empirical backing. The difficulties confirm the Keynesian belief in the volatility and waywardness of investment, but contradict the idea of a reliable connection between demographic change and investment behaviour.

The main implication of Keynesian economics has turned out to be the unimportance of demographic change for macroeconomics, rather than its importance as a cause of investment. Keynesian modelling acknowledges the macroeconomic inefficiency of permanent unemployment and, unlike neoclassical economics, sees this as being normal to capitalist economies. Unemployment in neoclassical theory derives only from the frictions and imperfections that obstruct the smooth functioning of the market system: a frictionless economy could attain permanent full employment. From a Keynesian perspective, unemployment is integral to the system and makes life more comfortable for employers by strengthening their bargaining power, raising the profit share in national income, and easing the recruitment and dismissal of employees. Contrary to the neoclassical view, employers would find it harder to function smoothly in a 'frictionless' economy at full employment than in one with mass unemployment where labour is readily hired and fired. A government pursuing Keynesian demand management policies can in principle attain or get near to full employment, but practical examples of thoroughgoing Keynesian intervention are rare. Few governments, even nominally Keynesian ones, have put into practice the policies that Keynes envisaged. Early on, Kalecki (1943) foresaw this and argued that capitalists would never permit the state to secure full employment through Keynesian demand management and so diminish their bargaining power and control over employees.

Kalecki's version of Keynesian economics gives prominence to the distribution of national income between wages and profit and to the related topic of class interests (Sawyer, 1985). The resulting theory is allied to Marxian economics in its reliance on class and its recognition of permanent unemployment, which becomes a structural feature of capitalist economies and forms common ground between Marxian structural ideas and Keynesian disequilibrium. An economy with unemployment operates with a working population much larger than the current demand for its services, causing a slackness that cushions demographic changes. Under these circumstances, demographic changes cannot be said to create a special burden of dependency, when the normal functioning of the economy creates dependency all the time. The dependency of the unemployed is best understood as being endemic to capitalist economies, a view expressed long ago by Marx but equally consistent with a Keynesian outlook (Jackson, 1992a). There are no major obstacles to assimilating Keynesian views with Marxian and other non-neoclassical approaches. They have far more in common with each other than they have with neoclassical economics.

Non-neoclassical, disequilibrium modelling rules out demographic determinism. Changes in employment mediate the effects of changes in the age distribution: one cannot take for granted that an ageing population will cause a rising tax burden or a falling share of national income accruing to the working population (Jackson, 1992b). A higher proportion of old people may have an expansionary effect on aggregate demand and employment, which reduces the number of dependent unemployed and has an ambiguous effect on total dependency. The continuous movements of many other macroeconomic variables further complicate matters in reality, as these variables may have a much greater impact than population ageing on employment and dependency. The economy is open to many sources of instability and keeps a reserve of excess capacity and underutilized labour in order to absorb this instability. As a result, demographic changes have only a minor significance. Non-neoclassical modelling can yield similar conclusions to a neoclassical approach, but for utterly different reasons. In the general equilibrium model of Auerbach et al. (1989), demographic changes have a smaller influence than might be expected, because they are accommodated by a perfectly adjusted, smoothly equilibrating economic system with no slack. In a disequilibrium approach, demographic changes are accommodated by an economic system that is not perfectly adjusted to anything and has extensive slack to buffer it from, among other things, the influence of population ageing. One approach has a perfect market-clearing general equilibrium, the other is permanently away from general equilibrium.

With Keynesian arguments playing down the macroeconomic significance of demographic changes, the concerns over population ageing are, it might seem, a false trail. This may not necessarily follow if policy discussion moves from the macroeconomic level to a more specific, disaggregated, institutional level. Capitalist economies with chronic unemployment have no binding aggregate resource constraints in the neoclassical manner. Aggregate demand, not the economy's productive capacity, is what holds down current output and employment. In policy discussion, however, the relevant constraints are the financial ones associated with public pension schemes and social security measures. These are institutional in origin, created by a decision to record and balance a particular budget. Analysis of financial constraints requires more institutional detail than is customary in neoclassical economics, which often frowns on ad hoc models as spoiling the axiomatic purity of rational-choice individualism. Keynesian and non-neoclassical economics have less of a problem with institutional detail, since they are not based on individualistic first principles. A general non-neoclassical approach can coexist with smaller scale, ad hoc models set up to consider some specific policy issue. Keynesian economics, by reducing the significance of aggregate real resource constraints, can enhance the significance of specific institutional detail. One might then ask whether a general theoretical framework is necessary and whether an unsystematic, empirical approach might suffice. The next section considers this.

TOWARDS A LESS REDUCTIVE THEORETICAL FRAMEWORK

All the theoretical frameworks adopted in the discussion of ageing have their limitations, and none can provide an exhaustive account. Theorists have been wont to reduce the whole analysis of ageing to one aspect of reality, such as social structure, individual preferences or human biology, and neglect other aspects. Reductionist theorizing produces a blinkered view of the subject matter that may pick out a few relevant points but obstructs a full understanding. Many attempts at general theorizing in the social sciences have succumbed to reductive oversimplification and then hardened into a disciplinary orthodoxy. A possible response to this problem is to try to do without theory altogether and rely solely on unsystematic empirical work. The effort is futile, as investigators cannot avoid interpreting their empirical 'facts' theoretically: if they do not make the theory explicit, then it will still be implicit in the questions they pose and the conclusions they reach. What appears an atheoretical stance may be sustaining a narrow, restrictive view of reality. Abandoning theory for empiricism will produce a superficial and uncritical brand of academic research. An alternative response to reductionism is to be aware of the difficulties of theorizing and attempt consciously to theorize in a non-reductive manner. The structural and disequilibrium views outlined in the present chapter can, if handled carefully, underlie a non-reductive approach to ageing. Of particular importance is their capacity to relate social structure to individual behaviour through the concepts of culture and ideology. Successful analysis of ageing should rest on the interactions between human biology, individual behaviour and social structure.

The alternatives to neoclassical economics are consistent with the concept of ideology and can allow for the 'crisis' of ageing having an ideological character that exaggerates the real economic effects of population ageing. From this viewpoint, one should not look solely at the material consequences of ageing, but also at the social institutions defining old age and at the way in which social commentary has shaped the 'ageing crisis'. When considering ideology, it is helpful to distinguish material production, institutions and ideology, as in Figure 4.1. The three tiers are closely interrelated and resemble the Marxian scheme of

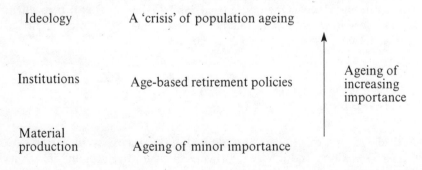

Figure 4.1 Ageing and ideology

technology, social relations of production and ideology, though they are not intended to be an exact application of Marxian categories. At the bottom tier of material production, the structural and disequilibrium arguments suggest that ageing has only a minor importance for the economy. As most people retire before they become physically incapable of work, there is slack within the individual life cycle. The individual's working life has not been stretched to its utmost, and the recent trend towards earlier retirement has made this increasingly obvious. At the aggregate level, permanent unemployment creates slack within the working population. Labour supply outstrips labour demand, and so the working population is not producing at its full potential. These slackness properties of capitalist economies shelter employers from changes in the size of the working population. Permanent unemployment may be inefficient, but it consolidates the bargaining power of employers and frees them from binding demographic constraints. Consequently, the physical ageing of individual workers and the age composition of the population as a whole have only limited effects on production.

The slack in production is due partly to measures based on age, notably a statutory retirement age. At the middle, institutional level, therefore, age has significance as an easily recorded characteristic by which the government and employers can classify and divide people. A change in the age distribution may necessitate adjustments in the institutional arrangements for public pensions and social security, even though its effect on real (as opposed to financial or monetary) variables is minimal. Age-based retirement policies are deceptive. They are actually reducing the real economic impact of individual and population ageing, yet they give an institutional importance to age that belies its small economic importance.

At the top, ideological level comes the image of an 'ageing crisis' demanding urgent remedial action by governments. The 'crisis' hangs mainly on institutional matters such as pension finance, but the terminology of 'dependency burdens' and 'resource constraints' merges financial and real issues. Under the (often implicit) assumption of full employment, ageing can be depicted as imposing a physical constraint on an economy that uses its working population to the maximum extent. The apparent existence of a tightening demographic constraint on the economy is a valuable rhetorical tool for libertarians, because it makes public budgetary retrenchment seem inevitable. Proponents of laissez-faire can invoke demographic change as a pretext for cuts in welfare provision. If the ageing 'crisis' appears severe enough, the public may tolerate measures that they would otherwise regard as harsh and undesirable. Population ageing can be blown out of proportion and manipulated to serve the interests of the dominant economic and social groups.

Neoclassical economics is poorly equipped to tackle ideological issues, as it omits ideology from its basic theoretical model and has a predisposition to endorse laissez-faire. The neoclassical insistence on individualism blocks a proper appreciation of the institutional and ideological levels of analysis. Alternative theoretical approaches are less reductive and more awake to ideology, class interests and the social construction of old age. They can provide a richer account of ageing and a better chance of finding a critical standpoint.

Ageing is a broad yet intricate subject that can be discussed at many levels. Theories of ageing have generally picked out for special attention one of five main levels: human biology, individual agency, technology, social institutions and ideology. Biological theories concentrate on the fundamental physical processes of ageing that lie beneath everyone's experience of old age and apply in all societies at all times and places. Even here, however, it may be difficult to separate the 'pure' genetic content of ageing from the various environmental influences on the physical capabilities of old people. Most biological theorizing is located outside the social sciences, in natural science or medicine, though it has an obvious relevance for social scientific work on ageing. Individualistic approaches to ageing stress the role of individual agency and subjective experience. Examples are those case-history studies adopting a largely atheoretical, interpretative method founded on the biographical experiences of particular individuals. Alternatively, individualism can be built into a general theoretical structure, as with neoclassical economics, such that social outcomes derive from fixed assumptions about individual behaviour. Technologically based approaches give pride of place to technology as the foundation of all social conditions, including old age, and the driving force behind all social change. Modernization theories, for instance, regard the current low status of old people as the product of a long-term evolution towards capitalist forms of production. Material concerns also animate Marxian accounts of social change and the post-Fordist arguments about growing flexibility and decentralization. An institutional perspective dwells upon the social context of human behaviour and the way that social conditions mould and constrain individual experience. In the study of ageing, such a perspective has come to the fore with the structured dependency approach and the 'social construction of old age'. Finally, an ideological view discusses general cultural attitudes and their effect on people's experience of ageing. Negative images of old age are seen as having their own powerful influence, independent of any other factors. These five levels suffice to show the complexity of ageing, and they are by no means exhaustive: each level could be further subdivided, and additional levels could no doubt be identified.

A starting point when analysing ageing is to recognize the stratified, multilayered character of the ageing process. Theorists on ageing are presumably aware of the many possible layers, but most theoretical work nonetheless seizes upon one particular layer and accords it a higher priority than the rest. This selective focus can be defended as a form of abstraction, in which a single element is plucked from a complex whole and subjected to detailed analysis. If other theorists analyse other elements of the same complex whole, then the theories might perhaps come together to provide a more complete picture. Uncoordinated theorizing seems somewhat haphazard, however, and at variance with many theorists' claims to have found a general standpoint, a permanent abstraction that can inform subsequent theorizing and empirical work. Neoclassical theory is the classic example of this in economics, but many non-neoclassical theories could fulfil a similar reductive role. In avoiding an overcommitment to neoclassical methods, one should also avoid becoming committed to an alternative, equally restrictive orthodoxy. Non-neoclassical methods have the key advantage of greater diversity, which lets theorists take account of many factors absent from neoclassical economics. When discussing ageing, a reasonable stance would be to presuppose a single, complex object of enquiry (thus rejecting a thoroughgoing relativism), while accepting that no single model can encapsulate this reality and that pluralistic theorizing is required. Some theories would be incompatible with each other, but others could be complementary abstractions within a wider theoretical framework. Instead of rejecting theory outright, one would be cautious of the explanatory power of any single theory and encourage a constrained diversity of theories that together might explain reality.

The conclusion, then, is that theory can still have value, as long as it takes a non-reductive form. Much social-scientific theorizing has rested on a single grand abstraction; several exist in the discussion of ageing, such as disengagement, modernization, structured dependency, and neoclassical individualism. The abstractions tend to become permanent presuppositions that dominate thought about old age, giving a reductive view that overlooks important aspects of its subject matter. Other abstractions are needed. One cannot do justice to a subject as broad and complex as ageing without borrowing ideas and abstractions from several academic disciplines in both the social and natural sciences. A general theoretical framework will have to be open and non-reductive, capable of encompassing human biology, individual agency and social structure. Such a framework is nearer to a general statement of non-reductionism than a detailed theoretical system. This approach will not on its own uncover the mysteries of ageing, but it can guard against the reductionism so prevalent in the social sciences. More detailed theorizing about ageing can be undertaken through various coexisting abstractions aimed at different facets of what is, after all, a highly intricate subject. A guiding principle of constrained theoretical diversity recognizes the need for diverse ways of trying to understand a single complex reality. Some ways may be better than others, but no single way is ever going to provide a perfect understanding. Constrained theoretical diversity is hard to detect in the methods of neoclassical economists. It is discernible, at least as an implicit stance, in the interdisciplinary work of non-neoclassical economists, social gerontologists and sociologists.

5. Productivity and employment

Much of the disquiet over population ageing has been based on the expected fall in average productivity as the population ages. For economies with long-term unemployment, the fears about rising dependency ratios may be misdirected: total productivity depends on employment and economic activity, which vary cyclically and respond to many factors other than demographic change. Population ageing can influence productivity through the age composition of the employed population as well as through the dependency ratio. This suggests that one should move down from the aggregate level to discuss individual productivity, skills and wages.

The age composition of the working population changes slowly as in each period a birth cohort completes its full-time education and starts to look for employment, while an older cohort reaches the statutory retirement age and enters retirement. Individuals differ in the timing of their entry to and exit from the working population, but the age composition of the working population as a whole closely reflects the relative sizes of birth cohorts. If unemployment rates vary among age groups, there may be a discrepancy between the age composition of the employed and working populations, although changes in the age composition of the working population will usually carry through to employment. The key issue is whether a rising average age of the employed population has detrimental effects on the economy. To address this issue, one must consider the productivity of older workers.

PRODUCTIVITY

If all workers were perfect substitutes, regardless of their ages, there would be no need to worry about the age composition of the employed. Younger workers would be interchangeable with older ones, and the ages of the employed would be significant only in so far as the numbers retiring had an effect on total employment. For age to be relevant to productivity, employees of different ages must differ systematically in their attributes.

Old people differ from the young in having undergone the degenerative process of biological ageing, which diminishes their physical strength and sometimes also their mental capabilities. They become increasingly vulnerable to external shocks, until eventually their survival is threatened: biological ageing culminates in death. Reduced physical and mental capabilities may render them less productive as employees, especially in strenuous manual work, and less adaptable to new methods of working. A rising average age of the working population should, by this criterion, reduce average productivity. Old people also differ from the young in another way, which may offset biological ageing. Age is a prerequisite for experience, and the old have an advantage over the young in the longer period they have had available for learning. This applies both to job-specific skills and the more general skills acquired from a longer exposure to the various difficulties that arise in life. When an economy grows rapidly, job-specific skills can soon become outmoded and regarded as an impediment to further economic growth. Experience is not always a valued commodity. General skills should, nonetheless, have value for any kind of employment. When brought together, the opposed effects of old age produce ambivalence. Can old people, with their reserves of knowledge and experience, overcome the adverse physical effects of biological ageing? Finding a reliable empirical answer to this question has proved notoriously difficult.

Biological ageing manifests itself through the physical decline of people in advanced old age. A degenerative ageing process exists at all times and places, but its effects vary with social and economic conditions, and in developed countries it may have little relevance for productivity. Biological ageing, which is only imperfectly understood, seems to involve programmed and unprogrammed elements (Hendricks and Hendricks, 1977, Chapter 4; Bond, Briggs and Coleman, 1993). The programmed element rests on each person's genetic inheritance; individual differences occur within a basic pattern of ageing common to all. People have an internal biological clock that determines their growth until they reach adulthood, whereupon growth ceases and a gradual physical deterioration begins. Programmed ageing is usually seen as fulfilling an evolutionary function by ensuring that human beings grow till they are capable of reproduction. Once a generation has reproduced itself, it becomes expendable in evolutionary terms, and so growth comes to an end and physical decline with old age sets in. The unprogrammed element of ageing derives from susceptibility to random events internal to the individual, such as errors in the replication of genetic material or toxins produced by normal metabolic processes. It has no evolutionary interpretation, but adds to the physical deterioration of old people. Age-related disease is a further detrimental influence, distinct from biological ageing and correlated with social conditions (Wilkinson, 1986). The list of age-related diseases and disabilities is lengthy and well documented, including heart disease, cancer, impaired physical strength, loss of hearing and vision, and problems with memory. All of these become commoner in old age, though they are widespread in developed countries only among the 'old old', that is to say, people of 75 or more who are well above the normal retirement ages. Biological ageing and age-related diseases do not produce serious physical disabilities for most people of working age. This raises the possibility that the advantages of greater learning and experience may compensate or even outweigh the disadvantages of biological ageing.

As people get older, they undergo psychological ageing that may cause declining intellectual performance and shortcomings relative to younger people (Hendricks and Hendricks, 1977, Chapter 6; McPherson, 1983, Chapter 6). The ageing process has a marginal influence on mental capabilities, as is evident among the 'old old', whose basic intellectual functioning may be impaired. Up to this age, however, most people maintain a fairly constant intellectual performance, overlaid by learnt abilities, repertoires and practical intelligence (Coleman, 1993). One can acquire learnt abilities only through experience, and here lies an advantage for the old over the young. Old people can draw selectively on their wider experience, which enables them to interpret and simplify what younger people may perceive as a mass of unrelated and perhaps contradictory information. The ability to take a broader view and transcend apparent contradictions may reduce old people's perplexity in the face of uncertainties and help them reach more dispassionate and reflective decisions. This can, in principle, give them better judgement than younger people; it may be the wisdom that has traditionally been ascribed to the old. Wisdom, unfortunately, is difficult to define and test empirically, and the evidence for the wisdom of the old remains anecdotal.

Memory loss with age threatens the use of experience by the elderly. It seems to have its greatest effect on the retention of meaningless numerical information, as against true knowledge that has been fully learnt and interpreted (Cohen and Faulkner, 1984). The effect on wisdom may therefore be small, and serious deterioration of memory is, in any case, confined largely to people well above the statutory retirement ages. When the elderly become aware of disadvantages such as memory loss, they can follow new routines to compensate, for example, by resorting to written notes and reminders. Compensatory routines often ensure that the old are at least as reliable as the young in keeping appointments and carrying out prearranged tasks. The developmental approach to psychology adopts a life-span view of intelligence that regards old people as having a more integrative outlook than the young, which makes them less reliant on pure reasoning and better able to exploit intuitive feelings and understanding (Erikson, 1965; Riegel, 1973; Schaie, 1978). Most intelligence tests pass over integrative concerns and instead focus on the reasoning abilities characteristic of younger age groups. Formal testing assesses the elderly by criteria favourable to the young and places them at a disadvantage. Consequently, although most empirical work indicates a slow decline in mental functioning with age, the overall picture is more complex and may involve some qualitative advantages for the elderly. Only empirical study of particular occupations can resolve whether productivity does indeed decline with age, and the results obtained may not generalize to other occupations.

Empirical studies of work performance have suggested that old people can attain a productivity comparable with that of the young. In the UK the labour shortages of the late 1940s and 1950s stirred interest in later retirement and the work performance of older age groups. Researchers in occupational psychology began to investigate the age–productivity relation, with a view to finding out whether old people are capable of full-time work. Interest was such that the research constituted a separate discipline of 'industrial gerontology'; Dex and Phillipson (1986) describe the period as a golden age of interest in older workers. The empirical results were generally optimistic about the working potential of the elderly. Experimental studies discovered that age correlated only weakly with work performance (Welford, 1958; Riley and Foner, 1968, Chapter 18). Old people could adjust successfully to the detrimental effects of ageing and match the productivity of their younger counterparts (and their earlier selves). Furthermore, studies of working conditions in industry found that older workers were subjected to an institutionalized age discrimination that had little grounding in their work performance (Heron and Chown, 1967). They were allocated to less skilled work duties merely because of their age and not because of any inability to carry out the work. Apparently, they were victims of the negative attitude of employers, an attitude without a proper rationale but well entrenched.

The results of industrial gerontology implied that old people were being unjustly treated in the current organization of production and that, if desired, they could take on more complex work duties, retire later and make a bigger contribution to production. The positive conclusions were in tune with the case for later retirement put forward during the 1940s and 1950s, but from the 1960s onwards unemployment started to rise in the UK and technical change undermined the employment opportunities of unskilled and semi-skilled manual workers. Interest in the working potential of old people diminished, as did the official support for empirical work in the area; industrial gerontology virtually ceased to exist as a discipline in its own right. Only a handful of independent researchers have undertaken any subsequent work on the age–productivity relation (Welford, 1976). The initial findings of industrial gerontology have gone largely unchallenged and, if anything, have been ratified by later research, so that current knowledge of the age–productivity relation more or less coincides with the results of the postwar research activity (Charness, 1985). In short, it seems that old people do on average experience a decline in certain mental and physical abilities, but that these abilities are either irrelevant to most types of work or amenable to compensatory routines. Variation within the older age groups implies that many old people can match, or even surpass, the productivity of the young.

Recent research on the employment of old people has concentrated on the institutional difficulties they face. A desire to encourage earlier retirement has replaced the desire to extend people's working lives. Early exit from the labour force has accompanied the collapse of full-time employment beyond the statutory retirement ages, and it is becoming harder for old people to stay in employment, even when they have the ability and will to do so. Their work experience is constantly depreciating under rapid technical change and may eventually be perceived negatively as a commitment to old-fashioned working practices. They become the preferred candidates for redundancy and, at a time when the supply of unskilled jobs is limited, have little choice but to exit early from the labour force. The elderly are the losers from economic growth as their once-valued characteristics fall out of favour. True physical disabilities among the old are mainly irrelevant to these developments. Economic growth, improved living standards and reduced mortality can cause an increase in average disabilities at any given age, owing to the longer life expectancy of people with chronic disabilities (Verbrugge, 1984). Such trends strengthen adverse perceptions of the elderly, but have only a tenuous connection with the employment experiences of particular older workers. Much more relevant are rising unemployment and rapid technical change, which have led to the elderly being regarded as the most expendable section of the working population.

Productivity depends on a complex mixture of social and physical factors, and output per head in any job varies with the organization of production. Few work activities are at a true productive optimum constrained only by the personal attributes of the employees. The slight physical and mental decline that occurs with age is of only minor significance. Productivity cannot be separated from the organization of production, which is a feature of the economic regime as a whole. The variability of productivity in most jobs permits old people to adjust their ways of working so as to uphold their work performance and offset the detrimental effects of ageing. Widespread assumptions that old people are less productive may amount to a form of ageism, in which employers exaggerate the effects of age on work performance and use them to justify reorganizations of production motivated by other, institutional concerns. The internal structure of the labour market, not the physical capabilities of workers, determines many age differences in employment. When trying to explain the discrepancy between the weak age–productivity relation and the stark contrasts in treatment of workers at different ages, one has to look at the demand side of the labour market and the causes of age discrimination.

WAGES AND EMPLOYMENT

Under perfectly competitive conditions the real wage equals the marginal physical product of labour, and the age–productivity relation decides the variation in earnings with age. If age is unrelated to productivity, then the wages of all people in the same employment should be equal, regardless of their age. If, on the other hand, age is negatively related to productivity, then the wages of older workers should be lower than those of the young. Competitive labour markets create an immediate bond between physical productivity and wages, such that physical decline and lower productivity with age should lead to a downward sloping age–earnings profile. This is sometimes observed in manual work, but upward sloping age–earnings profiles are more common, especially at the earlier stages of a person's working life. The standard competitive explanation of earnings rising with age hails from the long-term investment framework of human capital theory (Becker, 1964; Mincer, 1974). Older people have higher productivity through the positive influence of experience and training on skilled and non-manual employment; a rising or hump-shaped age–earnings profile portrays accurately the age–productivity relation. To explain observed earnings patterns on competitive lines, human capital theory argues that the greater work experience of old people outweighs their physical decline. A genuine rise in productivity with age suggests that an ageing labour force would improve average productivity and create few difficulties for employers.

Empirical testing of the link between wages and marginal productivity is subject to obstacles similar to the ones encountered in investigating the age–productivity relation. It is difficult to measure the productivity of an individual worker in a collective enterprise involving hundreds of other workers, along with managers, machinery, technical know-how, and so forth. It is also difficult to assess whether workers are receiving their marginal product, as would happen under perfectly competitive conditions, or whether their earnings differ significantly from their productivity. If rising age–earnings profiles do not represent productivity differences based on differences in experience, then older workers may be receiving wages above their productivity and younger workers receiving wages below their productivity. This implies privileged treatment for older workers, in other words, positive discrimination by age. In neoclassical economic theory, discriminatory practices deviate from perfectly competitive assumptions and are normally explained as the result of either tastes or market power (Becker, 1971). According to the taste theory, employers have a taste for discrimination, even though it reduces productivity and profits, and are willing to indulge their taste despite the costs incurred. According to the power theory, the privileged social group acts collusively and raises its earnings by excluding other groups from the best employment opportunities.

Neither the taste nor the power theory is well suited to explaining the position of older workers. Few if any economists have argued that employers have a taste for recruiting older workers (the opposite seems more plausible) or that old people are somehow acting collusively to raise their wage payments. Older workers may not be in a privileged position at all. They often receive higher wages than younger workers, but if they become unemployed they have little or no chance of finding new employment. Retirement practices effectively exclude many of them from paid employment, and their seemingly privileged position does not extend to those who are retired or unemployed. Matters are more complicated than a simple positive discrimination by age. Older workers typically have a rising age–earnings profile ending in a large and abrupt reduction in earnings upon retirement or early exit. This does not amount to clear-cut age discrimination and has to be explained using a different theoretical approach.

An alternative argument is that age–earnings profiles originate in the non-competitive structure of labour markets: wages could then be unrelated to productivity without any age discrimination by employers. Rising age-earnings profiles, coupled with mandatory retirement, may be a consequence of an internal labour market sheltered from competition. To encourage their employees' commitment and discourage rapid turnover of staff, firms may establish their own hierarchical career structures, in which earnings increase with age and employees are rewarded for length of service. The positive age–earnings relationship need not be based closely on productivity. Newly recruited workers may have wage rates below their marginal revenue product, but if the age–earnings profile is steeper than the age–productivity profile their earnings will eventually catch up with and overtake their productivity. During the later years of employment, workers can be seen as receiving deferred pay to compensate for their previous low earnings. Participation in the internal labour market finishes with mandatory retirement and the payment of an occupational pension, another reward for long service with a particular firm.

Neoclassical theorists have modelled these institutions formally as the outcome of market-like, mutually beneficial interactions between a firm and its workers (Lazear, 1981, 1990; Ippolito, 1991). Alternative views have stressed the divisions within labour markets. A dual labour market approach juxtaposes the internal or primary labour market with a secondary labour market operating competitively (Doeringer and Piore, 1971; Edwards, 1979). Internal labour markets hive off a privileged segment of the labour force and reward it with job security, a well-defined career path and a generous pension scheme. The labour force is divided into a primary sector that identifies closely with the employer and carries out managerial duties, and a secondary sector that has little loyalty to the employer, is at the mercy of competitive labour markets and makes frequent moves (via periods of unemployment) between firms. The primary/secondary division rests on factors other than age, and the theory makes no reference to age discrimination. Older people in primary labour markets will do rather well, but in secondary labour markets they will suffer if they cannot match the work performance of younger generations.

The expected effects of population ageing differ between the competitive human-capital approach and the less competitive internal markets approach. An ageing population should not create special problems for a competitive economy. Workers receive their marginal product, and changes in the age distribution causing a change in productivity or labour supply will bring about appropriate adjustments in real wages. An older population could have an adverse effect on the economy's overall productivity, but this is an unavoidable external restriction that can be dealt with efficiently through market pricing. Neither the government nor employers need to respond specifically to population ageing: competitive pressures take account of any changes that have to be made. Falling productivity could be detrimental to living standards, but market forces will accomplish the necessary retrenchments and share them out in accordance with the prevailing distribution of income and assets. The changing sizes of cohorts induce the right labour market adjustments. Easterlin's work on relative generation sizes predicts that the members of a large ('baby-boom') cohort will be exposed to fierce competition in the labour market resulting in low real wages and poor job security (Easterlin, 1980). This corresponds to an efficient market adjustment, though it may have far-reaching social repercussions, including delays in marriage, lower fertility, and higher divorce rates. A small ('baby-bust') cohort can, by contrast, reap economic and social benefits throughout its life cycle because of its favourable position within labour markets. The influence of generation size is thought to be greatest under ideal competitive conditions when the economy is continuously at or near full employment.

Population ageing during the first part of the twenty-first century will arise from the entry into old age of the 'baby-boom' cohort born in the 1940s and 1950s. This large yet prosperous cohort would seem on casual empirical grounds to contradict the relative-generation-size hypothesis. Nevertheless, formal empirical studies have claimed that the negative effect of cohort size on earnings is well established (Easterlin, 1980; Berger, 1985; Ermisch, 1988; Martin and Ogawa, 1988; Wright, 1991). Several studies have found that the the cohort-size effect is strongest among certain social groups (chiefly university graduates) and that its long-run implications for the working population as a whole are significant but small (Freeman, 1979; Welch, 1979; Murphy, Plant and Welch, 1988; Klevmarken, 1993). The general conclusion is that, other things being equal, an ageing population will flatten out the typical age–earnings profile and increase the earnings of younger relative to older generations. A few empirical studies have investigated the relation between cohort size and unemployment or job security. As with the earnings relation, it seems that large generation size may have had a detrimental effect and increased unemployment among certain age groups, but there remains doubt about the strength and generality of the relationship (Bloom, Freeman and Korenman, 1987; Zimmermann, 1991; Schmidt, 1993). Because cohort-size effects are weak, other influences on earnings can easily outweigh them.

Easterlin, Macdonald and Macunovich (1990) argue that the baby-boom generation has attained its high living standards by changing its behaviour patterns away from those of earlier generations: by staying single, delaying marriage, having fewer children and enjoying the fruits of two-income household units. If these changes were due to adverse labour market conditions associated with the large size of the baby-boom generation, then the Easterlin theory may be consistent with the prosperity of recent large generations. But the changes in behaviour may have other origins, and the role of cohort size in influencing behaviour is difficult to isolate. Alternative generational theories, such as the intergenerational conflict approach described in Chapter 2, contradict the Easterlin theory. In a democratic society, a large generation may be politically stronger than smaller ones and better able to protect its interests by political means. The Easterlin theory takes an essentially competitive view of

labour markets, and the changes foreseen are the ones that come 'natu-
rally' from efficient market adjustments: a large generation brings an
exogenous increase in labour supply which in a competitive labour
market reduces real wages. The problems confronting large generations
are merely the correct market responses to generation size and a symptom of the competitive economy's putative success in coping with
demographic change. Members of large generations may be unlucky in
bearing the brunt of market readjustments, but the logic of market efficiency dictates their predicament.

The scene becomes more complex outside the ideal case of competitive
labour markets. If spontaneous market adjustments cannot efficiently
accommodate demographic change, then there may be grounds for policy
responses by employers or the government. In an internal labour market
with a positive age–wage relationship, the general assumption is that
older workers are paid more than their marginal product and younger
workers less. The deferred pay received in the later stages of the life cycle
appears on a cross-sectional basis as a subsidy to older workers at the
expense of the young. Under steady-state conditions with a stable age distribution this would be sustainable and consistent with a constant rate of
profit. When the population ages, however, employers may be unable to
maintain the current age composition of their labour force and end up
with a higher proportion of older workers. Even if some employers
manage to preserve the current age composition, this will not be possible
for all employers collectively. An increased ratio of old to young employees will increase the wage bills of firms with rising age–wage profiles. If
older workers are paid more than their marginal product, then employers
suffering lower profitability have an incentive to seek other institutional
arrangements (Blanchet, 1993). The predicted consequences depend on
the gap between the wages and productivity of older workers, about
which little is known with certainty.

Employers can cut their wage payments by flattening out the age–wage
profile and narrowing the productivity–wage gap, as Figure 5.1 illustrates.
Assuming that similar proportional adjustments are made throughout the
life cycle, the age–wage profile will rotate clockwise about the point
at which wages equal productivity, and the curve denoting the productivity–wage gap will rotate anticlockwise about the equivalent point. Wages
converge with productivity and the subsidy from young to old diminishes.
A flatter age–wage profile raises the relative earnings of the smaller,
younger generations and thus mimics the wage adjustments that would
result from competitive markets.

Employers are in a dilemma. On the one hand, they could preserve the
current age–wage profile and retain the organizational benefits of the

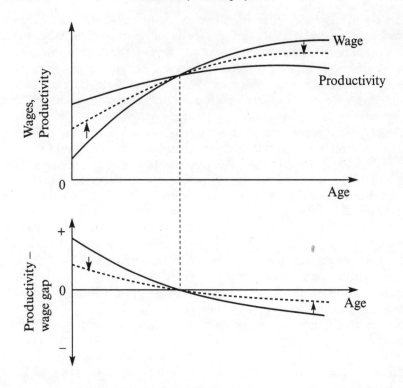

Figure 5.1 Flattening out the age–wage profile

internal labour market, but pay the penalty of the productivity–wage gap for younger workers no longer being sufficient to subsidize the wages of older workers. The shortfall would come from profits, reducing profitability. On the other hand, they could flatten out the age–wage profile so as to cut the wage bill and increase profits, but this would reduce the effectiveness of the internal labour market. In the limit, with wages again in line with productivity, there would be a reversion to competitive conditions. The trade-off is between the short-term benefits of cutting the wage bill and the long-term benefits of keeping intact the internal labour market. The practical relevance of this argument is unclear, given the problems in defining and measuring productivity. But whatever the productivity and efficiency implications of ageing, an ageing population will raise the wage bills of firms with a positive age–wage relationship. Current arrangements within internal labour markets will come under increasing strain, though they may be secure enough to withstand the demographic pressures.

Employers also have an incentive to lay off well-paid older workers and replace them, if at all, with less-well-paid younger ones. When older workers are not replaced, the main burdens of adjusting to an ageing population will fall on the social security system: employers are evading their own adjustment problems and passing on the main costs to the state. When younger workers replace older ones, this narrows the earnings gap between old and young, as it raises the demand for the services of the already scarce young and reduces the demand for the services of the old. The resulting tensions within internal labour markets should cause a movement to a more competitive outcome. In practice, employers often lay off older workers during periods of rising unemployment when labour markets are at their least competitive. Early exit is regarded as a painless way of laying off workers, with the incidental result that it alters the age composition of the labour force. Younger workers replacing older ones has at times received official public support, for example, through the Job Release Scheme introduced in the UK in the late 1970s. Officially, such policies aim to improve the job prospects of young people during a recession and simultaneously reduce recorded unemployment. The policies leave implicit any intention to remodel the age composition of the labour force and do not present themselves as being a response to demographic change. They do, all the same, provide a surrogate market response. Older workers are in excess supply, their employment status becomes insecure, and younger workers are available to take over their work at lower rates of pay.

Once age becomes a factor in determining employment, the road is clear to a more general ageism in society. Employers may not be discriminating by age as a matter of taste, but age-related employment practices will influence public perceptions of old people. Internal labour markets give ageing an institutional importance unrelated to its effects on productivity. The sudden cessation of work that characterizes internal labour markets widens the distance between old people and the rest of the population. A plunge from the upper reaches of an organization's hierarchy to complete retirement reinforces the idea that people above a certain age have nothing to contribute to production. The arrangements are never fully rationalized and have little connection with biological ageing, in view of the meagre evidence for a negative age–productivity relation. Early exit, encouraged by the growing financial burdens on employers as the labour force ages, has brought forward the institutional age limits on employment to affect younger age groups. Even if the statutory retirement age remains unchanged, people who are approaching it may be seen as having outlived their usefulness to employers. Generous pension schemes and other financial inducements might sometimes act as compensation, but early exit will always weaken the standing of the elderly in the labour market. Age restrictions on recruitment usually accompany age limits for existing employees. If the older unemployed are debarred from work on account of their age alone, then their early exit will be irreversible. The reluctance of prospective employers to recruit them ratifies their previous employer's decision to relinquish their services. Age has rendered them unemployable.

TRAINING

Training and retraining are germane to the problems of population ageing if they can raise the productivity and employability of old people. From the human capital perspective, special policies to train older workers may be unnecessary: human capital models already incorporate a positive age–productivity relation in the guise of on-the-job learning and post-school investments. Older workers will not have to be retrained if they can stay in their current jobs and benefit from their accumulated experience. This optimistic view should be tempered by the empirical doubts about the true nature of the age–productivity relation and the possibility that other models, such as those based on internal labour markets, depict reality more accurately. An internal labour market approach is less sanguine about the fortunes of old people: their earnings advantage over younger workers may not be founded on a true productivity advantage and they may be vulnerable to the financial reorganization of firms adjusting to accommodate population ageing. Technical change may cause a rapid depreciation of the skills that older workers have acquired in the past. As more and more workers exit early from employment, they are increasingly finding themselves unemployed and short on marketable skills. A possible response to this would be to reverse the usual assumption that training schemes are for the young and consider the case for training and retraining old people.

The scope for training policies depends in part on the character of the work being considered. Unskilled work, by definition, precludes formal training. Most jobs will require some skills, but if the skills are easily and quickly learnt the experience of older workers will have little value. People in low-skilled manual jobs, particularly jobs demanding physical strength, fare badly as they age. Biological ageing sets in, their earnings start to decline and they become susceptible to layoffs. Once unemployed, they cannot realistically expect to re-enter their previous employment, and their chances of securing alternative unskilled jobs are slim. Training policies to upgrade their skills and open up a wider range of job opportunities may provide the only hope of renewed employment. Workers in skilled employment fare better: they often have a rising age–earnings profile, together with higher wages and greater job security than unskilled workers. Internal labour markets protect many skilled workers from the immediate impact of fluctuations in economic activity. With the growth of early exit and the rearrangement of internal labour markets, however, skilled workers too are becoming vulnerable to losing their jobs. Once unemployed, they cannot in general stay in their own profession, and any new employment will almost certainly require new skills. By contrast with the unskilled, for whom retraining could bring a delayed upgrading to skilled work, this could entail a move to less skilled work, an effective downgrading of their skill levels and social standing.

Technical change may act against the interests of older workers by devaluing their human capital and giving an advantage to younger workers trained in new techniques. Recent developments, which have witnessed population ageing combined with rapid technical change, can seem menacing to the elderly. Other factors offset a purely pessimistic view. The position of older workers depends on the length of the training period as well as on the rate of technical change. They will normally do best in industries with little technical change and skills that are slow to acquire and slow to depreciate. This increases the age gap between workers at the end of training and those at the beginning, and ensures that the skills acquired from training endure over a person's full working life. Older workers can preserve a long-term advantage over the young. In the extreme case, when technology is constant and skills never depreciate, younger generations can match but never surpass the old, and employers should be ready to take a favourable view of ageing. As technical change speeds up, the skills of older people depreciate more quickly and may ultimately become worthless, giving younger generations trained in more modern techniques an advantage over their older counterparts. A short training period can increase the adaptability of the older worker. If technical change is very rapid, then skills depreciate fast and training periods have to be short, otherwise skills may erode in value before the training period is completed. This helps older workers because it increases their chances of recovering their appeal in the labour market. The elderly will benefit most from technical change when skills are quickly acquired and quickly depreciate; workers nearing the end of their statutory working lives can then be retrained and re-employed. Since everybody's skills are soon outdated but soon replaced, the elderly cannot be written off as being irrevocably committed to old methods and unable to take up new ones. By this argument, technical change may be neutral to the interests of older workers. If the pace of change is very fast, then all skills become transitory and the differences between old and young workers are subsumed in a permanent revolution.

For older workers to hold their own against the young, they need the skill acquired through training to be either invariant, so that the young might eventually catch but not overtake them, or constantly being revised, so that neither young nor old can gain any advantage from a skill differential. A steady replacement of skills is the least attractive possibility for older workers, since their hard-won experience continuously depreciates as they progress through their working lives, up to the point where they are laid off and replaced by younger workers with newer skills. Actual technical change will involve a mixture of cases: some industries will have perennial, slowly acquired skills that give older workers an advantage; others will have rapidly changing, easily acquired, low-grade skills that place older and younger workers on the same insecure footing; still others will see the skills of older workers being slowly but steadily devalued, to the detriment of their earnings and job security. The effect of technology on employment can take many forms, and the fate of older workers will vary among industries and occupations.

Policies to retrain older workers are subject to the problems of the old in learning new skills and the short time horizon over which they can put their new skills to use. The belief that old people cannot learn new skills is related to the more general arguments about their declining productivity and, as with the more general arguments, has little or no empirical foundation. If anything, older workers perform better in jobs that require skill than in jobs that are unskilled and require only physical effort or manual working at a fixed pace (Welford, 1958). New skills can equalize the current positions of older and younger people, as both are without prior knowledge or experience, and allow older people to prove their adaptability. Employers have found that older workers are capable of learning new skills and outperforming younger workers in areas such as reliability and punctuality (Davies and Sparrow, 1985; Warr, 1994). To assert baldly that old people are untrainable is a harsh judgement on their abilities. Employment trends in most developed countries have seen a shift from manufacturing to services and from manual to non-manual work. The newly created non-manual jobs have been in areas like retailing that demand few specialized skills and only short periods of training. Older workers should benefit from these trends and, given the chance, should perform well in many of the expanding sectors of the economy. It remains true that older workers are rarely recruited to the newly created jobs, but this is not because of their low productivity or difficulties in learning new techniques. High unemployment and the growth of early exit have meant that old people, irrespective of whether or not they are trainable, face declining work opportunities.

The other obstacle to retraining, the short future working life of old people, has more substance. If skills are costly to acquire in terms of time and monetary expense and intended to endure over a full working life of 40 years or so, then older workers are at a disadvantage in realizing the full returns to their investment in human capital. Retraining for employment with the highest skill levels implies embarking on a new long-term career in later life, which will normally be unfeasible. Most retraining, however, concerns lower skill levels and shorter time horizons. When the relevant time horizons are reduced to, say, 10 or 20 years, the retraining of old people becomes a more viable proposition. The old can extend their careers by working beyond the statutory retirement ages, and those prepared to undergo retraining should be keen to continue working as long as possible in order to receive the full monetary returns. Older workers have a shorter future working life than the young, but this should not be accepted as a definitive argument against their being retrained. The recent post-Fordist emphasis on flexible employment suggests that the opportunities for retraining should be expanding. As statutory retirement ages become less significant, older workers should have more leeway to retrain, start new jobs and prolong their careers. This assumes that flexibility offers workers a choice of retirement dates and a greater diversity of career patterns. Currently, it is early exit rather than retraining and longer working lives that has been replacing formal retirement at the statutory age. Flexibility has been confined largely to employers, who have chosen to relax the usual statutory guidelines and encourage people to retire early. With chronically high unemployment, older workers have had few openings to retrain and renew their working careers. The problem is not the short time horizon of the old (which is actually quite compatible with an era of flexibility, impermanence and diversity), but the absence of work opportunities for anyone who does undergo retraining.

Employer attitudes can be a major impediment to the retraining and continued employment of older workers. Age discrimination appears either directly as a visible restriction on recruitment of the elderly or indirectly through measures that adversely affect the elderly without being overtly biased against them (Drury, 1994). Direct age limits excluding older workers from jobs or training can be made illegal if governments introduce anti-discriminatory legislation, but on its own this is unlikely to secure equal treatment for older workers. Indirect discrimination will still be possible if employers adopt recruitment policies with an asymmetric impact on the young and old. Examples of indirect discrimination are arrangements encouraging early 'voluntary' retirement by older workers and schemes that assist the elderly to bridge the gap between early retirement and retirement proper. Measures like these, which at face value benefit the elderly, can also reduce expectations about old people's work performance and confirm the prevailing view that the old are less productive than the young. Ageism goes well beyond the overt restrictions placed on old people to include the general presuppositions about age that underlie social and economic behaviour (Bytheway and Johnson, 1990). Removing ageism and lifting the employment restrictions on old people will require a gradual process of cultural change, as well as the more obvious measures banning age discrimination.

Empirical research on employers' attitudes to the older worker suggest that, although they ascribe certain positive qualities to the old (such as steadiness and reliability), they have a strong preference for younger workers (Taylor and Walker, 1994, 1996). A low average age of the labour force will generally imply a low average age of the people making recruitment decisions and, along with that, a reluctance to recruit older workers. Age biases perpetuate themselves unless something happens to jolt recruitment practices out of their long-standing rut. Employers' prophecies about older workers will often be self-fulfilling: low expectations about work performance discourage the retraining of older workers, which consigns them to less skilled, less modern working methods and prevents them displaying their ability to cope with new techniques (Taylor and Walker, 1994). Older workers will become identified with low-skilled, low-wage service employment that supposedly best suits their limited abilities. A vicious circle of low expectations and limited opportunities can be broken only by concerted attempts at improving information about the capabilities of the elderly and breaking down employers' prejudices. In recent years, governments have been more sympathetic than employers to the continued employment of older workers (Guillemard, Taylor and Walker, 1996). While employers have persisted in their preference for early retirement during a period of prolonged unemployment, governments worried about the future costs of public pensions have been readier to contemplate an extended working life for those who want it. Employer attitudes now lag behind official government attitudes, in the sense that employers prefer single-date early retirement to a greater diversity of working practices. A compromise between these attitudes could improve the welfare of older workers if it does indeed restore some of their work opportunities. Reduced age discrimination will count for little, though, if chronic recession holds down the number of jobs on offer. Real progress on the employability of older people will require a substantial increase in economic activity and employment.

The level of economic activity has influenced attitudes to retraining. In times of mass unemployment and early exit, the case for retraining older workers appears weak. Recent unemployment has been so high that the smaller sizes of the cohorts reaching the school leaving ages have not guaranteed them employment. With joblessness prevalent among the younger age groups, the use of resources to retrain the old seems misguided and wasteful. Public resources for training become concentrated on the younger unemployed with a full working lifetime ahead of them. Retraining of older workers is restricted to particular firms which, despite the overall excess supply of labour, have had difficulty obtaining the skills they require among younger age groups and turn to older workers as an alternative source of labour. More widespread re-employment of older age groups will happen only if there is an upturn in economic activity in the developed countries and a reversal of the trend towards early exit. Otherwise younger generations will remain the focus of training initiatives. The outlook for older workers is highly sensitive to economic activity: with full employment, population ageing will encourage retraining of older workers and produce longer working lifetimes; with continued high unemployment, it will discourage retraining and consolidate early exit. At present, continued high unemployment seems more probable. Older age groups have the potential to be retrained to cope with new technology, but this potential will remain unfulfilled if chronic unemployment persists.

EMPLOYMENT AND LABOUR FORCE PARTICIPATION

In most developed countries, the salient employment trends during the postwar period have been the rise in female labour force participation and the emergence of early retirement and early exit. Each successive birth cohort has seen a higher proportion of females entering the labour force. In some countries, such as the UK, the proportion of female labour force entrants has levelled off, but the proportion of females in the working population will continue to rise until the younger cohorts have completed their full life cycles (Ermisch, 1983, Chapter 4). The growth in female employment has been concentrated in low-paid, low-skilled, often part-time jobs and, combined with declining male employment, has been associated with the changing character of work. Early retirement and early exit have also become well established over the last few decades. The trends towards earlier retirement and rising female employment are interrelated. A simultaneous rise in female part-time work and fall in the employment of older males at the top of an earnings hierarchy indicate a movement to greater flexibility and less structured working practices. Changes in the labour force participation of older workers are part of a more general pattern of change.

Older workers have not been retiring early entirely by choice. Retirement at a certain age is a condition of some people's employment contracts that is binding both on those who would have liked to retire earlier and on those who would have liked to carry on working. Formal retirement conditions are most commonly found in highly regulated employment, for instance, internal labour markets with occupational pension schemes and fixed ages at which employment ends and retirement begins. Mandatory retirement often occurs at the statutory retirement age, though this is by no means inevitable. In less regulated, more competitive labour markets the statutory retirement age is a guideline usually adhered to, but evadable when external pressures are strong enough. Firms wishing to reduce their labour forces may nominate workers approaching the statutory retirement age as the prime candidates for laying off. People who will soon retire anyway may be happy to leave employment a few years early if offered financial incentives; external events and the actions of the employer may strongly influence their 'voluntary' decisions to retire early. Whether such decisions should be regarded as voluntary is a moot point. The person retiring has made a constrained choice equivalent to the choice behaviour analysed in neoclassical economics, and yet the employer has manipulated the choice, perhaps to the extent that it coincides with the employer's own wishes. When this happens, the outcome is voluntary only in the sense that people are free from a strictly binding constraint; they are not free from external inducements to opt for particular alternatives. Few retirement decisions are unadulterated by extraneous influences, and most fall somewhere between the extremes of being wholly voluntary and being dictated by employers or the state.

The partly constrained, partly voluntary nature of early retirement gives rise to several pathways from employment to economic inactivity. Typical experiences vary within a single country and between countries (for the UK, see Casey and Laczko, 1989; Laczko and Phillipson, 1991; Atkinson and Sutherland, 1993; for international comparisons, see Guillemard, 1989; Jacobs, Kohli and Rein, 1991; Smeeding, 1993; Rainwater and Rein, 1993; Rein and Jacobs, 1993). Older workers who leave employment before reaching the statutory retirement age must bridge the gap between the loss of wage income and the receipt of public retirement pensions. Important income sources are unavailable, and alternative arrangements are needed. Broadly speaking, there are four main ways of bridging the gap: occupational pensions, a publicly supported pre-retirement period, unemployment benefits, and disability benefits (Laczko and Phillipson, 1991, Chapter 4). Each of them merits more detailed discussion.

Occupational pensions blur the distinction between early exit and early retirement. Workers entitled to occupational pensions can safely leave employment before reaching the statutory retirement age and still receive a pension, the size of which depends on their previous earnings. Any losses are confined to their reduced pension receipts from retiring early and their ineligibility for a public pension until they reach the statutory retirement age. Occupational pensions are a standard feature of secure, well-paid, non-manual employment within internal labour markets. People with occupational pensions are, on the whole, financially comfortable in old age, and the period between early exit and official retirement should not create major difficulties. Even this privileged group of workers cannot always choose early retirement: some occupational pension schemes give their members a right to retire early if they so wish, but others place early retirement at the discretion of employers. An occupational pension scheme makes it easier for employers to use early retirement as a means of reducing the size of their labour force. Whenever the employer wants to shed labour, the range of early retirement options offered to employees will be greater and the pension levels higher. Some employers may be prepared to pay early retirers a full pension in order to alleviate the firm's adjustment problems and avoid compulsory redundancies. While occupational pensions provide financial security for workers in the transition between work and formal retirement, they are also a tool by which employers can influence the retirement behaviour of their employees and guide decisions that at first sight seem voluntary.

An officially sanctioned pre-retirement period arises when the state financially supports workers who exit early from employment. This is the public counterpart of a private employer creating financial incentives for early retirement. The state, unlike private employers, normally wishes to reallocate rather than reduce employment, and public funds will be contingent on the replacement of the early retired with newly recruited younger workers. In the UK, for instance, the Job Release Scheme operating from 1977 until 1988 permitted certain older workers to retire early and receive public pension benefits, subject to their being replaced by unemployed school leavers. Because the scheme offered the early retired only the basic flat-rate public pension, its coverage was restricted mainly to low-paid workers. The arrangements were further restricted by being conditional on the employer's willingness to take on young recruits. Other countries, such as France, Germany and the Netherlands, have implemented similar schemes, and as in the UK the prime purpose has been to reallocate employment in times of recession and raise the chances of young people finding jobs. Providing additional retirement options for older workers has been only a secondary consideration. Since pre-retirement schemes rely on age to determine eligibility, their mode of operation resembles formal retirement policies and can be viewed as another instance of structured dependency. Several of the schemes have now been withdrawn, which implies that there was no real desire for a permanent, state-supported pre-retirement period (Guillemard, 1989). Pre-retirement schemes have encouraged short-term reallocations of employment, without going as far as to become institutionalized. They are too rigid and formal to be fully compatible with the new flexibility in employment, and for this reason it seems unlikely that that they will ever be a permanent feature of retirement practices.

When there are no occupational pensions or public pre-retirement schemes, workers who exit early from employment have often financed themselves until retirement by declaring themselves unemployed and claiming unemployment or social security benefits. Their hopes of regaining employment are minimal, and they may turn into 'discouraged workers' who stop actively looking for jobs and may well leave the working population altogether. People in this predicament have seldom given up working voluntarily. 'Unemployed' accurately describes their status, yet they are sometimes reclassified as 'retired' . Governments may for the sake of appearances delete them from the register of unemployed and treat them as having officially retired. Older unemployed workers in the UK have been allowed to keep their former pension and benefit rights without having to maintain the semblance of seeking work; these people have an equivocal status somewhere between the working population and the retired but officially belong to neither group. Their pre-retirement-by-default is financed at the low level of social security and unemployment benefits. When asked to classify themselves, older unemployed workers frequently prefer the more respectable label 'retired' to the less palatable 'unemployed'. In their self-perception, they may already have entered retirement, even when they are not officially recognized as retired and still counted among the unemployed. They have an uneasy identity divided between unemployment, retirement and a possible third category of pre-retirement. Few workers in this position will be pleased with their lot, but they may uphold their self-respect by saying that they would have chosen retirement in any case. Unemployment benefits bestow on employers a greater freedom to dispense with the services of older unskilled workers; they do for unskilled workers what occupational pensions do for skilled and non-manual workers. Several European countries have made special arrangements for the older unemployed, which guarantee continuous receipt of benefits up to the statutory retirement age and give unemployment-cum-retirement a semi-official status (Guillemard, 1989). The arrangements underscore the right of older people to receive transfer payments, but at the same time damage their employment prospects and imply that they have little hope of ever working again. The distinction between unemployment and retirement is blotted out, so that unemployment becomes perceived as retirement in everything but name. This rather confused situation will probably endure, unless an upsurge in economic activity brings increased employment of older workers.

A final route between early exit and official retirement is through registered disability and the receipt of disability benefits. In recent years, alongside the rise in unemployment, the number and proportion of old people classified as disabled has been increasing (Piachaud, 1986). This could be partly due to a genuine rise in disability among the old. Improved survival rates may permit more of the disabled to survive into old age, producing an apparent worsening of health, despite the fact that on an individual basis health has improved at all ages. The upward trend is combined with cyclicity, which seems to be caused by changes in the reporting of disabilities. Most methods of registering disability leave room for flexibility in the attitudes of disabled people and the interpretations of disability by doctors and other professionals. When unemployment is high and jobs are scarce, those with marginal disabilities have an incentive to declare their disability and get themselves registered as disabled instead of unemployed. The incentive is strengthened when, following standard practice, disability benefits are paid out at a higher level than unemployment or social security benefits. Older people may also regard disability as being more socially respectable than unemployment and having a lower probability of attracting censure. As with unemployment benefits, some governments have given disability benefits a semi-official status as a path between work and retirement (Guillemard, 1989). Eligibility criteria have sometimes been widened to entitle people with only minor disabilities to disabled status and the receipt of full disability benefits. This effectively acknowledges an 'economic disability' based only on age and unconnected with any physical disabilities. Access to disability benefits has been extended both by flexible interpretations of existing disability criteria and by changes in the criteria. Disability has now become an established method of crossing the employment–retirement divide.

The several types of early exit and early retirement imply that there is no set pattern of retirement covering all workers. The experience of older workers is becoming increasingly fragmented, except for the single dominating trend towards early exit before the statutory retirement age. Virtually all developed countries are experiencing this trend, with some variation among countries in the rapidity and extent of change and in the means by which early exit is accomplished (Kohli et al., 1991). Of the alternative routes between work and retirement, some have a special importance in certain countries but are much less important in others. Rein and Jacobs (1993) classify developed countries into two groups: 'high early exit' countries, such as France, Germany and the Netherlands, and 'low early exit' countries, such as Japan, Sweden, the UK and the US. Workers in the 'high early exit' countries experience a rapid fall in labour force participation as they enter their late fifties and early sixties, accompanied by a permanent transition from full-time work to unemployment or retirement. Early exit has occurred mainly through structural programmes that are often publicly supported and let older people receive unemployment or disability benefits until they reach the statutory retirement age. This pre-retirement period is a surrogate for real retirement: once people have exited early from employment, their prospects of re-employment are negligible. Benefits in 'high early exit' countries are relatively generous, and older people have little incentive to search for part-time or full-time work.

The 'low early exit' countries have much higher (but still declining) rates of labour force participation and employment among the older population. Early exit is less prevalent and less sudden than in 'high early exit' countries, and the incidence of gradual retirement and part-time work among the elderly is greater. Arrangements for early exit are not as structured or standardized, leading to more variation in experience between countries and between individuals within a country. Rein and Jacobs (1993) look at the contrasting examples of partial retirement in Sweden, lifetime employment in Japan, and the deregulated approach of the US.

The Swedish partial pension scheme was an attempt to replace a single, statutory retirement age with more flexible retirement. Workers could reduce their working time gradually, and a partial pension compensated the fall in their wage income. The scheme produced a higher rate of part-time work among old people than is common elsewhere, together with a lower reduction in their net incomes. Raising the labour force participation and employment of old people, and thus reducing spending on unemployment benefits, was one of the scheme's explicit objectives (Delsen, 1990). Although the scheme was successful, this may have been because of its generous provision, which could prove difficult for other countries to emulate in the current economic and political climate.

Retirement arrangements in Japan have given greater prominence to employers. The traditional system of lifetime employment with a single employer normally involved mandatory retirement at a fixed age (usually 55) below the statutory retirement age of 60. Firms had an informal responsibility to help their employees pass from the end of lifetime employment to the start of retirement proper: this could be done by extending the original employment contract, offering part-time or less intensive work at a lower salary, or arranging alternative employment with an affiliated company. Older people had a strong incentive to enter part-time work in order to cover their living expenses (Shimowada, 1992). Effectively, the traditional practices were a privately organized system of partial retirement. Recent developments have seen an increase in the mandatory retirement age from 55 towards 60, which lengthens the period of lifetime employment and narrows the gap between lifetime employment and retirement. If the partial retirement period vanishes, the arrangements will converge on those of the 'high early exit' countries, but the statutory retirement age will have a greater importance in the Japanese system.

Unlike the structured arrangements of Sweden and Japan, partial retirement occurs in the United States through a deregulated approach. Most US workers have private pensions that create a wide variety of retirement experiences. Public pensions are low, and so it is difficult for those without private pensions to sustain their living standards unless they work beyond the usual retirement age. As a means of increasing the employment chances of old people, the government has legislated to ban age discrimination in employment and prevent employers imposing mandatory retirement on their employees. This should yield flexible, unstructured retirement practices, with the state's activity reduced to the provision of a social security safety net and the enforcement of rules debarring age discrimination by employers. The prior expectation might well be that, compared with the more structured approach of other countries, the US approach would generate a higher incidence of partial retirement. In fact, only a minority of the working population has stayed in work beyond the statutory retirement age. For the majority, the effect of occupational pension schemes predominates; retirement takes place at a single date and entails an immediate switch from full-time work. Despite the limited state involvement, US retirement practices retain the structural properties observed in other countries. A unifying feature of retirement in the 'low early exit' countries is the redefinition of work for people employed beyond the usual retirement ages: their continued employment is sharply delineated as an interim period between full-time work and complete retirement. Partitioning of the life cycle by age is still important.

The diverse routes from employment to retirement show that there is no neat, stylized institutional framework applicable to all countries. On some interpretations, this is a symptom of the general change in employment practices from Fordism to post-Fordism (Guillemard and van Gunsteren, 1991). The Fordist starting point has firms operating on a large scale, producing standardized goods for a mass market and organized on highly structured, hierarchical principles that keep management strictly separate from labour. Managerial and skilled employees belong to an internal labour market with restricted entry, a rising age–earnings profile and mandatory retirement, whereas unskilled workers have less job security and a less hierarchical career pattern. Employment (especially within internal labour markets) is 'chronologized': recruitment and retirement take place at fixed ages and earnings are strongly correlated with age. Alongside large-scale firms, Fordism brings large-scale government, with interventionist macroeconomic policy on Keynesian principles and an extensive welfare state including public retirement pensions (Jessop, 1994). The welfare state too is 'chronologized' by having a statutory retirement age that must be attained before public pensions are paid. An institutionalized importance attached to age is a defining characteristic of Fordism, creating what can be termed the 'Fordist life cycle' (Myles, 1990).

Post-Fordism entails a fundamental change from mass production to newer industries based on information technology. Firms are no longer committed to standardization, so they can be smaller in scale, more flexible, and organized on flatter, less hierarchical principles. The internal labour market, with its rising age–earnings profile and mandatory retirement, is superseded by shorter-term arrangements in which employees no longer pursue a lifetime career with a single firm. Early exit and the various versions of a pre-retirement period supplant official retirement, which has diminishing importance. Changes in employment practices may spill over into the welfare state and force a reconsideration of formal retirement. The trend is towards the 'dechronologization' of the life cycle, and a person's age will have less significance than it did in the era of binding, statutory retirement arrangements. Post-Fordism suggests a movement away from fixed retirement patterns towards greater decentralization, flexibility and diversity. People will no longer have the same unified, centrally regulated experience of ageing.

Post-Fordism and 'dechronologization' seem to accord quite well with certain recent trends, but they are open to question. The greater diversity of employment practices need not imply that arrangements are becoming less structured at the individual level. Most workers still exit suddenly from employment, to enter retirement or a well-defined pre-retirement period: this remains a structured pattern of work. Employers are structuring their employment practices in different ways, so that early exit does not happen at a single, standardized age. Greater diversity reduces the role of the statutory retirement age, but it does not remove the effect of age on individual life chances. People still face (semi-) compulsory with-drawal from the labour force upon reaching a certain age, even if the timing of the change varies. The trend towards diversity can be seen as a privatizing and diversifying of structured ('chronologized') practices, rather than a 'dechronologizing' of the life cycle.

Further doubts about the post-Fordist approach concern the part played by technology. Post-Fordism is normally assumed to be founded on information technology and the passage from mass production to more decentralized arrangements. Such technical changes have only a tenuous link with the changes affecting the elderly. It is tempting to argue for a direct connection between new technology and early exit: older workers cannot adapt to rapid technical change and so employers are dis-pensing with their services earlier. This argument has little empirical foundation. Studies of productivity show that older workers can adapt smoothly to new methods and, if anything, the switch away from routine manual work should be in their favour. Early exit and a pre-retirement period are not inevitable consequences of information technology, and other interpretations of events are possible. Many post-Fordist develop-ments can alternatively be viewed as a reversion to a less regulated capitalism, a step backwards rather than forwards. In this view, the Fordist welfare state was only a temporary outbreak of public interven-tion in a longer-term capitalist framework. Post-Fordist privatization and decentralization may simply be old laissez-faire policies revamped and repackaged. If so, the new employment practices affecting the elderly have more to do with changes in political and economic climate than with changes in technology.

Beneath the surface post-Fordist diversity, most countries have a common, well-established trend towards early exit from employment. As economic activity has stagnated, employers have discovered that the early exit of older workers is a convenient way of reducing their labour forces; the initially short-term arrangements may well become permanent. In vir-tually all countries early exit has been a response to low economic activity and only vaguely linked with the characteristics of old people or the intro-duction of new technology. For the foreseeable future, notwithstanding the smaller birth cohorts entering the working population, it seems that older workers will be experiencing early exit and an extended pre-retirement period that may eventually become merged with official retirement.

6. Pensions and retirement

The economic literature on population ageing gives more attention to pensions than to any other issue, with the possible exception of labour supply (the interest in which is stimulated by pension policy). Economists have frequently treated pension finance as a narrow, technical matter unrelated to the wider concerns about demographic change. Pensions cannot, however, be separated from other aspects of ageing; they are entangled with retirement and with the living standards and social status of old people. A discussion of pension finance in isolation may be relevant to short-term political debate, but a thorough evaluation of ageing should consider the real, long-term effects of pension arrangements.

An ageing population heightens the controversies over pensions and retirement that would exist even in a demographic steady state. When pensions are financed from tax revenues, population ageing will put pressure on public budgets. The policy problem mimics, in financial terms, the binding aggregate resource constraint assumed in discussions of economic dependency. It may have a firmer foundation than the dependency approach, to the extent that financial constraints may indeed be binding (irrespective of chronic unemployment) if the government chooses to regard them as such. The problem has its socially created side, thanks to the social origins of the financial constraint, but the connection between population ageing and rising burdens on taxpayers is more direct than with a real dependency burden. Financial considerations broached by pensions are at odds with some of the broader social considerations surrounding old age. Later retirement can, for example, ease pension finance, and yet it has often been seen as a socially regressive change. A full treatment of the relation between pensions and population ageing should be aware of both financial and social matters. The present chapter will first look at the debate over pension finance and then assess the wider issues of retirement and the social status of old people.

TYPES OF PENSION SCHEME

Pension schemes can have many alternative characteristics. They can be financed from a fund of previously accumulated assets or on pay-as-you-go principles from the current contributions of the employed. They can be organized privately on an occupational or personal basis, or publicly. Participation in pension schemes can be voluntary or compulsory. Pensions can be paid on defined benefit principles, where benefits are set in advance of contributions, or defined contribution principles, where contributions are set in advance of benefits. Pension levels can be based on previous earnings or independent of earnings. These alternative characteristics are logically distinct from each other and can be combined to give numerous possible pension systems, many of which are rarely if ever observed. Most policy discussion addresses just a few widespread combinations of characteristics but omits other combinations that might be pursued (OECD, 1988b; Minns, 1996). A standard simplifying framework distinguishes three chief sources of economic security in old age, termed the 'three pillars': public pension and income maintenance schemes (further subdivided into contributory national insurance programmes and non-contributory, means-tested social assistance); occupational pensions, usually sponsored and organized privately by employers; and personal saving schemes, usually entered into voluntarily by individuals with no direct involvement by employers or the state (Schulz, 1996). Most people living in developed countries rely on one of the three pillars to finance their retirement. Some authors have argued that part-time work after the statutory retirement age should be added as a 'fourth pillar' that will become increasingly important as work and retirement become more flexible (Kessler, 1988; Giarini, 1990; Reday-Mulvey, 1990). A 'four pillars' approach branches out from income maintenance to consider the connections between income, employment and retirement. Even the simplified three or four pillar frameworks still leave a huge range of possible approaches to pension policy. The following discussion concentrates on population ageing and makes no attempt to evaluate pensions comprehensively. Of the characteristics mentioned above, the only one concerned directly with relative generation size is the choice between funded and pay-as-you-go financing. This has been central to the literature on pensions and demographic change.

Under a funded pension scheme, people pay part of their earnings while employed into a fund of financial assets which eventually finances their retirement pension. The scheme resembles private saving or private insurance in that people pay for their own pensions, so that on average they break even over the life cycle. Uncertainty enters the calculations because any particular person's age at death is known only approximately. Actuarial statistics provide a reliable indication of life expectancy; funded pensions are designed to be actuarially fair, ensuring that the average person will draw out of the pension scheme during retirement an amount equivalent in value to what they paid into the scheme during employment. People living longer than average will do better than just break even over the life cycle, and people who die prematurely will do worse. Funded pensions inevitably redistribute from the short-lived to the long-lived, but apart from this they are intended to be non-redistributive. Since nobody expects to be made worse off under actuarially fair funding, the pension scheme can in theory be organized on private, voluntary principles. Funded pensions are sometimes viewed as being synonymous with private pension arrangements, although they can also be publicly organized.

A pay-as-you-go pension scheme accumulates no fund and instead finances the pensions of the retired from the taxes paid by the working population. In place of the life-cycle reallocation of a person's income, there is a cross-sectional income redistribution from taxpayers to pensioners. This creates an intergenerational transfer often described as an implicit contract: each generation finances the retirement pensions of the previous generation on the understanding that its own pensions will be financed by the next generation. Because the contract is only implicit and extends over many decades, the risk of future taxpayers breaching it is always present. Economic growth will alleviate the burdens imposed on the next generation and may secure for the retired a higher living standard than would be available under a funded pension scheme. Pay-as-you-go financing does not in general satisfy the insurance principle that all people will on average break even over their life cycles. When taxes are progressive, pension finance brings about systematic income redistribution. The need for compulsory income transfers and the absence of an earmarked pension fund means that pay-as-you-go pensions are normally implemented through the state's power to levy taxes. Private, occupational versions of pay-as-you-go are technically feasible but uncommon and open to abuse if the pension contributions of employees become merged with the employer's general income.

The relative merits of funding and pay-as-you-go have long been debated, and each has points in its favour (Dilnot et al., 1994, Chapter 3). Laissez-faire economists have commonly preferred a funded approach. If a funded pension scheme operates on a voluntary basis, with individuals choosing their own pension levels, it can claim to represent the rational individual preferences on which neoclassical arguments for market efficiency depend. Competitive markets could then, in theory, offer the types of pension scheme demanded by consumers; a public pension scheme organized on either funded or pay-as-you-go principles would be superfluous. Funded pensions are also argued to increase aggregate savings, compared with pay-as-you-go, and therefore to raise investment and economic growth (see Chapter 3). A problem with a wholly private, funded pension system is free riding behaviour: people who do not make pension contributions and subsequently find themselves destitute in old age can still, on humanitarian grounds, receive non-contributory benefits. Free riders can force an unplanned income transfer from taxpayers to themselves, and even a minimal social security safety net would destabilize a voluntary private pension scheme. Free riding is avoidable only by legislating to compel participation in either private or public pension schemes, a curtailment of voluntary decision making. In economies with high unemployment, many of the working population face job insecurity and long periods spent unemployed, which prevent them from accumulating sufficient pension rights to cover their retirement. Under these conditions, it is doubtful whether a wholly private, funded pension system could ever be feasible.

Pay-as-you-go financing is better placed than funding to cope with economic change and uncertainty. An example of this is the impact of unanticipated inflation on funded pensions. Persistent inflation causes uncertainty about the future real returns to private savings, given that future inflation rates are unknown. The uncertainty applies to all assets collectively, and the risks on one asset cannot be offset by lower risks on other assets. Private insurers could suffer disastrous losses if they offered pension schemes guaranteeing a minimum real income in old age. As a result, they are unable to offer fully indexed pensions unless the assets accumulated in pension funds are index-linked and underwritten by the state. Pay-as-you-go financing is immune from this problem, because it uses the state's ability to impose cross-sectional income transfers through taxation. There is no stock of assets to be eroded by inflation, and pensions are financed from the current incomes of the working population, which increase automatically as part of the inflationary process. Provided that the economy grows sufficiently rapidly, the government will have no problems in guaranteeing the real incomes of pensioners against inflation.

Pay-as-you-go has the further advantage of giving old people a bigger stake in the benefits of economic growth. Under a funded system, they receive pensions tied to their previous contributions, whatever is happening to the incomes of the employed. When real incomes are declining this may be desirable, but real incomes are more likely to be on a long-run upward path arising from economic growth. As real wages increase, the fruits of economic growth accrue immediately to the employed, whereas the retired must depend on pension funds with a fixed monetary value. Faster economic growth swings purchasing power towards the younger, working generations and away from the old; the consequences for intergenerational equity and the social status of old people may be unpalatable. Pay-as-you-go financing is protected from these regressive redistributive effects, since tax contributions increase proportionally with real incomes and the replacement ratio for pensions stays approximately constant. Moreover, taxation can be progressive, and the government can, if it wishes, set its tax and pension levels so as to attain a more equal intergenerational distribution of income. The standard conclusion, following Samuelson (1958, 1975) and Aaron (1966), is that pay-as-you-go financing becomes more desirable relative to funding the faster is the rate of economic growth.

Population ageing is usually seen as causing greater adjustment problems for pay-as-you-go than funded pension schemes. In a funded scheme there are no intergenerational transfers of income, and relative generation size is of little consequence. A large generation makes greater contributions to pension funds during its working years and accumulates a larger stock of assets from which it can draw pension payments during its retirement. The only financial adjustment required is to accommodate changes in life expectancy. Where population ageing derives partly from falling mortality, a funded pension scheme must raise contributions or reduce benefits if it is still to break even on average over an individual's life cycle. Funded financing, organized on individualistic principles, has only to respond to individual rather than population ageing. As changes in fertility, not mortality, have caused the bulk of population ageing, the necessary adjustments in funded financing are marginal. With pay-as-you-go pensions, on the other hand, population ageing has direct implications for the ratio of contributors to pension recipients. Maintaining current pension and contribution rates will move the pension scheme from an initial break-even position into deficit. To restore a balanced pension budget, contributions will have to be raised or pensions reduced. The choice is an unpleasant one: higher contributions mean higher taxation and worries over disincentive effects and intergenerational conflict; pension cuts may increase hardship among old people and widen the income difference between young and old generations. Some such readjustment is inevitable when a pension scheme balances its revenues and payments: the economy is out of steady state and fixed budgetary arrangements cannot be sustained indefinitely. Given that steady-state outcomes are seldom observed, a balanced-budget pay-as-you-go system must be adjusted continually in response to demographic and other changes.

The pensions literature often assumes that funded schemes are private and pay-as-you-go schemes are public. A preference for funding as seemingly the best way of meeting demographic change can easily be translated into a more general preference for private pensions. Policy commentators can enlist population ageing as a reason to expand occupational pensions or personal saving schemes and move from public pensions to a 'multipillar' system (World Bank, 1994). The arguments based on demographic change are usually part of a wider case for privatization including non-demographic factors such as the supposed efficiency gains from a competitive environment and the avoidance of political interference in commercial decision making. Population ageing could only ever be a minor element in the broad economic and political debates over the role of the state, and as a reason for advocating funded private pensions it is not particularly convincing.

One difficulty is that funding cannot be introduced at a stroke: it requires a lengthy transition period during which the currently employed have to finance the pensions of the currently retired (who have not previously accumulated pension funds) and simultaneously contribute to their own pension funds. Until the funded scheme has matured, the financial burdens on the working population will be greater than they would have been if the previous pay-as-you-go arrangements had been retained. In the short term a transition to funding will actually increase the financial pressures created by population ageing (OECD, 1988a, Chapter 9; OECD, 1995).

A further difficulty is that funding has no unique link with private pensions. The government is by no means restricted to pay-as-you-go methods and can organize public pensions on funded principles through a national pension fund or personal schemes (Minns, 1996). A transition to funding as a response to population ageing need not entail the privatization of pensions. Population ageing has only a tenuous connection with privatization, and the people who play up this connection are generally those who already hanker after private arrangements and are searching for additional reasons to justify them. The main implications of population ageing for pensions revolve not around the private versus public issue but around funding versus pay-as-you-go.

If one considers the effects of population ageing on the real economy, as against pension finance, the advantages of funding are less clear cut. Barr (1979) argues that the supposed benefits of funding are based on a fallacy of composition: for an individual it may be possible to redistribute assets and spending power over time, but for society as a whole this option is unavailable. Few consumption goods are stored over long periods, and most goods produced when the dependency ratio is low cannot be saved and consumed later when it is high. Funded pensions transfer purchasing power from the past so as to make pensioners financially independent of the working population, but the inactive elderly remain dependent on the working population for the goods and services they consume. Tensions over pension finance may be reduced or removed, only to be replaced by tensions over the distribution of real resources. In a pay-as-you-go pension scheme, population ageing creates a visible clash between the working population's desire to keep tax rates down and the elderly's desire to preserve the value of their pensions. These financial claims also reflect conflicts over entitlements to real goods and services: decisions concerning pension finance affect the relative purchasing power of the working and retired populations. In a funded pension scheme, the purchasing power of the retired depends instead on their past pension contributions, which are fixed independently of the current size and tax payments of the working population.

As the population ages, pensions and taxes may be unchanged, while the real dependency burden on the working population must have increased. When total purchasing power exceeds the value of current output at the prevailing prices, a general price inflation will bring them back into line. The retired elderly with funded pensions have financial claims on real goods and services, but these claims are worth little if the working population cannot produce the goods and services demanded. Rising prices will choke off the excess demand, and the elderly will face a cut in their real pensions, despite having constant money pensions. For any given rise in the dependency ratio, the implications for production will be the same under funded or pay-as-you-go pension financing: the only difference is that with funding any cuts in living standards are accomplished through price adjustments, whereas with pay-as-you-go they appear explicitly as a renegotiation of pension and tax levels.

It is debatable which method of making cutbacks should be preferred. If people suffer from 'money illusion', they may be sensitive mainly to their money incomes and oblivious of reductions in their real incomes caused by price increases. The funded approach may have the advantage of reducing real incomes without any fall in money incomes or pensions, thus minimizing the risks of intergenerational conflict. One might, however, welcome the visible adjustments required under a pay-as-you-go system on the grounds that it is better to settle these redistributive matters by democratic decision making than by haphazard price adjustments. Conflicts between age groups may be intensified, but this at least ensures that redistribution is being addressed consciously and directly. The apparent advantage of funding in dealing with population ageing may, from this perspective, be a disadvantage.

The argument that funding and pay-as-you-go are equivalent in real terms has weaknesses, as it implicitly assumes full employment and treats the financial constraint on pensions as if it were a real resource constraint on the whole economy. The focus of concern becomes the aggregate dependency burden rather than pension finance. Full employment means that the size of the working population constrains the economy's output; such an assumption is ill suited to economies with high and long-standing unemployment. While the working population produces most (but not all) the material goods and services consumed at any one time, only the employed part of the working population undertakes the relevant economic activities. The notion of a mass of physical goods somehow being transferred from their 'producers' – the entire working population – to the 'dependent' elderly is artificial and oversimplified. More relevant to pension finance is the institutionally defined ownership of assets, embodied in financial and monetary variables like pension entitlements, social security benefits and taxes. A financially based approach, for all its narrowness, has the virtue of recognizing (consciously or otherwise) that the real economy does not face binding demographic constraints. The attention devoted to financial issues can be justified, as a demographic constraint on pay-as-you-go pensions does exist if the government wishes to record and balance the pension budget. When a balanced-budget constraint is being adhered to, there is a direct effect of population ageing on pension finance. For the real economy, by contrast, population ageing has only a muted influence, whatever the method of pension finance. Funding and pay-as-you-go are similar through the unimportance of population ageing, not through a common set of important real effects. This leaves their financial implications as the main point of interest when comparing funded and pay-as-you-go pensions.

FINANCING PAY-AS-YOU-GO PENSIONS UNDER POPULATION AGEING

Strictly speaking, a government financing pensions on pay-as-you-go principles has no need to balance the pension budget each period. It could let temporary surpluses and deficits even out over time, or finance a deficit on pensions from surpluses elsewhere in the public budgets, or simply tolerate a deficit and perhaps not even bother to record a separate pension budget. The economic significance of budget deficits is controversial. Neoclassical economics views an increasing public debt arising from repeated budget deficits as a real burden on future generations, who will eventually have to make sacrifices to pay off the debt. According to this logic, budget deficits are best avoided, and sound finance implies balancing the budget at all times. Correspondingly, budget surpluses benefit future generations by reducing public debt and accumulating assets that can finance future consumption. Partial funding of pensions, creating a temporary surplus in social security budgets, has been suggested as a sensible approach to dealing with population ageing (Aaron, Bosworth and Burtless, 1989; Hagemann and Nicoletti, 1989). The accumulated fund can tide the government over the medium-term difficulties of an exceptionally high dependency ratio. A budget surplus can alleviate the financial burdens on future taxpayers and, it is claimed, reduce interest rates, raise investment and boost the economy's productive capacity. As with other arguments about ageing, this approach melds financial and real considerations: it sees a stock of financial assets as a guarantee that material goods will be available for future consumption.

A large pension or social security fund cannot on its own ensure that future pensions will maintain their real value, and much depends on the use to which the fund is put (Asimakopoulos, 1989). Of greater importance than public budgets or deficits is the economy's productivity, which relies on high levels of economic activity and investment. To attempt to cut public budget deficits and achieve surpluses has a deflationary effect on the economy, reducing economic activity, discouraging investment, and ultimately threatening productivity. A large pension fund will do nothing for the elderly or anyone else if the policies required to accumulate it have harmed the economy's productive capacity (Wray, 1991). The idea that decreases in budget deficits or increases in surpluses are always beneficial should be treated with caution. A balanced pension budget is by no means a policy imperative and may have a detrimental effect on the economy.

Suppose, nevertheless, that a government wants to balance the pension budget during a period of population ageing. This can be interpreted as an internally generated, socially created condition on policy, without implying the existence of a binding material resource constraint or the necessity for 'sound finance'. Many governments impose this constraint on their own finances, and so it is relevant to consider the alternative ways in which the constraint can be satisfied. There are three main alternative ways of balancing the pension budget. The first is to keep current pension arrangements as they are, and increase the taxes paid by the working population. A government unconscious or neglectful of pensions will find itself adopting this stance. The second alternative is to reduce the monetary (and perhaps real) value of pensions in order to protect the incomes of the working population. Cuts in pensions require a conscious pension reform by a government worried about the political or economic ramifications of higher tax rates. The third alternative is to raise the statutory retirement age or introduce policies that will persuade the elderly to stay employed for longer. Pension expenditure can thus be curtailed without reducing the incomes of old people, albeit at the expense of a shorter retirement period (and on the assumption that old people can secure or retain employment). All three alternatives involve unpleasant cutbacks, but their impact will be softened if the economy is undergoing rapid growth of productivity and real incomes. The alternatives are not mutually exclusive, and a government wishing to even out the effects of the cutbacks could combine all three. For convenience only, the following discussion regards them as separate and distinct policies.

A government aiming to preserve the current value of public pensions as the population ages can do so in either absolute or relative terms. If the real pension level is held constant, the retired elderly are sheltered from a decline in their purchasing power, but may still lose out in comparison with the working population, whose real incomes should be increasing through the benefits of economic growth. A widening gap in living standards between the elderly and the rest of the population might be considered intolerable. To avoid this, pension levels can be fixed in relation to the average real disposable incomes of the working population, so that the replacement ratio remains constant and pensioners are allotted a fixed share in the returns to economic growth. A deepening division between the retired and working populations is prevented, at the cost of higher tax rates. The policy can be illustrated by means of a simple model. Let N denote the total population, with R retired and $N - R$ in the working population; the dependency ratio can be defined as $D = R/(N - R)$. Pensions are financed on pay-as-you-go principles, such that the pension budget balances at all times. The average pension level B is given by:

$$B = \frac{tM(N - R)}{R} = \frac{tM}{D}$$

where t is the tax rate and M is the average real income of those in work. The dependency ratio D rises exogenously as the population ages, and the pension budget can stay balanced only through compensating movements in B, t and M. When pensions are held constant in absolute terms, B is fixed, and t must rise if M/D falls. Population ageing requires a rise in taxes whenever the proportional rise in the dependency ratio exceeds the proportional rise in the real incomes of the working population. If real income growth is fast enough, a rising dependency ratio can be combined with a falling tax rate: this underlies the argument that economic growth can relieve the problems of pension finance (Midwinter, 1989). Consider now the case where pensions are held in a constant proportion to the disposable incomes of the working population, so that $B = b(1 - t)M$ with a constant replacement ratio, b $(0 < b < 1)$. For the pension budget to balance it must be true that:

$$\frac{t}{1-t} = bD$$

Since b is constant and the left-hand side of the equation is positively related to t, a rise in D will necessitate a rise in the tax rate, regardless of any movements in incomes and productivity. The index-linking of pensions to other incomes means that productivity gains are absorbed by higher real pensions and cannot be used to reduce the tax payments of the working population. Economic growth no longer eases pension finance, and an ageing population implies higher taxes whatever the economic growth rate.

The main advantage of holding pensions constant in absolute or relative terms is the income guarantee it offers the retired. If the aim is merely to provide a subsistence income, then pensions can be set at the lowest socially acceptable level; anything less would create officially recognized hardship among the elderly. In times of economic growth, constant absolute pensions are an unambitious goal that may well be attainable under population ageing without the need to increase taxes. Concern over the relative social status of the elderly may motivate the index-linking of pensions to disposable incomes. A long-term decline in pensioners' real incomes compared with those of younger people could cause relative poverty among the old and jeopardize their (absolute) capability to participate fully in society (Sen, 1983; Townsend, 1985). Index-linked pensions place a higher burden on taxpayers, although real pensions will increase only if productivity growth rises sufficiently to pay for them (and real pensions will fall if productivity and real incomes are falling). Even when the population is ageing and the tax rate is rising, the employed and the retired enjoy an identical proportional change in their real disposable income which, it might be argued, provides an equitable share out of the benefits from productivity growth.

The main disadvantage of absolute or relative income guarantees to pensioners is the possibility of higher tax rates and resistance from taxpayers. Resistance takes the forms considered in Chapter 2, namely disincentive effects and breaches of the intergenerational contract. Disincentives are a mainstay of the economic discussion of population ageing. Higher taxes are commonly believed to have deleterious effects on labour supply, savings and investment, notwithstanding the scanty empirical evidence for these effects. If disincentives do pose a threat to productivity and national income, then decisions to maintain the absolute or relative value of pensions may bring about lower productivity growth: in the model, the income variable, M, will be a negative function of taxes, t. A breach of the intergenerational contract arises if future taxpayers vote against the higher taxation required by guaranteed pension levels. This does not per-force have major effects on productivity or national income, but it stops the government redistributing income to pensioners: in the model, t may become stuck at some politically determined limit. Whether the conflict between age groups over pensions could generate a full-scale tax revolt is uncertain. A chronic rise in productivity, common to most developed countries, will in general yield higher living standards for the working population. They are not experiencing real income reductions, even if the tax rate does increase as the population ages.

The second alternative policy stance, the opposite of the first, is to hold tax rates constant and adjust pension levels. The previous model can again show the consequences for pensions and taxes. Pensions satisfy the relationship:

$$t = \left(\frac{D}{M}\right) B$$

where t is now held constant. If D rises proportionally faster than M, then pensions must be reduced to maintain a balanced budget. Should productivity and real incomes grow quickly enough, a rise in D may still be compatible with a fall in D/M and a rise in pensions. The equivalent relationship between t and the replacement ratio b is given by:

$$\frac{t}{1-t} = Db$$

For a constant t, the left-hand side of the equation is fixed, and a rise in D requires a fall in b if the budget is to remain balanced. When produc-tivity grows quickly enough to reconcile constant tax rates with rising pensions, the real incomes of pensioners will still be falling relative to those of the working population. Holding taxes constant while the popu-lation ages means that the relative incomes of old people must suffer, but not necessarily their absolute incomes.

The usual rationale for holding taxes constant is apprehension over the effects of raising them. Disincentives might be so strong that no increase in tax rates can be contemplated. Future generations might renege on current promises to finance retirement pensions and thereby break the implicit intergenerational contract. The resulting unanticipated cut in pensions would be a severe blow to pensioners who had expected a more substantial public pension and planned accordingly. It would be better, so the argument goes, for the government to reduce promised pensions now, allowing people to anticipate the reductions and build them into their long-term plans. On the assumption that cuts in pensions are unavoidable, the elderly will benefit most if the cuts are executed in a conscious, properly planned fashion rather than haphazardly. The case against this approach (apart from the doubts about the significance of disincentives and intergenerational conflict) centres on its harsh treatment of old people and its failure to maintain their living standards. Holding taxes down while the population is ageing may reduce the absolute incomes of old people and will almost certainly reduce their incomes relative to those of the working population. The adverse consequences of population ageing are being diverted towards the elderly, even though a (probably temporary) rise in tax rates could share out the proceeds of productivity growth more equally. In the formal model of Smith (1982), constant pensions with variable taxes are preferable to constant taxes with variable pensions as a source of social insurance against demographic risks. A ceiling on taxes would obstruct the best method of redistributing income in response to population ageing.

The third alternative policy stance is to raise the retirement age so as to offset the effects of demographic change on the dependency ratio. In principle, a rising retirement age could exactly counterbalance the growing relative size of the elderly population. The boundary between the retired population R and the working population $N - R$ could be continually redefined to leave the dependency ratio $R/(N - R)$ constant regardless of the age composition of the population. The budget constraint could then be rewritten as:

$$B = \left(\frac{t}{D} \right) M = cM$$

where $c = (t/D)$ is a constant, given that D is held steady by a rise in the retirement age. Pensions are a fixed proportion of the incomes of the working population, and as incomes rise, pensions rise with them. Because the adjustment of retirement practices keeps the dependency ratio constant, the economy remains in an artificial demographic steady state that obviates any adjustments to pay-as-you-go pension schemes. Unlike the first two approaches (fixity of B or t), fixity of D minimizes the revisions of financial arrangements under population ageing.

Later retirement can dispense with tax and pension changes. As the population ages, a balanced pension budget can be combined with constant taxes and pensions. If the existing pension level is regarded as optimal, then this will be the most efficient way to accommodate population ageing; in a simple utilitarian framework without disincentive effects or administrative costs, a change in the retirement age is socially preferred

to lower pensions or higher taxes (Jackson, 1989). By conventional efficiency criteria, adjusting retirement practices provides the optimum
response to population ageing. A further advantage of later retirement is
that the relative incomes of the retired and working populations are
unchanged, and so tensions over the income distribution (if not the
employment distribution) should be reduced. Neither the working population nor the retired are the clear losers from the policy adjustments.
What happens is a redrawing of the boundary between the two groups,
rather than a worsening of the circumstances of either.

Later retirement also has disadvantages, such as the continually changing retirement ages and the shortening retirement period. It would be far
from straightforward to manipulate retirement ages so as to offset demographic changes exactly and preserve a constant dependency ratio. Such
'fine tuning' could be achieved only by having mandatory retirement rules
for the whole population, but in practice most retirement arrangements
have a degree of flexibility and decentralization. Unless constraints on
retirement were tightened, a planned change in retirement behaviour
would be difficult to implement. Attempts to induce later voluntary retirement would normally require changes in tax or benefit levels and would
not therefore be distinct from the other main policy approaches. A continually changing retirement age would create problems for people planning
their retirement: unanticipated jumps in the retirement age would disrupt
work, consumption and saving. The other chief concern is about the
intrinsic demerits of later retirement. Most developed countries have seen
a long-run trend towards earlier retirement, which is often thought to
reflect a general desire for more leisure time as material prosperity
increases. Encouraging later retirement seems to be a socially regressive
policy that delays the arrival of expanded leisure opportunities. With
chronic unemployment, old people will in any case be hard pressed to stay
employed long enough to reach the new, higher retirement age. Longer
working careers can generate higher incomes in return for the loss of
leisure time, but this applies only if sufficient employment is available. A
combination of early exit, age restrictions on employment and later retirement could widen the uncomfortable gap between the end of employment
and the beginning of officially recognized retirement.

The simple model outlined above can be adapted to allow for variations in tax and pension arrangements. Creedy and Disney (1989a)
introduce VAT alongside income taxation and find (as one would intu-
itively expect) that it reduces the rate of direct taxation needed to finance
pensions and makes the direct tax rate less sensitive to the dependency
ratio; Blankart (1993) obtains similar results in the context of a public-
choice framework. Other possible refinements to the model are to add

means-tested pensions, permit the taxation of pensions, and differentiate between income and payroll taxes (Creedy, 1992; Creedy and Disney, 1992; Creedy and Morgan, 1992); these changes further reduce the adjustments required under population ageing and weaken the links between population ageing and specific institutional responses. When extra details are added even to simple models, the general theoretical framework can rapidly become algebraically intractable, forcing the analyst to resort to numerical simulations (Creedy and Morgan, 1992). Actual pension arrangements are complicated by many other considerations, such as earnings related components to pensions, disparities within the population in the timing of retirement, and changes in the proportion of people with funded occupational pensions (Schmähl, 1989, 1990). Pension policy also interacts with wider policy issues, including employment, labour force participation, economic growth and migration, which may assist in spreading the costs of ageing (Gillion, 1991). Simple theoretical models can depict only a few key features of pension financing, given that so much depends on the institutional background. A full treatment of the consequences of demographic change for pensions in any one country has to be based on a more detailed, quantitative investigation of the pension scheme in question.

Governments have usually combined two or more of the alternative adjustment methods, and the balance between them has changed with economic conditions and political climate. The UK, for instance, has at different times in the last 50 years adopted each of the three alternatives as the main plank of its pension policies. During the 1940s and 1950s, official concern over the effects of an ageing population on pension finance and economic performance lay behind calls for later retirement and increased economic activity in old age (Beveridge, 1942; Phillips Committee, 1954). Attempts to encourage later retirement were largely a failure and died out during the 1960s when economic growth slowed down and unemployment started to rise. By the 1970s, population ageing had fallen away from political prominence, and pension policies were reformulated without much discussion of future demographic changes.

The State Earnings Related Pension Scheme (SERPS) was introduced in 1975 with all-party agreement as a long-run approach to public pensions. SERPS offered more generous public pensions, making them comparable with private ones, and was designed to remain in place until well into the twenty-first century. It corresponded implicitly to the first of the policy alternatives discussed above: maintaining constant pension and retirement arrangements and raising taxes as the population ages. By the early 1980s, economists were analysing the full implications of SERPS and raising doubts about its long-run feasibility

(Ermisch, 1981; Hemming and Kay, 1982). Barely ten years after SERPS was introduced, the political will to sustain it began to dissolve. The new Conservative government would not tolerate the higher taxes implied by the pension promises of the 1970s; echoing the public sentiment of 40 years earlier, the official views again warned of the problem of population ageing (DHSS, 1984). This time round, the preferred policy option was to cut pensions rather than promote later retirement. SERPS, it appeared, might be abolished, but the eventual outcome was a reduction in the pensions offered by the scheme (Creedy and Disney, 1989b). Cutting pensions corresponds to the second policy alternative discussed above, and hence on different occasions UK policy makers have plumped for all three policy alternatives. Some recent changes in UK pension and retirement practices have involved later retirement, notably the equalization of male and female retirement ages at 65, which entails a rise in the female retirement age from 60 to 65. The policy resulted mainly from a wish to remove discrimination, but the choice of later female retirement was made with an eye to financing pensions under population ageing. Policy has come full circle and, despite much higher unemployment, returned to the recommendations of 50 years ago for later retirement.

Economists agree that pension finance is important chiefly because of its effects on the real economy, but having made this observation they differ widely in the conclusions they draw from it. Neoclassical economists, especially those of a laissez-faire persuasion, suspect that pay-as-you-go pension schemes depress aggregate savings, restrain investment, and weaken the real productive basis of the economy. They prefer funding, which has apparent immunity from the need to make regular adjustments to accommodate demographic change. The same strand of argument can promote private saving and the accumulation of a social security surplus that unbalances the pensions budget in a 'favourable' direction. The accumulated capital stock would bolster the economy's productivity, so that it could more comfortably support an ageing population (Kessler, 1990). Such reasoning has informed proposals for social security reform in the US in the 1980s (Aaron, Bosworth and Burtless, 1989). From a Keynesian standpoint, however, a budget deficit is more beneficial than a surplus, as it will maintain aggregate demand and encourage investment, whereas a surplus will have a depressing effect on the economy. Both sides of the debate accept the importance of real productive potential and the unimportance of preserving a strictly balanced social security budget, though one side advocates a surplus and the other a deficit. It is clear, all the same, that a religious adherence to a balanced pension budget has little backing from economists. A discussion conducted on the assumption of a balanced budget may be relevant when the government in power imposes such a constraint, but not necessarily otherwise.

The policy options considered in the pension financing debate have wider social consequences. Choosing a statutory retirement age raises fundamental issues about the economic and social status of old people. Superimposed on the discussion of short-term adjustments to pension schemes is a broader debate on the long-term future of the retired elderly as they become a larger proportion of the population.

ATTITUDES TO RETIREMENT

Earlier retirement and shorter working hours have frequently been seen as inherently desirable. For many people, the argument goes, work has only an instrumental value as a means to the end of earning money and so gaining access to goods and services. People have limited choice among alternative types of work, and their chances of deriving satisfaction from work are small. The decision to supply labour is heavily constrained by institutional circumstances and does not indicate a strong desire to partake in work for its own sake. Workers will avoid work wherever possible and try to reduce working time for a given wage income (whereas employers gain by increasing it). Most workers are offered a restricted choice of full-time work or nothing, and their choosing full-time work gives no assurance that they are content with current working hours or retirement arrangements. Earlier retirement and reduced working time might be a beneficial move away from the dominance of work, even if this implied a loss of wage income. Early exit too might have a progressive side, inasmuch as it modifies the typical patterns of work and swings the balance towards increased leisure time. A similar argument applies to the distribution of work. Early retirement might improve the job prospects of younger workers, particularly school leavers hoping to secure their first jobs. An officially lower retirement age could redistribute work from old to young and encourage an equitable sharing of working time; it would be preferable to unemployment as a means of accommodating the long-term decline in working time occurring in most developed countries. The trend towards earlier retirement seems, from this perspective, to be favourable, and any reversal of the trend in response to population ageing would be throwing away hard-won gains.

Earlier retirement can be combined with rising or stable consumption levels only if productivity growth outstrips the growth of consumption per head. Fewer workers are then required to produce the current national income, and aggregate working time declines. A chronic decline in working time can be viewed negatively as a waste of productive potential and a cause of hardship; falling demand for labour will create long-term unemployment and poverty for certain sections of society. As unemployment is concentrated among the lower socioeconomic classes, the people with the greatest need of full-time work have the greatest amount of enforced leisure. Attempts to reallocate a fixed total number of working hours may not be the best answer to this predicament: it might be better to raise the total working time available. By influencing aggregate demand and encouraging the appropriate kinds of investment, the government can potentially reverse the downward trend in total working hours and keep the economy at or near full employment without major changes in working practices. Keynesian demand management policies can always expand total working time, and working hours are not subject to an inevitable long-term decline that creates chronic unemployment. The remedy for economic stagnation, according to this view, is not to reallocate employment through earlier retirement or shorter working hours, but to stimulate demand and provide sufficient employment to make full-time work available for all.

A more positive response to reduced working time is to welcome it as a desirable consequence of productivity growth. Higher labour productivity can be accommodated either by keeping the same working hours and consuming more material goods and services or by holding material prosperity constant and reducing working hours. Usually, the benefits of productivity growth have been realized through a simultaneous rise in consumption and fall in working time. As people have become materially better off, their leisure time has become more and more valuable to them, until they are content to have shorter working hours and earlier retirement at the expense of some material consumption. Maintaining full employment under current working practices is not necessarily the best long-term strategy; a more moderate expansion of production and a gradual reduction of working time may be preferable. As long as employment is distributed evenly so as to avoid large-scale unemployment, the change could be said to benefit the whole population. If working time is distributed unevenly, then society may become polarized between those with skilled, full-time employment or unearned incomes and those excluded from full-time employment and living on social security benefits. To reap the full social gains from reduced working time would require more equal access to unearned incomes and well-paid employment, in other words, a rethinking of employment, ownership patterns and the organization of production (Gorz, 1989). Otherwise, under existing conditions, reduced working time divides those with access to employment from those excluded. Early exit and retirement exemplify this division. For some, early exit is the threshold of a lengthy, prosperous and comfortable retirement, while for others it is a premature end to their working career and a cause of poverty in old age. Without an extensive reorganization of production, the benefits of earlier retirement and reduced working time will be unevenly distributed and perpetuate existing social inequalities.

The case for later retirement hinges on the difficulties encountered with reduced working time. Traditional arguments for later retirement and longer working hours are associated with employers, who can raise their profits if they extend working time for a given total wage bill or if a smaller labour force performs the same tasks with higher work intensity and longer hours. Besides the sectional benefits to employers, later retirement might have more general social benefits. It is hard to foresee a time when work no longer constitutes the major source of income and unearned incomes are evenly distributed so as to share out the returns to technical change. A fundamental rearrangement of property rights seems utopian, and a more realistic stance would be to talk about policy options compatible with the current distribution of work, income and property. If many people are without unearned retirement incomes, then staying employed may be the only way they can maintain their living standards. Hence, the supposedly progressive trend towards shorter working lifetimes may cause poverty among the retired elderly. The wish to prevent poverty explains why proponents of the structured dependency approach have been critical of early retirement that generates income losses, reduced social status and financial dependency (Walker, 1981). Later retirement can be defended on the pragmatic grounds that it provides incomes for the more vulnerable members of society, and to this end it may be beneficial to let people stay in employment as long as they like.

The perfect liberal angle on retirement would be to have complete flexibility such that people can choose their own timing of withdrawal from work. Between the extremes of mandatory retirement and complete flexibility comes a wide range of possibilities. Flexible retirement is sometimes distinguished from gradual retirement: the former refers to a choice among single retirement dates, the latter to retirement in stages (Parker, 1982, Chapter 8). A retirement scheme can be flexible without being gradual, if people must retire at a single date but can exert an influence on this date, or gradual without being flexible, if retirement occurs in stages that are fixed and outside people's control. Gradual retirement can also differ in the smoothness of the withdrawal from work. Continuous reductions in working time would give a smooth, even retirement, whereas discrete reductions would give a jerky, stepwise retirement divided into several stages. Figure 6.1 shows the main alternative modes of retirement, with a dotted line denoting a choice available to the retirer and a solid line denoting the absence of any choice. Case (a) corresponds

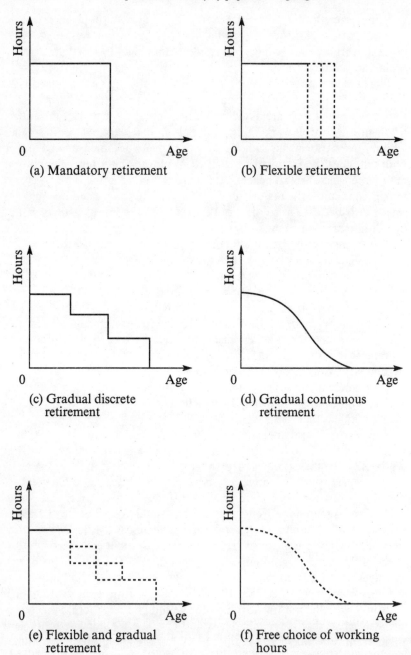

Figure 6.1 Alternative modes of retirement

to the familiar situation in developed countries, where most people work until they reach the statutory retirement age and cease to work thereafter. Case (b) provides the retirer with a choice among single retirement ages but disallows gradual retirement; it resembles certain cases of early exit, where the people exiting from employment can influence the timing of their exit (usually in conjunction with employers). Cases (c) and (d) offer gradual retirement without a choice among alternative pathways; (c) has retirement occurring in a few discrete stages, (d) has a continuous reduction in working hours towards zero. Case (e) combines flexible and gradual retirement, offering retirement in discrete stages along a number of alternative routes. Finally, case (f) permits complete flexibility, the opposite of case (a), where people are free to choose their own working hours and retire steadily from employment at their own pace.

From any given starting point, the flexible retirement in cases (b), (e) and (f) could lead to earlier or later retirement, depending on individual decisions. There would be no centrally determined retirement age, and changes in retirement would evolve gradually through decentralized decision making. In cases (e) and (f), people would have the additional option of retiring slowly and avoiding the lurch from full-time work to no work at all. A free choice of working time, as in case (f), must be the best option for the individual, but may impose costs on others. Fully decentralized retirement might not produce the best collective outcome. Employers would find it awkward to get to grips with continuous variability of working hours: taken to an extreme, this would imply changes in working time on a day-to-day basis. The more variable is working time, the higher are the administrative costs of recording and coordinating the activities of the labour force. Usually there will be restrictions on the choices available to workers, in order to make working and retirement arrangements more manageable. The government would also have problems with a fully flexible retirement system, as individuals would overlook the social consequences of their decisions about working time. Under a pay-as-you-go pension system, for example, earlier retirement might necessitate higher tax rates or lower pensions. Individuals would not as a rule be conscious of these collective outcomes when deciding on their own retirement. The government of a democratic society acts as an outlet for collective decision making. Alongside individual views, a collective view of retirement is required, and to implement it the government would normally have to restrict or steer individual retirement behaviour.

Flexibility of retirement in practice means a managed flexibility, in which a formal retirement scheme limits the range of options. The most extensive proposals for flexibility still entail only a partial lifting of the restrictions currently imposed on older workers. Several European countries have experimented with flexible and gradual retirement, on the basis of case (e) in Figure 6.1, and such policies will probably be extended in future years (Delsen and Reday-Mulvey, 1996). Flexible retirement has attracted widespread support both among politicians and the general public, but seems destined to fall short of complete flexibility and thus to play the secondary role of permitting variations on a common theme. Retirement will continue to be socially structured by measures that constrain or manipulate individual behaviour. Individual choices will continue to be influenced by social and cultural pressures, financial incentives, and so forth. Flexible retirement might seem to avoid the planning dilemmas of deciding between earlier or later retirement ages: individuals are free to make their own decisions, and the timing of retirement emerges spontaneously. True spontaneity divorced from external constraints or social pressures is unattainable, however, and it is salutary to acknowledge this. A formal framework of managed flexibility renders visible the external influences on retirement, instead of letting them operate tacitly in what purports to be a wholly flexible system.

PENSION AND RETIREMENT POLICIES

The growing instability of employment has motivated much recent discussion of pension policy. How can pensions can be reformed so as to accommodate shorter employment spells and more frequent changes of occupation? The discussion is not immediately concerned with population ageing but it does impinge on the arguments about demographic change.

One point of contact is the case for funded occupational pensions. From the narrow perspective of public finance, a switch to funded pensions can assuage the budgetary difficulties of public pay-as-you-go pension schemes under population ageing. Expanding funded pensions may not, however, be the best method of responding to the increased instability and 'flexibility' of employment. Indeed, the customary argument declares that pay-as-you-go is better than funding at coping with the dynamic issues of inflation, economic growth and structural change. Debates over funded pensions have been concerned largely with how their financial arrangements can be reconciled with flexible employment. At present, funded occupational pensions are located mostly within internal labour markets and tied to the older, hierarchical lifetime employment now being replaced by the new flexibility. Occupational pensions have normally operated on the defined benefit principle, whereby people's final salaries (or years of service) determine their pension entitlements. Pension schemes so financed encourage a long-term relationship between employees and employers, especially when the age–earnings profile slopes upwards and the final salary represents a maximum. The main alternative method of organizing funded pensions is on the defined contribution principle, whereby people's total contributions to the pension fund determine their pension entitlements. Compared with the defined benefit principle, this should reduce the uncertainties faced by the employer and permit pensions to be more portable, in other words, more easily transferred between employers (Bodie, Marcus and Merton, 1988). For funded pensions to become flexible, so the argument goes, they should be converted from a defined benefit to a defined contribution form. It may nevertheless be possible to increase the flexibility of defined benefit schemes without converting them (Disney, 1995).

The literature on pension reform is inconclusive, given that defined benefit schemes need not be inflexible and pay-as-you-go arrangements can be at least as flexible as funded ones. A drawback of this literature is its passivity: it takes for granted the trend towards flexible employment (and the corresponding growth of early exit) and hopes to see pensions reformed accordingly. The resulting policy proposals, if implemented, would affirm and strengthen the trend towards flexibility. To assess pensions more thoroughly, one has to raise the prior question of how flexible employment (and thus retirement) should be.

Crucial to any assessment of pension and retirement policies is the prevalence of early exit from employment. In many developed countries, early exit is fast becoming the norm and, despite never having been planned by the state, seems to be almost an institutionalized stage of the life cycle. Governments for the most part did not foresee the growth of early exit and have not adapted their pension and retirement policies to come to terms with it. Attempts to give official support to a pre-retirement period have been sporadic and temporary. The costs of early exit have fallen mostly on individuals, particularly unskilled manual workers without private pension arrangements (Laczko et al., 1988). The combination of de facto early retirement and public unease about pension finance presents the prospect of a lengthening 'private retirement' period before 'public retirement' begins. Arbitrary private arrangements give rise to large differences in experience among income groups. Prosperity during the pre-retirement period depends on a person's earlier employment history: stable, well-paid, skilled work provides occupational pensions and financial independence from the state; unstable, low-paid, unskilled work without an occupational pension scheme leaves a person reliant on social security measures never intended to cover a lengthy pre-retirement period. Early exit magnifies the existing income differences among the working population and confirms the low social status of lower income groups. In an era of flexible employment ('no jobs for life'), the risk is of greater job insecurity causing ever earlier exit and meagre pension entitlements. A concerted public response to early exit could counteract this risk. The basic options are to give greater support and recognition to the pre-retirement period, or to improve the employment chances of old people and reduce the incidence of early exit; these options are not mutually exclusive, and a mixture of them may be the best approach.

An overhaul of retirement practices would have to address the relation between early exit and official retirement. Merging them could clarify the position of many old people. One way to accomplish this, as well as increase the flexibility of retirement, would be to widen the range of formal retirement ages. A single retirement age could be replaced by an age band within which people can start their retirement and receive their retirement pension: some authors have proposed a 'decade of retirement' that would allow variations in the timing of retirement between the ages of 60 and 70 (Fogarty, 1975; Schuller and Walker, 1990). Governments could select a wider or narrower age band according to how much control they wish to exercise over retirement behaviour. If the lower age was sufficiently low, then a piece of what is presently counted as early exit could be reclassified as formal retirement and treated as such. The flexibility of retirement within the age bands would depend on arrangements between employers and employees: employers wanting to reduce their labour force could turn to formal retirement rather than early exit. Without changing existing patterns of early exit and retirement, it would be possible to eliminate much of the unpleasant pre-retirement period experienced by many people. As well as weakening the early exit/retirement distinction, banded retirement would have other benefits. It would provide a simple way to remove the differences in male and female retirement ages by applying the same band of retirement ages universally. It would also blur the distinction between the elderly and the rest of the population; for the first time some of the formally retired would be younger than some of the working population. This would weaken the worker/pensioner, young/old, dependent/independent dichotomies and dilute the significance of the single, statutory retirement age.

Banded retirement can be a practical possibility only if old people can find employment. Otherwise retirement would converge on the lowest official retirement age, and early exit would reappear. Flexible retirement schemes have a reasonable chance of providing a genuine work/retirement choice only in economies close to full employment. Within an existing pool of jobs, removing age barriers to employment can improve opportunities for the elderly. The direct approach to this issue, adopted in the US

and several European countries, is to ban age discrimination in job adver-
tisements, recruitment, the promotion and training of current employees,
and the conditions of retirement; it has become illegal in most areas of
work for the employer to impose mandatory retirement at a single age.
Prohibiting age discrimination might seem to resolve old people's problems, but the results of the US measures have been disappointing: early
exit and age discrimination have persisted despite the anti-discrimination
laws. This may be partly because many old people are ignorant of the
laws and have not asserted their rights. New laws alone are not enough to
prevent discrimination: there has to be knowledge of the legal framework
and a change in the cultural climate to make the laws binding.
Nonetheless, laws against age discrimination are a valuable declaration of
intent. To increase their effectiveness, the government should publicize
them and monitor age discrimination in recruitment and employment
practices; it should also invite employers to declare their commitment to
the equal treatment of older workers. Age discrimination rules are no
panacea, but they can foster a more enlightened attitude to the capabilities of old people.

If flexible retirement were introduced, a formula relating the pension
level to the age of retirement would be required. By the insurance principle, early retirers would have a smaller stock of accumulated
contributions and receive a lower pension on retirement. The pensions
paid under a flexible retirement system would be positively related to the
age of retirement: the later the retirement, the higher the pension. On
average, with actuarially fair arrangements, people retiring at different
ages would either break even or make equivalent net losses or gains from
the system. A difficulty with such a formula is that it sets up persistent
income disparities among old people who survive long beyond the retirement age; early but long-lived retirers on low pensions would be
penalized. Alternative pension arrangements could prevent this. One possibility would be to pay the same pension to all employees in similar
circumstances, independently of their age of retirement. This would
reduce income disparities among the retired, but would favour early
retirement and provide a disincentive to working beyond the minimum
retirement age. A compromise, suggested by Fogarty (1990), would be to
pay early retirers a temporarily lower pension, which is then increased to
the standard level once they pass the age of, say, 70. Income differences
among pensioners would be reduced, but not removed entirely. Another
option would be to pay partial pensions to part-time workers over the
minimum retirement age. By breaking down the customary retirement
condition on pensions, a partial or gradual retirement system could take
the edge off the arbitrary division between the elderly and the rest of the

population. Differences in pension levels would be contingent on the con-
tinuation of work rather than the age of retirement alone; all fully retired
individuals, whatever their age, would receive the same pension.

With or without changes in retirement policy, early exit from the
labour force is already introducing flexible retirement on a random
basis. Retirement practices are no longer standardized and vary substantially among occupations and employers. It would be better for the
retired if this variation could be within formal retirement policies that
clarified the retired status of those who currently exit early from work.
The problem with flexible retirement is that it is a two-sided arrangement affecting both employees and employers: what appears as
flexibility on one side of the arrangement appears as a restriction of
choice on the other. Complete freedom for employees to determine the
mode and timing of retirement would make it awkward for employers
to plan their recruitment, training and work practices; conversely, complete control of retirement and early exit by employers would cause
severe difficulties for employees nearing the end of their working career
and trying to plan a smooth transition to retirement.

A formal public framework of flexible retirement could establish a
compromise between the two sides. Retirement, instead of being decided
by local circumstances and the bargaining strength of management and
workers, would conform to a range of well-defined, generally available
options. Flexibility in retirement would be recognized officially and
upheld on principle. The reversion to formal retirement rules might perhaps be criticized as a throwback to the Fordist welfare state that has no
place in the new era of post-Fordism. If, however, the concept of official
retirement is to be retained and combined with flexibility, then this can be
accomplished only by centralized government action. A centralized
approach offers the only way of giving people standardized choices and
thereby producing greater equity in retirement options. The chief obstacle
to such a policy is the lack of job opportunities for older workers – a
government wishing to guarantee a genuine choice among work and
retirement options must also guarantee a sufficiently high level of
economic activity. Flexible retirement becomes entwined with macroeconomic issues.

A formally flexible retirement system would not end the financial
difficulties of public pension schemes. The financing of a pay-as-you-go
scheme would still depend on intergenerational transfers and would still
have to be adjusted under population ageing if the government insisted
on budgetary balance. Formal flexibility does help pension financing in
one respect, though, by giving the government some novel adjustment
options. The options of raising taxes or reducing pensions are unchanged,

but there are now two alternative versions of later retirement. One alternative is to have adjustment within the current retirement bands by giving people financial or other inducements to work longer. The government can respond to demographic change without recasting the whole pension and retirement system. Some limited government manipulation of 'voluntary' individual decisions might accommodate population ageing. If this approach proved inadequate, the government could adopt the second alternative of revising the band of retirement ages on offer. A higher minimum retirement age would ensure a rise in labour force participation by compelling those wishing to retire as soon as possible to work longer. Because retirement takes place within a formal framework, the government can impose changes in behaviour directly. Formal flexibility of retirement is a hybrid of fully flexible and fixed retirement regimes that allows the government to influence individual behaviour by either manipulative or administrative means. The policy options resemble those found in other forms of regulation, namely full flexibility, managed flexibility and fixity. A system of formally flexible retirement corresponds to the managed flexibility alternative and is essentially a compromise between the extremes of unregulated retirement and a single, fixed retirement age. It reconciles flexibility with a stable, regulated framework open to active government intervention when necessary.

7. Health care and social services

As people grow older their needs for health care and social services increase, owing to biological ageing. A rise in the average age of a population and a higher proportion of old people will bring greater total and average expenditures on health and social services. When services are publicly financed, this raises issues similar to the ones raised by pay-as-you-go pension schemes. A government pursuing a balanced budget has to choose between preserving current services and increasing taxes or cutting services and keeping taxes constant. It can lessen the tax burden by transferring resources from other public activities, switching to private finance, reducing unemployment, or increasing productivity.

Health and social services raise some additional, more specific issues. The relation between age and health has a biological core, unlike the institutional relation between age and retirement. Health care expenditure will depend on the future health and longevity of old people, an area about which we know little despite its obvious importance. The effect of age on health goes beyond the subject matter of the social sciences to encroach upon the territory of biology and medicine. Health care and formal social services differ from pensions in being real activities, not just payments of monetary benefits. Higher living standards and preventive health care measures can reduce the needs of old people for medical treatment; improvements in medical care can uphold current treatment standards at lower cost and reduce the financial burdens stemming from population ageing. The effectiveness of health care also relies on the appropriate allocation of old people between the intensive, specialized care provided in hospitals and the less specialized care provided in other institutions or in the home. The implications of ageing for health and social services are more complex than a mere extrapolation of current expenditure patterns to estimate the total burdens imposed by ageing: they depend crucially on changes in the future health of old people and advances in the technical and organizational efficiency of health care. The present chapter is concerned with the special characteristics that distinguish health care and social services from pensions. The next section discusses the effects of biological ageing on health. Later sections consider the efficient organization of health care and social services under population ageing.

THE RELATION BETWEEN AGE AND HEALTH

Ageing diminishes the body's capacity to resist disease; illness becomes ever more likely until at some point death occurs from an identifiable disease or natural causes. Human longevity is subject to a biological upper limit, and the deterioration of health with age can safely be regarded as a biological fundamental at all times and places. It is helpful to distinguish between life span, as the period for which a healthy person will live before dying of natural causes, and life expectancy, as the period for which on average a person can expect to live. Life span exceeds life expectancy, because most people die of illnesses before completing their natural life span. Disease-free lives are so rare that nobody has yet been able to pin down the life span of a typical, perfectly healthy human being. Even if a well-defined life span exists, life expectancy varies with social factors such as nutritional standards, work practices, sanitation, and the availability of medical care. Improved social conditions have brought an increase in life expectancy for both developed and developing countries. In any given country, mortality and morbidity figures are strongly correlated with social class, and the highest death rates and incidence of disease are concentrated among the poorest social groups (Wilkinson, 1986, 1992; Marmot and McDowall, 1986; Fox, 1989). Medical statistics show that life expectancy is capable of wide variations that may have significant consequences for the future of medical care.

Could improved health offset the difficulties of adjusting health care policies to accommodate an ageing population? Medical opinion on this question has generally been pessimistic. The fact that life expectancies are increasing suggests that people are dying prematurely, before attaining their natural life spans, of illnesses that may require costly medical treatments. Developed countries have passed through a major change in the causes of death, summarized by the theory of epidemiological transition (Omran, 1971). Prior to economic development the main causes of death were infectious diseases and famines, so that mortality rates were high compared with current levels and susceptible to periodic crises. As economic development took place, famines and other mortality crises became less common and most deaths resulted from degenerative rather than infectious diseases. Life expectancy increased, but people became vulnerable to chronic illness and disability in old age (Olshansky and Ault, 1986). Poor historical data have hampered assessment of this theory, and certain aspects of it – notably the presumed low incidence of degenerative diseases prior to economic development – are speculative.

The causality behind the epidemiological transition is normally ascribed either to improvements in living conditions, nutrition and sanitation or to advances in medical care: the most popular explanation has singled out improved nutrition, though this does not preclude a more complex, multicausal explanation (McKeown and Record, 1962; McKeown, 1976). Whatever the precise causality, the degenerative diseases of ageing, such as heart disease, cancer, diabetes, osteoarthritis, emphysema and Alzheimer's disease, have so far proved incurable and, unlike infectious diseases, often produce prolonged disability during which the elderly patient requires intensive care. Many of the 'old old' over the age of 75, notwithstanding their longevity, suffer chronic degenerative illnesses. People who would previously have died young of infectious diseases are now surviving into old age and dying later, after costly hospitalization, of the diseases of ageing. The critical demographic trend, according to the traditional pessimistic view, is the growth rate of the 'old old', who account for a disproportionate share of health care and social services (Denton and Spencer, 1975; Carstairs, 1981; Russell, 1981; Johnson and Falkingham, 1988). At best, the increased longevity will merely postpone a given period of illness until later in a person's life: the average intensity of care will then stay approximately constant (Fuchs, 1984). At worst, the greater needs among the 'old old' will create a growing intensity of care and compound the difficulties engendered by population ageing.

Against this pessimism has been set a more optimistic view based on recent trends in life expectancy (Fries, 1980, 1983, 1989; Fries and Crapo, 1981). Mortality statistics can be depicted by a survival curve that plots the percentage cumulative survival of a birth cohort against its age. At age zero the cohort has a 100 per cent survival rate, which then declines with increasing age until it reaches zero at an age when the entire cohort has died. Survival curves have 'rectangularized' over time, flattening out at a high survival rate in the earlier years of the life cycle and then falling away as the birth cohort enters old age. More people are surviving into old age but then dying within a narrowing band of ages in their seventies and eighties (see Figure 7.1). According to Fries and Crapo (1981), the rectangularization of survival curves shows that people are beginning to reach their full natural life span: their life expectancy and life span are converging. The culmination of this trend will be a rectangular survival curve such that virtually everyone will survive until they have lived out their life span, at which point they will have a disease-free natural death. Because the life span is biologically determined, there may be random variations among individuals, but the average natural life span should vary little over time or among societies. Current estimates of the age of natural death remain uncertain: Fries and Crapo set it tentatively at around 85, a figure that has empirical backing as an upper limit to attainable longevity (Olshansky, Carnes and Cassel, 1990). Most people

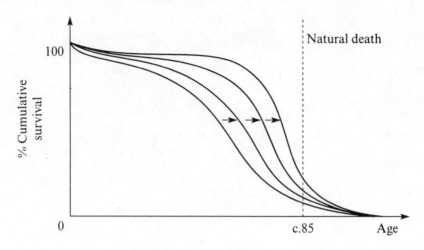

Figure 7.1 The rectangularization of the survival curve

might ultimately live longer than this, in which case the age of natural death could be revised upwards without substantially changing the theory's implications.

Besides the rectangularization of the survival curve, the other main component of the optimistic view is the compression of morbidity. The optimists assume that internal biological mechanisms, not diseases or disabilities, bring about natural death. On attaining the age of natural death, the body ceases to function properly and death occurs from natural causes or after a brief illness. Natural death implies the end of the diseases of ageing that produce chronic disability and are now the main causes of death in developed countries. Morbidity will be compressed against a 'biological wall' situated at the limit of the natural life span (Figure 7.2). People will become healthier during life, but will be unable to live longer than their biologically determined life spans. The 'optimism' resides in the promise of a disease-free life and declining demands for hospital care. Less uncertainty surrounding life expectancy might also be desirable as an aid to life-cycle planning, although a too-precise knowledge of their approaching date of death could bear heavily on old people.

The optimistic view has been controversial because it plays down formal medicine and replaces a stress on the cure of disease with a stress on prevention. At present, formal medical knowledge is powerless to cure the diseases of ageing, and it is doubtful whether cures will be discovered in the near future, if ever. Preventive measures, such as improvements in diet and reductions in smoking, seem to offer a better chance of tackling

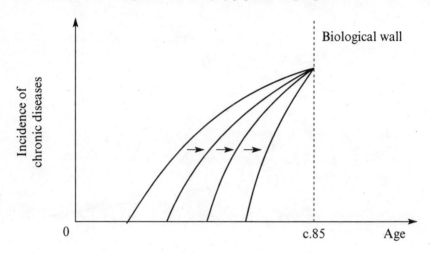

Figure 7.2 The compression of morbidity

the diseases of ageing. These measures would divert attention away from formal medical care to the activities of the population itself. The tacit conclusion is that formal medicine and the medical profession are of declining importance: most curable diseases have already been conquered and the ones without cures can best be dealt with by preventive activities outside the official framework of medical care. Another source of controversy is the suggestion that an ageing population will require no additional resources for the health services. If ageing means that more people are attaining their natural life span, then it may lead to static or falling per capita (and perhaps total) expenditures on health care for the elderly. By this argument, an ageing population is a symptom of success in preventing degenerative diseases and curtailing medical expenditures. Improved health among the old, valuable in itself, might have the further advantage of raising the perceived social worth of old people and breaking down presuppositions about age-related dependency (Wilson, 1991). Societies with rectangular survival curves and natural death at a predetermined life span would have only a weak connection between age and medical care. The chief activity of the medical profession would be to look after people during their short period of illness preceding natural death. Elaborate health care facilities and high medical expenditures would be superfluous.

As yet, the optimistic view amounts to little more than conjecture and has little grounding in experience; its empirical standing is too flimsy to justify changes in health care policy. Most developed countries have seen some rectangularization of survival curves, with more people surviving into old age and dying within a narrower age range. Survival curves are becoming flatter during most of the life cycle and steeper towards the end of it, though they may never become truly rectangular at a fixed natural life span. Rectangularization is consistent with a rising average age of death among the elderly and is not, therefore, conclusive evidence of natural death at a universal, biologically determined life span. The other component of the optimistic view, the compression of morbidity, has hardly any empirical support and stands merely as a hypothesis that may or may not be borne out by experience. Limited knowledge of the diseases of ageing makes the relative merits of preventive and curative approaches hard to assess. Curative medicine is at present unable to counteract these diseases, but breakthroughs in medical technology are always conceivable and cannot be dismissed. Preventive measures may apparently have a better chance of success, but they will not necessarily be so successful as to give people a disease-free existence until natural death. What seems likely is that advances in both curative and preventive techniques will mitigate the effects of the diseases of ageing without transforming old people's health. For practical purposes of health care planning, it is safer to take the pessimistic view that present morbidity patterns will persist. Empirical evidence on the medical history of the elderly goes against a compression of morbidity and vindicates the traditional pessimistic standpoint (Bromley, Isaacs and Bytheway, 1982; Manton, 1982; Schneider and Brody, 1983; Grundy, 1984; Brody, 1985; Bebbington, 1988). In drawing conclusions about health care provision, the compression of morbidity rather than the rectangularization of the survival curve is the more relevant consideration. Cautious optimism for the long-term future may be warranted, but the existing links between age, health and medical care are set to endure over current planning horizons.

POPULATION AGEING AND HEALTH CARE EXPENDITURES

The causality underlying the relation between age and health care expenditure is complex. Population ageing depends on health care, since a primary purpose of health care is to prolong life and thereby influence the age distribution. Health care also depends on population ageing, since medical treatments will have to be provided for the growing numbers of old (and especially 'old old') people. Population ageing causes increasing health care per capita, while increasing health care causes an ageing population. This dual causality can be illustrated as in Figure 7.3.

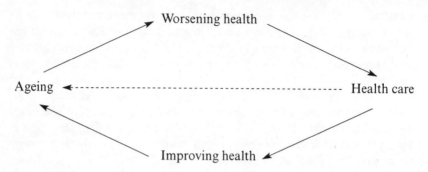

Figure 7.3 Ageing and health care

The standard assumption is that population ageing will produce worsening health and an increase in health care activities. Causality goes in one direction from ageing to health care. But successful treatments allow people to regain their health and live longer, so health care will, to a minor degree at least, cause population ageing. In some cases, longer life may be achieved without improved health, if people survive only at the cost of severe disabilities and a low quality of life. This would create a direct reverse link between health care and ageing, bypassing the intermediate stage of improved health (shown as the dotted line in Figure 7.3).

The circular causal relationships can produce paradoxical outcomes. A person cured of serious ailments during the early stages of life may survive into old age and fall victim to the diseases of ageing. Successful treatments among younger age groups may in the longer run raise the average incidence of chronic illnesses and disabilities. This has happened in developed countries, where the major infectious diseases have been virtually eliminated (Gruenberg, 1977). As people are now avoiding premature and, in terms of medical expenditure, 'cheap' deaths from infectious disease, they are surviving long enough to suffer the chronic diseases of ageing and incur higher medical expenditures; better treatments may give rise to a higher average morbidity rate in what is now an older population. Medical expenditures on curative treatments for the 'young old' may call forth additional expenditures devoted to the less curable ailments of the 'old old'.

A full intertemporal planning framework would take into account the consequences of successful curative medicine. Planners would be aware of more people surviving into old age and requiring further medical treatment, and there would be no surprises at the outcome of earlier policy decisions or regrets that certain decisions were made. The development and adoption of cures would imply a willingness to embrace their consequences for future health care. In reality, neither governments nor individuals have perfect foresight. Cures are adopted because of their desirable short-run benefits, and the less palatable long-run consequences are overlooked or only dimly perceived. On balance most cures would probably still be desirable when their impact on ageing and future health care is taken into account, but the financial costs might be much higher than expected. The putative 'crisis' of health care spending reflects the failure to recognize the full effects of earlier planning decisions. A perfectly planned approach would acknowledge the endogeneity of population ageing and allow for the influence of policy measures on people's future health and longevity. Most policy discussion is less ambitious than this: it assumes population ageing to be exogenous and looks only at responses to externally determined needs.

The organization of health care services has a strong influence on the relation between ageing and medical expenditures. Particularly important are the use of services by different age groups and the efficiency of services once they are being used. Biological ageing might be expected to yield a clear-cut pattern of health care provision increasing with age: as old people become more prone to disease and disability they require more intensive medical care. Matters are not quite so simple in practice, and the demand for medical care depends on many factors other than biological ageing. Variations in demand by people with the same physical illnesses and disabilities have a significant effect on medical treatment and expenditures. The initial contact between the elderly patient and the medical services is partly a matter of choice, especially for less severe complaints. Seeking medical care is an individual or family decision, culturally influenced and specific to a person's social background. Among people with the same medical condition, those in higher social classes and with more education will usually demand more assistance from the medical services. Under private health care systems, a bias towards the higher social classes derives from their greater ability to purchase health care. The same bias occurs in public health care systems, even when their express intent is to provide equal access (Le Grand, 1982). The higher socioeconomic classes are generally better informed about public services and quicker to demand medical care.

As average real incomes increase and people move into skilled, non-manual employment, the demand for health care rises independently of the incidence of disease among old people. A greater propensity to seek medical treatment counteracts the effects of higher living standards and improved health. The trend towards increasing health care use rates will be strengthened if policy changes reduce the costs borne by the public: the Medicare scheme in the US is an example of this (Fuchs, 1984).

Higher use rates are ambivalent. They may indicate a more comprehensive health care service covering a higher proportion of genuine ailments and offering better standards of care. They may, on the other hand, indicate a growth of unnecessary treatments, along with inefficiencies in the treatments provided. A rise in use rates is welcome when it removes gaps in the coverage of the medical services and ensures that treatable medical conditions get treated, but not when it causes overprovision of medical care for some patients and creates a skewness in the types of patients and medical treatments covered.

These alternative cases are difficult to distinguish from each other on the basis of the available medical data. Most health care services rely on doctors to act as agents for 'consumers' who have scant knowledge of their own ailments and may be so ill that they cannot make rational decisions. Under clinical freedom, doctors are empowered to recommend the best possible treatments irrespective of financial or other restrictions. They have no incentive to recommend wasteful or unnecessarily expensive treatments (as may be the case under fee-for-service arrangements), nor do they have an incentive to keep down the costs of medical care. They are left to act as neutral arbiters of health care use rates and medical expenditure per capita. Whether financial matters should enter into a doctor's medical decisions remains a contentious issue and broaches the further issue of health care efficiency.

For a given use rate of medical services, health care spending depends on how efficiently the services are organized: unsuccessful or inefficient treatments will waste resources and prolong the treatment period. When several successful treatments coexist, the efficient option by cost-effectiveness criteria is the one that offers the desired level of health care at least cost. Few health care systems could plausibly claim to have attained efficiency in the treatments they provide, and their prevailing inefficiency and organizational slackness influences the effects of population ageing on health care. Maintaining current practices implies accommodating demographic changes within an inefficient health care system. It is convenient, under the circumstances, to combine adjustments of the health care system in response to population ageing with reforms to increase efficiency. The resulting policy problem is more than a fine tuning of efficient practices to meet slowly changing demographic needs. Improved efficiency is desirable at all times and is associated with population ageing only if ageing has been the necessary spur to reform.

Efficiency in health care has a technical and an allocative aspect, corresponding to the customary theoretical distinction between technical and allocative efficiency. Technical efficiency maximizes the outputs of a productive activity for given inputs. In health care it pertains chiefly to the efficiency of the treatments and internal organization of the formal health care sector. An efficient health care service would choose the treatments and practices yielding the greatest output of health subject to a politically determined budget constraint. The main obstacle to attaining such efficiency is the definition and measurement of health: formal economic appraisal requires a quantitative yardstick by which alternative policies can be compared. Health economists have long sought an acceptable health output measure, but the topic has aroused controversy on both theoretical and ethical grounds (Broome, 1985, 1993; Bell and Mendus, 1988; Loomes and McKenzie, 1990). Allocative efficiency refers to the allocation of resources among different, technically efficient productive activities; it addresses the question of what to produce, rather than how best to produce it.

Health care requires allocative choices between many activities, for example, between alternative treatments of the same illness, between the treatment of different illnesses, between alternative locations of treatment, and between formal medical care and other, less intensive types of care. Decisions about alternative approaches to treating the same illness can be subsumed in the technically efficient treatment of that illness, but the other allocative choices are distinct from a narrow conception of technical efficiency. As with technical efficiency, a quantitative health output measure is a prerequisite for formally assessing allocative efficiency. Some allocative decisions involve distributing people among alternative care sectors, for example, the 'balance of care' decision to determine how to allocate old people between hospital, residential and domiciliary care (Mooney, 1978). Within hospitals, a prominent area of debate is whether old people should be treated in separate geriatric wards or integrated with other patients (Hall, 1988). Efficiency in health care has proved difficult to quantify at all levels, from the treatment of specific conditions to the organization of the whole health care system. An agreed quantitative notion of efficiency is needed, however, if one is to speak of optimum health care policies or reforms moving towards an optimum.

The efficiency concepts adopted by health economists to evaluate health care have normally been static and timeless, applicable only to existing, well-established treatments. Population ageing takes place over many decades, and medical technology will almost certainly have made advances during the time scale of demographic forecasting exercises. New medical treatments that are at first costly and inefficient may eventually turn out to be efficient once they have been perfected or, conversely, may fail to fulfil their initial promise and never replace earlier methods. The fundamental uncertainty about the results of medical research means that it cannot easily be depicted as a rational choice among existing alternatives. What now seems to make economic sense could with hindsight be revealed to be misguided, and the most thorough evaluations of current medical practices could still leave a loophole that might render the findings inappropriate. The hopes for a breakthrough with the diseases of ageing are slim, but they will be even slimmer if research activity and new treatments are restricted on cost-effectiveness grounds. An overzealous pursuit of cost-effectiveness in the short run could detract from the chances of major improvements in long-run health care.

Future health care developments can be forecast only tentatively. Estimates of the effect of population ageing on expenditures have to treat ageing as exogenous to the health care system and assume that there will be no radical advances in preventive or curative medicine. Use rates are held constant at present values or assumed to follow trends observed in the recent past. Under these assumptions one can take data on health care spending by age group, along with data on the age composition of the population, and construct projections of future health care spending. Studies based on this method conclude that health care spending will rise substantially in the immediate future (Ermisch, 1983, Chapter 8, 1990; Pearson, Smith and White, 1989). The increase is due mainly to the higher costs of medical treatments for all age groups and has little connection with population ageing (Heller, Hemming and Kohnert, 1986; OECD, 1988a). The separate contribution of demographic change is significant but insufficient to warrant its being singled out as the cause of a special health care crisis. Efforts to improve the efficiency of health care need to be directed at the system as a whole, not just at treatments for the elderly.

Simple extrapolations of current trends should err on the pessimistic side. If technical advances coupled with economic appraisal of health care permit more cost-effective treatment, then expenditures per head will be lower in the future than they are at present. Unfortunately, the formal evaluation of health care is still at a rudimentary level that makes this assumption unreliable: new technologies are introduced with an imperfect knowledge of their long-run impact on costs. Broadly based assessments of health care efficiency will continue to be precarious. Technical changes currently dominate increases in the cost of health care, and only some of these changes will be associated with improved efficiency. Population ageing will add marginally to the cost increases, but only as a secondary factor. Where demographic change does bring cost increases for an inefficient health care system, the resulting financial burdens have as much to do with the inefficiencies as with demography. The general organization of health care creates great uncertainties, far greater than the ones created by demographic change. Given these conditions, simple extrapolative prediction is a fittingly humble method: despite its inadequacies, it at least recognizes the impossibility of producing accurate theoretical forecasting models.

Prediction should ideally rest on time-series data, because the relevant information on health concerns people moving through their life cycles. Data on health and health-care spending by age are mostly cross-sectional, comparing different age groups at a single date, and so generational effects become mixed with the effects of ageing. A full longitudinal data set would trace a representative sample of people over their whole life cycle and observe their susceptibility to the diseases of ageing, together with their use of medical services. Such information would allow a reasonably well-informed (but far from perfect) planning of health care services that incorporates demographic changes. Longitudinal data on health have always been scarce, and the gap in knowledge is an obstacle to predicting future health care trends (Maynard, 1988). Much discussion of ageing and health care remains speculative, and reliable conclusions are hard to reach without proper clinical and budgetary information. When health itself is so difficult to pin down, the prospect of a perfectly efficient health care system adjusting smoothly and continuously to demographic changes seems misplaced. What does seem feasible is a tentative attempt to learn from past experience in order to derive approximate indicators of future demand for health care under demographic change. This could be done more accurately using time-series data, and collection of such data would contribute significantly to the informational content of health care planning.

AGEING AND THE BALANCE OF CARE

Serious illnesses and disabilities have to be treated in the formal medical sector as there are no real alternative sources of care. Much general care of the elderly is less specialized than this and can be provided in several different locations. Three main locations stand out: the homes of the elderly or their relatives, residential institutions, and hospitals. Care within the home, termed domiciliary or community care, can be undertaken formally by public authorities or private voluntary organizations, or informally by relatives and friends. The public accounts exclude informal care, but even so it imposes real economic costs on the carers; Chapter 8 will consider the informal sector in more detail. General care is also provided in residential institutions established for that purpose ('old people's homes'), which have their own paid employees and can be privately or publicly owned. They differ from hospitals in that they offer only general, unspecialized help with everyday activities. Intensive medical care has to be provided in hospitals, either general medical institutions or geriatric hospitals designed specifically for elderly patients. Hospitals normally treat only those with a diagnosed medical complaint, although even on this basis they undertake general as well as specialized care. How should the dependent elderly population be allocated among the three care sectors – domiciliary, residential and hospital? How, in other words, can we find the right balance of care? It would seem logical that the most dependent elderly should be cared for in hospitals, those with lesser disabilities in residential institutions, and the least dependent in their own homes. The actual allocation of old people among the sectors is often wayward. As with health care, population ageing has stimulated interest in improving efficiency and seeking a more consistent method of organizing care.

Assessments of efficiency must appraise both technical efficiency within care sectors and allocative efficiency between care sectors. The present discussion focuses on allocative efficiency, assuming that the internal organization of the sectors is either efficient or at an acceptable standard of efficiency. The usual techniques of economic appraisal should in principle be able to determine the optimum balance of care; old people could then be classified by their physical disabilities and assigned to the most suitable care sector (Mooney, 1978; Knapp, 1980). The prior expectation is that the costs of caring will increase with the patient's disability, but that domiciliary care will have a cost advantage at low dependency levels, residential care at medium levels, and hospital care at the highest levels (Mooney, 1978). Figure 7.4 illustrates this. The quality of care is assumed to be constant between the sectors, so that the sector with the lowest cost is unambiguously preferred. Under the expected cost structures, two threshold dependency levels, D_1 and D_2, will emerge: below D_1 domiciliary care has the lowest cost, between D_1 and D_2 residential care, and above D_2 hospital care. A policy planner with knowledge of D_1 and D_2 could allocate the elderly population efficiently among the care sectors. The policy issue is how, if at all, the thresholds can be identified and made operational.

The economic literature on care is expanding but far smaller than the equivalent literature in social policy. Several economists have attempted to analyse care within a framework of formal economic appraisal (Mooney, 1978; Wright, Cairns and Snell, 1981; Knapp, 1984; Wright, 1987a and b; Netten, 1993). The obstacles they have met resemble those met in the economic appraisal of health care, and the results obtained are similarly tentative. Evaluations of care involve two stages. The first is to measure output, which means assessing the physical dependency of the people being cared for. As a simplifying assumption, most economic

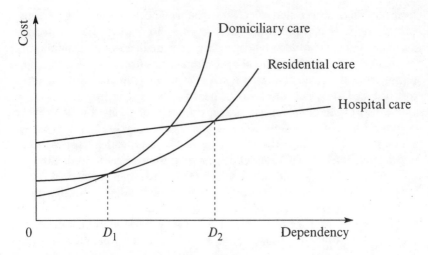

Figure 7.4 Dependency and the costs of care

appraisals are cost-effectiveness rather than cost–benefit studies: they hold the output of care constant and identify the option that minimizes the monetary costs. The method is to assess dependency and then compare the costs of the policy options in dealing adequately with each dependency level. Policy has the objective of caring, not curing, and so dependency remains fixed; unlike health care, general care has the limited aim of enabling old people to survive reasonably well with given incapacities. One way to measure dependency is by an ordinal scaling based on observable characteristics ranked in order of severity (Wright, Cairns and Snell, 1981). Increasingly severe disabilities are, for example, inability to go shopping, inability to perform household tasks, and inability to feed oneself; each of these yields a dependency level and, along with the absence of disability, they produce an ordinal scaling with four ranks. Once dependency has been measured in this way, a cost-effectiveness study assumes that every policy option can provide care to a minimum standard for persons at every dependency level: any excess of care above the minimum standard goes unvalued. The output of care is then held constant at the acceptable minimum.

The second stage is to evaluate the social costs of care. As with cost–benefit analysis, the costs should be expressed in monetary form but include all relevant non-monetary and opportunity costs incurred by carers. Shadow and imputed pricing is therefore necessary. For domiciliary care, the main costs to be evaluated are housing costs (when old people live in separate households), personal living expenses, the costs of formal caring services, and the costs of informal care. Evaluating informal care poses particular problems because it has no market prices or formal accounts. For residential and hospital care, the main costs are capital costs, personal living expenses, general operational costs (catering, cleaning, portering), and the costs of caring services (nursing, care assistants, and so forth). Fixed and operational costs, because they are aggregated over the whole institution, often conceal the separate cost of caring for each elderly resident. The method adopted is to either take averages or ask the institution's staff to estimate the caring costs for a typical person at each dependency level. When a full set of cost figures has been derived, covering all dependency levels in all caring sectors, the analyst can construct a quantitative version of Figure 7.4 and identify the dependency thresholds D_1 and D_2 that determine the efficient balance of care.

The results of formal studies have not in general reproduced the pattern of Figure 7.4. Mooney (1978) concentrated on people judged by social policy professionals to be near the dependency thresholds on both sides, but his numerical results did not clearly bear out the professional judgements. A problem was the variation in the quality of care on offer. As an unobservable variable, quality may disrupt the cost comparisons to the disadvantage of the options giving higher quality care at a higher than necessary cost. Wright, Cairns and Snell (1981) constructed cost-of-caring schedules for all dependency levels and ranked the policy options consistently in order of increasing cost as domiciliary, residential and hospital. This corresponds to the prior professional judgements at low dependency levels, but conflicts with them at high dependency levels. The variable quality of care and the omission of informal care from the cost estimates may have distorted the results. Both factors may exaggerate the cost-effectiveness of domiciliary care and understate that of residential and hospital care. When care varies in quality, the care provided in institutions may be of a higher quality than that provided in the home. If care could be restricted to a single uniform quality, the advantages of institutional care at the higher dependency levels might become more apparent. Economic appraisals of care seem to contradict current professional judgements on the balance of care, but it would be premature to conclude that major policy changes are called for. The inadequacies of the economic appraisal techniques, recognized by most economic practitioners, suggest that the judgements of social policy professionals may be at least as reliable a guide to allocating the dependent elderly among caring sectors. Formal quantitative modelling is still a long way from matching old people accurately with the best source of care.

Static economic appraisals do not show how well the various care sectors can adapt to the changing size and composition of the elderly population. Nor do they indicate how best to adjust a suboptimal starting point so as to move towards the policy optimum. These dynamic considerations complicate the analysis of efficiency and may overturn the findings of static economic appraisals. A policy favoured by static efficiency criteria may be less attractive if it proves rigid and inflexible or if the marginal costs of attaining it are excessively high. The policy problem is how to extend or adapt caring practices so as to meet the extra need for care resulting from demographic changes. Since existing practices are less than ideal, the problem must blend adjustment with reform, in the hope that policies aimed at coping with a growing elderly population will also swing the balance of care towards the more efficient care sectors. Expanding certain care sectors, or transferring old people between sectors, will incur costs distinct from those arising in the normal, steady-state functioning of the sectors. If any sectors have excess capacity it might be desirable to expand them up to full capacity in the short run even if they are not the least-cost option. Likewise, if the transfer of old people between sectors causes them hardship it might be better to leave them where they are, ignore the high costs, and delay the approach to long-run efficiency.

Despite the impression given by static economic appraisals, a perfect instantaneous match between the elderly population and the various sources of care is unfeasible. A thoroughgoing policy would have to look at the capacity constraints on care sectors, for instance, the availability of housing and carers in the domiciliary sectors and the physical capacity of the residential and hospital sectors. It would also have to bear in mind the frictional costs of transferring old people between sectors. Given the difficulties already encountered in matching old people with the appropriate source of care, these further difficulties will preclude exact quantitative planning. Formal economic appraisals of care are best seen as contributing to a larger decision-making framework, part of which must be informal.

A planned care system, with all its drawbacks, still offers the best prospects of accommodating demographic change. The alternatives to planning are unappealing: markets for care of the elderly can never be perfect, and a laissez-faire approach cannot be relied on to yield an efficient, equilibrium outcome. Laissez-faire will generate intensive formal care for those who can afford it, whether or not they need it, and for the rest an over-reliance on an informal care sector that receives no public support. Any objective assessment of need requires planning authorities to produce evaluations and allocate old people among care sectors. The distribution of the elderly population within a country will usually be uneven, and as a result some decentralization of planning may be desirable; the decision-making bodies would then be at a local or regional level, working to guidelines determined centrally. Planning of care has found acceptance even from policy makers normally following a market-based approach. In the UK, a laissez-faire administration conceded the case for a planning framework in which local government coordinates the care sectors and allocates the elderly among them according to assessed need (Department of Health, 1989). Other developed countries have adopted similar frameworks. Planning, despite the inherent difficulties, is a necessary but not sufficient condition for a more efficient and equitable allocation of caring activities. This has been generally appreciated: the most active area of debate is not the case for planning as such, but the precise nature of the planning and the role of competition in creating incentives within a planned system. Chapter 8 considers the main alternative approaches and their relationship with informal care.

INCREASING THE CAPABILITIES OF OLD PEOPLE

The balance-of-care literature presupposes that old people have a fixed dependency level unaffected by social policy provision. They are assumed to need care, and the only active policy question is what type of care they should receive. Undoubtedly, many old people are so dependent on care that they have no realistic hope of recovering their independence. Others, though, are on the margins of dependency, particularly the 'young old' who have hitherto been independent and are now poised on the threshold of joining the dependent population. According to the balance-of-care approach, all that should happen is that their declining physical capabilities should be monitored and beyond a certain point the appropriate type of care should be provided. Old people are viewed as helpless victims of ageing whose need for care rises inexorably. Such an approach may be too pessimistic. Ageing is a social as well as biological process, and the social aspects ensure flexibility in the onset of dependency.

A key issue, therefore, is whether dependency can be avoided. As in medicine, preventing or curing of a condition is better than merely coping with it. The medical literature has entertained an optimistic (if fanciful) strain of thought, and the scope for optimism about social care is at least as great: it is easier to envisage delaying physical dependency than preventing the chronic diseases of ageing. Measures to reduce dependency on social care merit more detailed consideration. Lower dependency levels would be intrinsically desirable if they resulted from old people's improved capabilities and would promote efficiency by removing superfluous care and releasing resources for other uses. The rising financial costs of social services have created pressures to introduce charges and transfer services to the private sector; if old people are paying for formal care, they have a further reason to maintain their physical capabilities and hence their independence. Dependency will increasingly be subject to financial costs on top of the physical costs of reduced capabilities and the social costs of dependent status. Delaying dependency would be valuable to old people but, more generally, would relieve the difficulties facing the provision of social care. The debate over financing care resembles in many respects the debate over financing pensions, but the opportunities to delay dependency are a point of difference. Expenditures on social care, unlike those on pensions, can be reduced through improvements in the efficiency of services – the balance-of-care question – or reductions in the need for services. These two issues are interrelated, as services provided to people who do not need them cannot be efficient, but much policy discussion assumes that social care is necessary and concentrates on what type of care should be provided. The prior issue is whether care could be avoided altogether.

Assessments of physical dependency among old people are supposed to be neutral and objective, yet almost inevitably they are in part socially determined. Unidimensional notions of dependency or disability have no fixed meaning, and the attempt to measure them in quantitative terms is fraught with difficulties (Bond, 1976). Economic appraisals usually assess physical dependency by considering the everyday activities that a person cannot perform without assistance. At the margins of dependency, where the important policy decisions are made, there is often doubt over whether a person should be classified as able to perform a particular activity. The subjective judgements of the assessors or the elderly themselves unavoidably influence marginal classifications, which are less clear-cut than they seem. The neat dichotomies of able/disabled or independent/dependent have more to do with administrative convenience than with the characteristics of old people: it is simpler to give people a label than to have a continuum of intermediate cases and mixtures of abilities and disabilities. Even when assessors formally evaluate dependency, they may still misallocate people among care sectors. Empirical studies of residential homes have found that a high proportion of residents (up to 40 or 50 per cent) have only minor functional impairments and are capable of self-care (Booth, 1985). The same applies to the domiciliary sector: empirical studies show that formal caring services are provided to people who have little need of them (Goldberg and Connelly, 1982).

Once a service is provided, for whatever initial reason, it will usually continue to be provided irrespective of changing circumstances. People are often assigned a dependent status according to whether they already receive assistance with daily activities, on the assumption that existing care tallies with objective physical needs. This means that the boundary between self-care and care provided by others, which determines the initial movement into dependency, has a special importance. If, as has commonly been observed, old people have a strong desire for independence, the design of caring policies should respect their wishes and assist them to stay as independent as possible (Townsend, 1986). It may not be feasible to produce a perfectly planned, optimal caring system, but it should be feasible to move in the right direction and reduce premature dependency.

The margin between formal dependence and independence turns on the private decision to approach the state and ask for assistance, and the public decision on whether assistance is warranted and, if so, what assistance should be provided (Qureshi and Walker, 1986). These decisions are often made separately, which creates a division between an earlier stage of self-care plus informal care by relatives and a later stage of formal care. Old people do without state assistance until some crisis prompts them to approach the state. At that point, assuming they are judged to require formal care, they switch suddenly from almost complete independence to a high level of dependency. There is little attempt at a smooth transition to increasing care; once a certain disability threshold has been reached, the old are deemed to be unambiguously better off receiving formal care. The imprecise method of decision making reinforces the division between dependence and independence without guaranteeing that all old people are treated consistently. It also sustains the idea that relatives (nearly always female relatives) have sole responsibility for providing care, until the difficulties become so severe that formal carers must step in and take over. At the critical threshold, formal care is transformed from being inappropriate to being the single best way to provide care. Policies aiming for a slower, smoother transition to dependency could reduce the abruptness of the change. Five examples of such policies will be considered here: preventive health care; measures to alleviate poverty among old people; provision of support for informal carers; measures to improve old people's accommodation; and coordination of care to give more consistent decision making.

Preventive health care is the most direct method of increasing old people's physical capabilities and prolonging their self-reliance. At present it stands as the only viable means by which we can hold at bay the chronic diseases of ageing and reduce average levels of disability among the old. The case for preventive care seems clear, but doubts remain about how it should be organized. Possible approaches differ according to the extent of formal public involvement.

The most activist approach is to screen the whole population for specific medical conditions that can be prevented when detected early enough. This has the advantage of providing comprehensive and equitable care, although it would be too expensive to implement across the whole range of preventable medical conditions. The returns to screening are greater for the young than the old (who have a shorter future time horizon), and screening programmes have often in practice been restricted to younger age groups, a form of age discrimination defended on cost-effectiveness grounds: younger populations generate a greater volume of quality-adjusted life years or other health output measures. Empirical evaluation of comprehensive screening programmes for old people has cast doubt on whether they have significant economic or medical value (Taylor, Ford and Barber, 1983; Freer, 1985).

An alternative, more selective approach is case finding, whereby general practitioners or health visitors monitor the health of the elderly population and formally screen only those people identified as being at the greatest risk (Freer and Williams, 1988; Sidell, 1995, Chapter 7). The high-risk groups can be identified by circulating questionnaires about health, by making an overall health assessment whenever old people visit their general practitioner, or by giving anyone over a certain age the right to regular health check-ups. Selectivity should ensure better targeting and lower costs than a comprehensive screening programme, yet the need for formal organization still implies a substantial real and financial cost.

The least centralized type of preventive care aims only to educate and inform the public, so as to change their behaviour and steer them towards a healthier lifestyle: anti-smoking campaigns and official advice on healthy eating are the main practical examples. With less involvement of the medical profession, the financial costs will normally be lower than the costs of centralized screening programmes (Fries et al., 1993). Traditionally, the medical and social policy professions have regarded this kind of behavioural approach with suspicion, as a possible excuse for governments to run down medical services, cut health care spending, and shirk their duty to provide high-quality curative medicine. At worst, governments could replace formal health care with decentralized preventive programmes and thus hold private individuals solely responsible for their own health. If used judiciously, however, a behavioural approach can accompany curative medicine and formal screening measures as part of a wider health care strategy. The ultimate goal of preventive health care should not be to cut medical spending and wind down formal medicine, but to work alongside other policy measures in sustaining the physical capacity of old people and postponing the onset of dependency.

Poverty exacerbates the difficulties confronting old people. Low incomes bring low nutritional standards, a poor quality of accommodation, and weakened resistance to diseases and disabilities. Any of these factors can increase the chance of a person becoming dependent on formal care. The chief income source for most old people is public pensions and social security benefits; other significant income sources are employment, occupational pensions, and private savings. Employment incomes are declining through the prevalence of early retirement and early exit, while occupational pensions and private savings are increasing in relative importance but still make up a lower proportion of pensioner income than state benefits (Johnson and Falkingham, 1992, Chapter 3; Walker, 1993b). The continued importance of state benefits ensures that public policy can have a large effect on old people's incomes. What remains less clear is the effect of higher incomes on dependency.

Empirical studies show that the lowest income groups among the elderly – usually those previously involved in manual work, who have had the highest incidence of unemployment and the lowest access to occupational pensions – are the most socially deprived: they spend a higher proportion of income on food and basic necessities, and are less likely to possess consumer durables such as central heating, telephones and washing machines (Townsend, 1979; Wright, 1988). A lower living standard normally causes higher dependency levels, and this too is found in empirical studies, where disabilities correlate with income, social class and other socioeconomic variables (Taylor and Ford, 1983; Taylor, 1988; Victor and Evandrou, 1987). On a cross-sectional basis, therefore, higher incomes seem to reduce and delay dependency, though their influence is interrelated with many other social factors and the precise quantitative effects remain uncertain. The obvious drawback of higher pension or social security payments is that they clash with the arguments to cut pensions in response to population ageing. If higher pensions can delay dependency, then the lower costs of social and hospital care will partly and perhaps wholly offset the rise in pension costs. Since the exact effect on dependency is unknown, the benefits of the policy are more uncertain than the known costs of higher pensions; this militates against the policy being adopted in practice. The case for higher public pensions and benefits is stronger than it may at first appear, but jars with the current climate of budgetary retrenchment.

An alternative approach to delaying dependency is through practical or financial support to informal carers, in the form of cash subsidies, assistance with caring activities, short-term respite care, or a longer-term sharing of care. Improved support compensates carers for the real costs of their caring activities and should increase the quantity and quality of the care they provide. If the increased supply of informal care can replace expensive formal care or postpone its onset, then the net effect on public expenditures will be ambiguous. The policy can also increase labour supply if it encourages informal carers who are presently working to stay in employment and combine work with their caring activities. Customary attitudes take for granted that public resources devoted to informal care would be better devoted to formal caring services or any other formal activities. Such attitudes derive from a neglect of the real benefits of informal care, and a more enlightened approach would seek a proper coordination of the informal and formal sectors. Formal domiciliary care is often regarded as a substitute for informal care, to be invoked only when problems have been encountered. But it may complement informal care; it consolidates the capacity of old people to look after themselves and backs up the efforts of informal carers. Formal care need not 'crowd out' informal care, and their strict separation is an artefact of policies forcing a decision between them. Empirical studies suggest that the supply of informal care is positively related to income and need not conflict with employment (Muurinen, 1986; Stone and Short, 1990; Boaz and Mueller, 1992). Practical assistance to carers raises both the supply of informal care and the labour supply of those carers who combine work with care (Chang and White-Means, 1995). The exact quantitative effect of public support may be unclear, but the directions of the expected behavioural changes are well established. Currently, public spending is restricted mainly to the institutional sectors of care, even though they cover only a minority of the elderly population. Diverting public spending towards domiciliary care could discourage premature movements into institutions and reduce the financial burden on taxpayers.

Suitable housing bolsters old people's living standards and enhances their ability to stay independent. A familiar place of residence often has a special significance, as they may have lived in the same property for decades and become so attached and well attuned to it that a movement into another property or an institution would cause severe difficulties (Sixsmith, 1986). According to some commentators, the preservation of the home, rather than the provision of care, should be the bedrock of social policy (Higgins, 1989). Along with its emotional connotations, the physical attributes of housing may have a prime influence on dependency. Poorly designed or maintained accommodation is inconvenient and dangerous for the old, and inadequate heating can be life-threatening. Problems with unsuitable housing can foster a more general dependency requiring intensive formal care; it would then be desirable to adapt the housing of old people so as to help them keep their independence. Housing policies can be crucial to the balance between dependence and independence. The housing problems of the old differ from those of the young. Most old people are already housed, and their usual difficulty is not homelessness but flaws in their current accommodation.

A possible response is to encourage sheltered housing schemes, whereby old people live in purpose-built properties under the surveillance of formal carers who monitor their well-being and deal with emergencies. The desirability of sheltered housing depends on the characteristics of the residents: for those with severe disabilities it can be a less institutionalized alternative to a residential home but for those with higher capabilities it may be an overprovision of care. The basic quality of accommodation frequently has greater relevance than access to formal care (Butler, Oldman and Greve, 1983). Sheltered housing schemes are more costly than ordinary housing and risk overstating and deepening the dependency of their residents (Wheeler, 1986); they have tended to be showpieces which could not easily be extended to all old people. Many residents of sheltered housing schemes could survive comfortably with less attention and in less specialized accommodation. It is sensible, therefore, to consider alternative approaches to finding the right accommodation for the elderly.

The main alternative to sheltered housing is to assist old people living in ordinary accommodation. Instead of constructing new, specialized housing, the aim is to adapt their existing accommodation to suit their changing needs. This could cover more old people at the same expense as sheltered housing schemes and allow them to live more independently. With public-sector housing, the costs of renovating properties would be lower than the costs of constructing and operating sheltered housing schemes: a policy change could be financed from the existing budget. With private owner-occupied or rented housing, the cost could be borne wholly or partly by the owners of the property. Many owner-occupiers are prosperous but living in properties too large for their current requirements or needing extensive repairs. Measures to assist elderly owner-occupiers to finance their own home improvements can counteract these difficulties. The simplest approach permits them to trade down, so that owners of large properties can purchase a smaller, more suitable property at a lower price and use the equity released to renovate the property and finance their retirement. Other arrangements can provide equity without the owner-occupier moving house; old people can remortgage their properties and receive a lump-sum income payment that can finance improvements to the property and other expenses incurred in old age (Wheeler, 1982; Gibbs, 1991). Public encouragement for these schemes could result in a better match between the needs of elderly owner-occupiers and the nature of their properties (Wheeler, 1986). Such a piecemeal, individualized arrangement, wherever feasible, can prolong the self-sufficiency of old people and reduce the financial and other costs of formal care. Sheltered housing and residential institutions can then concentrate on people no longer capable of self-sufficiency.

A final way to increase the capabilities of old people is to introduce more consistent decision making about the provision of care. Many deficiencies in the care of the elderly emerge from the mismatch between the services being provided and the characteristics of the recipients. Both underprovision and overprovision of care can cause unnecessary dependency. When care is underprovided, say through inadequate support for informal carers, then in the short term this reduces the care being offered and suggests a low dependency level; in the longer term, it may accelerate the onset of higher dependency levels and the provision of formal care. When care is overprovided, people are prematurely designated as being dependent and receive superfluous care services that may erode their self-reliance and diminish their physical capabilities. Avoiding a misallocation of care can benefit old people directly and reduce the waste of resources from overprovision. To improve the allocation of care requires better coordination between domiciliary, residential and hospital sectors, so that old people are located in the most suitable accommodation and receive the appropriate type of care. Commentators on social care have frequently urged this, but it has been difficult to achieve.

One might think that a general set of policy guidelines would be enough to secure coordination and collaborative working between the social service, health care and housing branches of the welfare state. On its own, however, an overarching policy on care cannot guarantee that the providers work together effectively: they may see coordination of care as a threat to their independence and a source of unwelcome difficulties in negotiating with other organizations (Hudson, 1987; Webb, 1991). A mere request by central government for cooperation between caring organizations is unlikely to bring perfect results: the agencies involved can find ways of pursuing their own objectives and watering down the government's policy (Dalley, 1991). Full cooperation may happen only after agencies are given an incentive to start working together, for instance, by providing additional funding as a reward for successful collaboration. The agencies then have a common interest in the success of the policy and, once collaboration has started, can develop the trust required in long-term working relationships.

Coordination of private and public care raises additional problems. Private, informal care goes unrecorded in the national accounts and unmonitored by any public bodies. It is extremely diverse and fragmented and, unlike public social services, does not have a unified administrative structure that would facilitate planning. If coordination of care is to include informal economic activities, then there must be a public authority with the power and ability to act as a lead agency and decide on behalf of old people the desirable allocation of formal and informal care. These decisions should ideally be based on reliable information about the full social benefits and costs of informal care, so that it is not treated as a free good and a cheap substitute for the formal alternative. The next chapter considers in more detail how informal care relates to the formal economy.

8. Informal economic activity

Conventional notions of old age are intertwined with notions of economic activity. People below the statutory retirement age are seldom described as old, and the chief mark of being old is to have retired from formal economic activity. The elderly are not officially expected to be working, and the categories 'elderly' and 'economically inactive' have become mutually reinforcing: people are elderly because they are inactive and inactive because they are elderly. This makes it tougher for old people to obtain formal employment and deters them from searching for it. When they do remain economically active, their activity is often restricted to the unpaid, informal sectors of the economy. Such activity, omitted from the national accounts, passes almost unnoticed in economic discussion but may, nonetheless, be a significant part of the national economy. Informal economic activities are a genuine form of production involving real opportunity costs. Changes in the boundaries between formal and informal economic activity have important implications for the organization of the economy and the perception of old age.

Theoretical and policy discussion has neglected informal care, even though it dominates the economic activity of the elderly and their total receipt of economic services. With no recorded accounts, informal activities cannot easily be included in quantitative assessments of policy; many assessments concentrate solely on what is quantifiable and hence abandon (often implicitly) any claims to comprehensiveness. Informal economic activity becomes a reserve category that can substitute for formal activities without ever being acknowledged in national income accounting. Paradoxically, the absence of informal activity from the accounts encourages governments to rely on it more heavily in the provision of care. A transfer of care from the formal to the informal sector appears in the accounts as a saving of resources. Governments have an incentive to promote informal care (usually termed 'community care'), while giving little or no support to informal carers and excluding informal care from the national income accounts. The willingness to rely on informal care proves that it has value as a real activity; it is worthy of standing in for formal care, but not worthy of a mention in the formally recognized resource allocation. Ultimately, one could end up with the entire burden of care being removed from the public finances, placed on the shoulders of informal carers, and presented as a triumph of public-sector efficiency and fiscal rectitude. This lopsided approach to care is the result of arbitrary accounting procedures, and a full economic appraisal should at least attempt to evaluate informal care. Recognizing informal economic activity would raise public awareness of old people as contributors to national output and recipients of vital but undervalued services.

The current chapter looks at informal services in an economy with an ageing population. After setting out the basic characteristics of the informal sector, the discussion moves on to consider the informal care of old people and the methods of evaluating it. The chapter concludes by addressing the policy issues surrounding informal care and its relation with the formal sector.

THE INFORMAL ECONOMY

Economic institutions are normally identified as economic through their connection with production, exchange and consumption. The sum total of all productive activity determines the size of the economy. A problem arises in aggregating the physical outputs of disparate activities, and to resolve it the outputs are expressed in monetary form such that the money value of outputs substitutes for the real output itself. Activities without an output valued in monetary terms, or without inputs that can be valued in the same way, have to be excluded from total output; they do not count as being economic and are omitted from economic discussion. But activities can be economic, in the sense of involving production, exchange and consumption, without having monetary outputs or inputs: domestic production and informal care are prime examples. If one defines these activities as economic, then the total economy is larger than the sum of activities with a monetary valuation. The total economy is split between a formal economy, which has an output measured in monetary terms, and an informal economy, which has no monetary measure of its output.

Both formal and informal economies can be divided into several sectors (Wheelock, 1992). A key distinction is between activities with marketed outputs and those without. In the formal economy, most activities are fully integrated into the market system, with their output sold on markets and their inputs purchased on markets, and are well suited to simple quantitative measurements of output and costs. They conform to the usual theoretical model of competitive private firms interacting through markets, and the extent of competition depends on the prevalent market conditions. Certain public-sector activities, notably nationalized industries, also have marketed outputs and inputs, although they have objectives other than profit maximization and fit less neatly into theoretical models of competitive efficiency. For accounting purposes, they are equivalent to private companies with marketed outputs and create no special problems in generating a formal, monetary measure of their output. The most difficult measurement problems arise when public-sector activities produce non-marketed outputs: the main examples are social services such as health and education. Unmarketed social services count as formal economic activities in the sense that they employ people and purchase factor inputs on competitive markets, but have no single output measurable in monetary units. The public accounts normally take the monetary value of the inputs into these services as a proxy for their outputs. Input-based valuations, while readily obtained, come strictly speaking from the wrong market and may be misleading: a rise in efficiency (same services produced with fewer inputs) shows up in the accounts as a fall in output, whereas a fall in efficiency (same services produced with more inputs) shows up as a rise in output. To avoid these unwelcome properties, one has to impute monetary valuations to non-marketed outputs.

All marketed outputs are legally required to be measured in taxable monetary units. Any informal markets are generally illegal because they stand outside the official framework of national income accounting and tax collection. By their nature these activities must be clandestine, and their true extent is unknown; they vary from large-scale illegal trading, corporate fraud and tax evasion to minor individual involvement in black markets and moonlighting. Informal markets mimic formal ones, as the participants have the same self-interested motivation and interact to reach voluntary agreements of mutual benefit. The objection to informal trading is not that it is unproductive, but that it goes outside the legally sanctioned formal system of markets. This demonstrates the institutional character of formal markets, which depend on the state to define their boundaries and enforce the property rights transferred when market transactions take place. Informal market activity closely resembles formal market trading, but evades its legal structure and thus stands as a rival, parallel market system.

Much of the informal economy has neither a marketed output (formal or informal) nor marketed inputs: there are no market transactions, and collective or altruistic goals may motivate behaviour. The disengagement from the market system indicates a difference of outlook rather than a desire to exploit loopholes in the legal framework of formal markets. Activities without marketed outputs or inputs can be divided into voluntary and domestic sectors (Wheelock, 1992). The voluntary sector comprises non-marketed activities taking place outside the household and often involving interactions between households. Non-trading, not-for-profit bodies have a well-defined institutional structure but pay no wages, so that their output cannot be proxied by the value of their inputs. More often, voluntary work is undertaken on a personal basis, without an institutional structure: care of the elderly is a good example of this. Whenever carers are relatives, friends or neighbours living outside the households of the people being cared for, their caring activities are classified as part of the voluntary sector. These care arrangements are specific to the households concerned; informality extends to the loose organizational structure as well as the absence of market transactions.

The domestic sector includes all informal activity occurring within the household. Most housework falls into this category, as does care of children and old people, when within the household. Many domestic work activities have no substitutes in the formal, market economy and constitute the dominant mode of provision. A few do have substitutes (for example, DIY activities, home-grown food and any home-made goods) and require the purchase of marketed inputs; in these cases the decision to produce the good or service in the domestic sector often entails an element of consumption. The main domestic economic activities are housework and caring, which largely reflect motives other than pure self-interest. As the domestic counterparts of formal public services with unmarketed outputs, they have an altruistic tone missing from market transactions. The formal and informal economies can both be subdivided into a market sector founded on individual self-interest and a non-market sector founded on collective or altruistic aims.

The resulting picture of the economy distinguishes four sectors according to whether economic activities are formally recorded and whether they have marketed outputs. Figure 8.1 illustrates this. Neoclassical economics depicts a modern developed economy as a neat, homogeneous, market-based system in which all economic activity is formally recorded and the outcome of rational, self-interested behaviour: the focus is on formal activities with marketed outputs, in the top left-hand corner of Figure 8.1. Some neoclassical theorists have appealed to externalities, public goods and increasing returns to scale as a justification for public social services (Barr, 1993). The specialist field of public economics has produced an extensive account of the formal, unmarketed sector in the top right-hand corner of Figure 8.1. Economists have paid far less attention to the informal economy in the bottom half of Figure 8.1. Topics such as domestic production and caring are seen as non-economic and therefore the province of social policy or sociology. Academic studies of the informal economy, despite being economic in subject matter, are conducted mostly outside economics.

	Output marketed	Output unmarketed
Formal	Legal markets	Public and social services
Informal	Illegal markets	Domestic and voluntary activities

Figure 8.1 Four sectors of the economy

The total economy incorporates both the formal and informal economies, along with the interaction between them. The two are rarely in direct conflict and often complementary. A purely formal economy, organized on competitive lines without an informal sector, would be unfeasible. All developed economies require diversity and impurity: by the 'impurity principle', planning or informal economic activities must accompany a system of formal markets (Hodgson, 1984, Part 2). What appears to be a pure market economy is a complex mixture of market arrangements, planning and informal activities that continuously interact and reinforce each other. The mixture varies between economies, as is clear from international comparisons (Hugman, 1994), or within a single economy over time, but the same components are present in virtually all cases. To stress only one component may seriously misrepresent the way in which an economy functions. Formal markets dominate capitalist economies, but the economies could not survive without the informal non-market activities of housework and caring. Hence, it is a mistake to ignore informal economic activities, as if they are somehow inferior to formal ones or of negligible economic value. Comprehensive national accounts that portray the full range of economic activities should include the informal economy and treat it on the same basis as the formal economy. Attempts to add informal activities to the national accounts are hindered by the lack of reliable information and as yet remain only approximate (Goldschmidt-Clermont, 1990, 1992). But whatever the difficulties, a proper recognition of informal activity is essential to an understanding of the total economy and its component parts. The interaction between the formal and informal sectors has a unique importance for old people, as most of their care is informal.

INFORMAL CARE OF OLD PEOPLE

Modernization theorists argue that economic development disrupted traditional family relationships and replaced informal care with formal
arrangements. The family in pre-industrial societies, according to this argument, was organized on the same hierarchical principles as society at large.
Old people stood at the head of multigenerational families, which meant
that younger family members were living in the same household and available to provide unpaid services for the elderly. Pre-industrial societies
apparently favoured old people through a generous provision of informal
care within extended families. Empirical backing for this view comes from
observed trends in household structure. The proportion of old people at
the head of a household and the proportion who live alone have been
increasing, though the increase has been concentrated in the last two
decades (Wall, 1984, 1989; Falkingham and Gordon, 1990). More
one-person households consisting of old people may indicate the decline of
the multigenerational household and (more speculatively) a dwindling of
informal care. As life expectancy has increased, children have been leaving
home at an earlier stage in their parents' life cycle, creating a longer 'empty-
nest' phase during which an older couple (and eventually a widow or
widower) lives alone (Grundy, 1991). The growing number of solitary old
people is due partly to population ageing, but it may also be due to weaker
family bonds and a growing fragmentation of society.

Recently the idea of a past 'golden age' for old people has come under
criticism. An immediate problem is that the old were numerically insignificant in pre-industrial societies: most families would have had no elderly
members and could not have been multigenerational (Johnson, 1982).
When elderly family members were in fact present, they were not necessarily given privileged treatment at the top of a hierarchy. Historical
studies have suggested that they did not have favoured status and that the
notion of the extended family is a myth (Anderson, 1971; Laslett, 1971,
1977). Changes in the living arrangements of the elderly have not fol-
lowed a simple unidirectional trend during industrialization. In the UK,
for example, the proportion of the elderly living alone fell during the
nineteenth century and rose during the twentieth, so that current living
arrangements are closer in some respects to those of a pre-industrial society than to those of the late nineteenth century (Wall, 1992, 1996). In any
case, old people living alone cannot safely be assumed to mean that intergenerational altruism must have collapsed. The old may be living
increasingly in separate households, but they often stay near to their
offspring and receive assistance from them. Studies of informal care
within families show that close (usually female) relatives are as willing to

offer informal care as in the past and that there is little evidence of a decline in moral obligations or duties (Shanas, 1979; Brody, 1981; Finch, 1989, Chapter 2). Informal care remains a vital service provided to old people, even if it is now more likely to occur between rather than within households. The proportion of old people resident in institutions has always been low and has been falling in recent years. Most old people receive care within their own homes, mainly from relatives, and because of population ageing the total amount of informal care is now larger than ever before. Under these circumstances, it is unhelpful to draw contrasts with a 'golden age' that probably never existed.

Another reason for the apparent decline of informal care has been the twentieth-century expansion of formal services, which might at first glance be regarded as having replaced informal activities. Modernization theory predicts that economic activities will be steadily formalized during economic development and markets or formal public services will take over from the previous informal, hierarchical arrangements. Formalization has had a minimal effect on domiciliary care, however, and most formal services have been provided in a residential or hospital setting. Formal domiciliary services were slow to develop and uneven in their coverage, with public authorities often passing responsibility to private voluntary organizations (Means and Smith, 1994, Chapter 2). The caution in developing formal domiciliary care suggests that the state was content with the role of informal care and reluctant to undermine the willingness of relatives to offer voluntary unpaid services. While formalization went ahead elsewhere in the welfare state, it hardly touched domiciliary care and did not replace the activities of informal carers. Until the last decade or so, governments have made little attempt to coordinate formal and informal care; the opposite was nearer the truth, as formal services were set up as self-contained entities and kept apart from the informal sector. The welfare state grew alongside but separately from the informal sector, and in no sense can be said to have superseded it.

The coexistence of formal and informal care is now an active policy issue. Politicians have become wary of formal, state-provided solutions to social problems and have instead promoted a 'mixed economy of care' in which care is shared between public and private sources. This pluralism of care has always been present tacitly, since the formal welfare state has never provided comprehensive social care: most care has been undertaken informally by relatives, and any formal domiciliary care has often been undertaken privately by voluntary organizations. The difference from earlier policies is that governments are now openly pursuing a public/private, formal/informal mix and not leaving it to emerge spontaneously from the gaps in public provision. There are now official efforts to integrate the private and informal sectors into public decision making so as to evaluate the balance of care more accurately and equitably. The new, explicit approach to the mixed economy of care can take several forms, depending on the relative importance of markets, planning and participation. Market-oriented versions stress competition between the sources of care, such that planners can choose the least-cost alternative and recontract when necessary (Le Grand, 1991; Le Grand and Bartlett, 1993). Other versions (sometimes called 'welfare pluralism') stress communal values and the participation of the users of care in decisions about the services provided (Hadley and Hatch, 1981).

Despite the differences, the common theme in much recent policy debate is a movement away from centralized provision towards diverse sources of care. Post-Fordist views regard technical change as the driving force behind the recent trends; information technology is permitting greater flexibility and decentralization in care, as it supposedly is in other economic activities (Hoggett, 1991). The post-Fordist interpretation remains open to doubt, however. Certain technical developments do ease communication between providers and recipients of care, and this is conducive to decentralization. Improved availability and quality of telecommunications systems and consumer durable goods should in the long term reduce the reliance of old people on caring services and help them to stay independent (Gershuny, 1983). Technical developments have contributed to recent social changes, but they are not the only relevant factors. The immediate driving force behind recent policy changes is as much political as technical, and one should steer clear of a reductive technological determinism.

Informal care sits rather uncomfortably in the general analysis of decentralization and post-Fordism. Formal services are gradually becoming more diversified, with a less centralized administrative structure, greater flexibility in provision, and increased private sector involvement. The same trends cannot be applicable to informal activity, which is already decentralized and provided on diversified ad hoc principles. Informal care is, if anything, moving in the opposite direction to formal care. The arguments for a mixed economy of care propose that informal activities previously separate from the formal economy should be brought within the same decision-making procedures as formal care. Centralized monitoring of informal care will counterbalance decentralization of formal care. The overall tendency cannot be characterized as a single movement towards decentralization: this may be happening with formal activities, but there are countervailing pressures on the informal economy. As informal care comes within the public sphere, policy makers will have to assess the relative merits of formal and informal provision and the desirable balance between them. Recent developments may have a technological underpinning that will become more apparent in the longer term, but their short-term consequences have been to increase the discretion of policy makers over the types of care being provided. Assessing formal care is difficult enough, as was observed in Chapter 7, and including informal care within the same assessment causes still greater difficulties. Much rests, therefore, on how formal and informal care are to be compared.

Informal care differs in several respects from formal care and is sometimes claimed to be superior. Its advocates point out the value of the personal relationships it reflects and creates, particularly when care takes place within the family. Old people may prefer to receive care from people they know and trust, instead of from anonymous professionals. The relatives of old people frequently accept that they have obligations to provide care and are happy to do so voluntarily. A voluntary caring relationship in which the provider and recipient know each other is, arguably, an ideal state of affairs. Informal care by volunteers from outside the family but within the local community may be the next best alternative. Voluntary, informal arrangements, inside and outside the family, are closer to the common perception of caring than is a contractual arrangement with a professional carer. The 'gift relationship' is lost as soon as an activity is incorporated in the formal economy (Titmuss, 1970). Informal care may, in addition, reduce feelings of dependency. Old people often fear the first contact with formal care as a step on the road to more complete dependency and eventual institutionalization. Such fears may be unfounded, but they demonstrate that, other things being equal, old people prefer care to be informal. The essence of informal care is that it emerges voluntarily, to the benefit of the recipients and providers alike. Once imposed on people, it becomes a less attractive proposition, effectively an unpaid version of formal, contractually-based caring. To preserve the character of informal arrangements, advocacy of informal care must stop short of imposing informal methods from above and be content with choosing informal approaches whenever a choice is available.

In other respects, formal care may be superior to informal. Professional carers have normally undergone training and are well prepared for the tasks awaiting them. Informal carers, by contrast, may have first-hand knowledge of the person being cared for but little knowledge of how to provide effective care. The poor quality of informal care can undermine its good intentions and genuineness, especially in cases where the dependency of an old person has started at a low level and then increased with age to culminate in severe disability beyond the capacities of the carer. Formal care is more amenable to the centralized monitoring of quality and, while centralization may seem unpalatable, it can assist the attainment of a uniform, satisfactory provision of care. Informal caring can be arbitrary in its availability. Those with a plentiful supply of younger, well-disposed relatives will benefit most from informal caring arrangements. Others with no relatives, or with relatives unable or unwilling to provide care, will be less fortunate.

An economy that relies heavily on informal care will have to tolerate large inequalities in the amount and quality of care received by old people. The only way to ensure that care is available to all, including those without informal carers, is to provide at least a safety net of formal care. The effects of informal care in raising welfare and reducing dependency are also questionable. Old people may feel less dependent when cared for by their family, but dependency relations within the family can bring their own difficulties. Informal care extended over long periods may cause a loss of good will; what started as a voluntary arrangement may end up as a source of conflict and ill feeling. When this happens, less familiarity between providers and recipients of care may be desirable. Once good will within the family evaporates, the caring relationship becomes involuntary and may threaten the quality of life of all the parties involved. As an old person becomes increasingly dependent, the burden on informal carers grows and they find it harder to cope without formal support; in virtually all cases formal care is eventually needed, if only in the form of medical care during the last stages of life. Few would argue for universal informal care. The problem is how to relate formal to informal care and find the right balance between them.

Financial considerations have influenced government attitudes to formal and informal care: transferring care from the formal to the informal sector reduces public expenditure and apparently improves efficiency, as if the previous output of formal care were now being provided at zero cost. A government anxious to cut taxes will be tempted to promote 'community care', even when formal care would be preferable on efficiency grounds. Official caring policy in the UK has long favoured the expansion of community care; both the main political parties have endorsed this, although the apparent consistency of policy masks a changing political climate (Walker, 1982b, 1993a). Informal care is prone to government manipulation: when other sources of care are run down or withdrawn, relatives will often feel obliged to provide informal care as a last resort. The moral sanction of duty can induce people to offer unpaid, 'voluntary' services, notwithstanding the unpleasantness of the tasks involved and the sacrifices of time and income they entail. A forced expansion of informal care will reduce its average quality as more reluctant carers are pressed into service. Informal care, as it expands, will be less attractive in comparison with the formal care it is displacing. Treating it as a cheap, second-best alternative to formal care is an unsatisfactory method of organizing caring activities. A proper evaluation of care should give equal standing to formal and informal approaches.

The disparity between formal and informal care is avoidable if intermediate approaches are exploited to the full. Informal care can be combined with formal services that cover the more difficult or specialized caring tasks: this relieves the burdens on informal carers and improves the general quality of care. Temporarily replacing informal with formal care can provide a respite period for informal carers and increase their effectiveness. Public subsidies for informal care can raise the supply of informal carers and strengthen their ability to offer good care. Weakening the formal/informal boundary can discourage a simplistic bias towards one or the other approach. Policy should be willing to take advantage of voluntary informal care, but only as part of a comprehensive strategy giving public support to informal carers and making consistent decisions about the right formal/informal mix. Consistent decision making gathers together all formal, informal and combined alternatives in a single framework; informal methods have to be 'formalized' analytically despite their absence from the national accounts.

ECONOMIC EVALUATION OF INFORMAL CARE

To evaluate care requires estimates of the real benefits and costs of informal care, which can be compared with the benefits and costs of equivalent formal activities. The appropriate techniques of economic appraisal are the ones used in cost–benefit analysis to quantify non-monetary social costs. They are far from perfect and the results should be viewed with caution, but it is better to try to gauge the benefits and costs of informal care than to ignore the issue or do without any sort of formal appraisal. Quibbling too much about the evaluation of informal care plays into the hands of those who would be only too pleased to exploit it as a substitute category of care that covers up for inadequate formal provision. Attempts to evaluate care have concentrated on the cost rather than the benefit side so as to simplify the analysis. Cost-effectiveness studies hold constant the benefits of the options being compared and identify the option with the lowest social costs: formal and informal care are assumed to provide similar services and generate similar social benefits. A complete cost–benefit analysis would recognize the differences between formal and informal care and evaluate their benefits separately; as yet, however, little progress has been made in appraising the qualitative benefits to the recipients and providers of informal care (Smith and Wright, 1994). The economic literature has generally assumed that the benefits of formal and informal care are equivalent and then considered how a social costing of informal care might be obtained.

The main costs imposed on informal carers are the loss of their time and the unpleasantness of the tasks they undertake. Many caring tasks are time-intensive. An old person at a high dependency level may need assistance with almost all activities, together with round-the-clock surveillance: for a single informal carer the sacrifice of time is complete. As dependency levels decline, so does the time taken by caring tasks. At the lowest dependency levels, care may be limited to assistance with a few activities on a weekly or irregular basis. Even here, informal carers provide services in kind and must be giving up time that they could have devoted to other things. One would expect to find a trade-off between informal care and employment, especially among females; empirical studies bear this out, though the strength of the relation remains a matter of contention (Wolf and Soldo, 1994; Ettner, 1996). Involvement in care mainly reduces working hours, while leaving labour force participation virtually unchanged, and has a larger effect for females than males (Arber and Ginn, 1995). Such results demonstrate the burdens being borne by many women who would otherwise work full time but are willing to combine informal care with part-time work. Time spent caring can alternatively be drawn from time spent in leisure activities, for example, when the carer is economically inactive or continues with the same employment as before.

Whether care displaces employment or leisure, it must have opportunity costs. If the care is voluntary, then it brings benefits that exceed its opportunity costs and imposes no net cost on the carer. In some cases, a carer might be willing to offer care but prefer a quantity or intensity of care lower than that now being undertaken. Carers, like many workers in the formal economy, face all-or-nothing choices: they can either look after a relative with a particular combination of disabilities or refuse any involvement in care. Part of their total caring time will be voluntary, that is to say, their first-choice activity, and the rest an involuntary excess of care. Evaluations of care should attach a cost only to the time spent on involuntary care. Normally, voluntary and involuntary care are not distinguishable by observed characteristics, and all care appears to be voluntary in so far as the carer has chosen the current caring activities in a constrained, all-or-nothing decision. The involuntary aspect of caring should be measured relative to the level of care that an unconstrained carer would choose, and this can be done only by inference from observed behaviour or by survey methods.

The costs of care depend on qualitative as well as quantitative factors, on the tasks being performed as well as the time spent performing them. Caring activities are often disagreeable: carers do not relish dealing with incontinence or performing personal tasks such as washing, dressing and feeding. Generally, the more unpleasant are the tasks, the greater are the costs, and the smaller is the proportion of carers willing to tolerate the tasks. As the recipients of care grow older, their dependency level increases, and with it the likelihood of their requiring more intensive care. Informal carers who were prepared to undertake routine caring tasks may find themselves undertaking far more intensive care than they had initially expected. Once committed to a caring role it can be difficult to withdraw, and carers may end up with an intensity of care well beyond what they would have freely chosen. Eventually the good will of carers may be whittled away to the extent of provoking a crisis and a transfer of the elderly person into formal care. An intensity of care above the ideal must be imposing a cost on informal carers that goes uncompensated by financial rewards. Assessments of the costs of informal care should allow for the nature of the tasks being performed.

Few economists have conducted a full economic appraisal of informal care of the elderly. There is an extensive academic literature on both formal and informal care, but this falls mostly within the discipline of social policy. Empirical studies in social policy seldom gather the quantitative information needed for economic appraisals and are satisfied with a less formal, qualitative stance. The economic appraisals of care that do exist confine themselves mostly to the formal sector where monetary data are more easily obtained. The studies by Mooney (1978), Wright, Cairns and Snell (1981), and Knapp (1984) centre on formal approaches; Wright, Cairns and Snell (1981) collected data on informal care but stopped short of deriving monetary costings. Economists who have appraised social care have generally been aware of informal care, but have had to concentrate on the formal sector because of informational problems. It is, nevertheless, reasonably clear what formal methods could be used to evaluate informal care if the necessary information was available (Wright, 1987a and b; Netten, 1993; Smith and Wright, 1994). The aim is to elicit measures of willingness to pay for change (or the absence of change) which express in monetary form the effect of caring arrangements on people's well-being. When carers are sacrificing other activities or performing tasks obnoxious to them, they would be ready to give up some income in order to relinquish or reduce their caring activities. A monetary measure of this willingness to pay indicates the approximate costs of involuntary care and can be compared with the costs of the formal alternatives.

A prior step before evaluating informal care is to identify the time spent involuntarily on caring. As informal care goes unrecorded in official statistics, this requires survey methods. Estimates of caring time differ according to whether or not carers and recipients of care live in the same household. When care takes place in a single household, many general chores (such as cleaning, cooking or shopping) are carried out in the same fashion with or without an additional elderly resident. Only those caring tasks specific to the elderly person entail a sacrifice of time. If, on the other hand, the recipient of care lives in a separate household, the informal carers may be replicating general chores, and the time devoted to these should be included in the imputed costs of informal care. Total caring time should, if possible, be disaggregated to take account of the various tasks involved. Data from surveys of carers will inevitably be approximate, since the carers themselves may be only vaguely aware of the time allocated to particular tasks. They are being asked to construct the equivalent of a formal time-accounting framework, even though they are working informally and probably without a strict time schedule. The results may be unreliable, but the nature of informal activities prevents accurate measurements. Further complications arise in specifying the degree to which care is voluntary. Some carers looking after close relatives will be reluctant to say that any of their activities are involuntary. A general assertion of one's willingness to provide care suggests that informal care is imposing no cost on carers. This will be true for only a minority of carers. To get a clearer view of attitudes to care, surveys should pose a range of questions and avoid asking baldly whether care is voluntary. Normally when carers admit to tiredness and strain or acknowledge difficulties with caring tasks, their care will have an involuntary element. Assuming that enough information can be collated on attitudes to care, the proportion of time allocated to involuntary care can be estimated.

The investigator can then attach a social value to this time. Opportunity-cost valuations depend on the alternative uses to which the time could have been put. Cost–benefit analysts often distinguish between work and leisure as alternative activities. If the carer would otherwise have been working, the time spent in involuntary care can be valued according to the earnings forgone. In these cases valuations are obtainable from the wage rates for the relevant types of employment. Unemployment reduces the social cost of lost working time, because the informal carer's former job may be taken by an unemployed person whose enforced leisure time has a low opportunity cost; with high unemployment, cost–benefit analysts use an adjusted shadow wage rate below the market wage. If care involves a sacrifice of leisure time, then alternative methods are needed. Leisure, unlike work, has no observable price, and a value has to be inferred from decisions affecting a person's free time. The commonest approach is to derive a value of leisure from decisions about modes of transport. A more rapid transport mode saves leisure time for people travelling to work, but is generally more expensive than a slower alternative. Other things being equal, the cost difference between them provides a monetary valuation of the leisure time saved. This procedure usually gives leisure time a value below that of working time, and so it becomes important to identify accurately the alternative uses of time spent on informal care.

A more thorough approach would go further than a tripartite division of time into formal work, informal care and leisure: each of these embraces many activities that could be valued differently. Single, catch-all valuations of working, caring or leisure time could give a misleading impression of the true costs of care. Informal carers will place a higher value on reducing time spent in unpleasant tasks, such as dealing with incontinence, than in less demanding tasks, such as shopping. When information is available on the activities of informal carers, cost–benefit analysts can weight time savings according to the intensity of care. One method of doing this is to obtain, through surveys, information on the tolerance of carers for distinct caring tasks (Wright, 1987a). The lower the proportion of carers willing to perform a certain task, the more unpleasant it is and the higher is the value of reduced time spent performing it. The weight attached to the task should be inversely related to the tolerance ratio. If, say, only 50 per cent of carers are prepared to perform the task, then an hour of the task will require approximately two hours supply of representative informal care: the task has twice the value of standard caring time (for tasks with 100 per cent tolerance). Empirical studies have found low tolerance levels of some caring activities: Sanford (1975), for instance, found a minimum figure of 16 per cent for activities requiring 24-hour observation and frequent disruptions of sleep; the resulting valuation of caring time is 6.25 (=100/16) times that of standard caring time. Given the large differences in valuations, disaggregation by activities could be crucial to the costing of informal care.

An alternative approach is to relate informal care to equivalent formal services. Whenever informal carers and public services provide the same care, the cost of the public services can be taken as a minimum social value of care: if informal care was withdrawn, this would be the cost of replacing it with formal arrangements. Formal and informal care are thus treated identically. The dearth of formal equivalents for many informal caring activities is a serious obstacle to this apparently simple approach. Informal care provided within a household demands a constant surveillance that has no public parallel outside residential institutions. Even if equivalent public services exist, they may be an imperfect match for informal care. Unobservable qualitative factors will always intrude and could work in either direction: informal care could be superior to formal care because of the personal relationships involved, or inferior because it is more amateurish and variable in quality. A further obstacle is that this approach cannot be used to compare the efficiency of formal and informal care, but only to evaluate the total costs of care relative to the costs of other economic activities.

If the government already provides financial assistance for carers or recipients of care, then this can be a yardstick of the social value placed on care. When a care allowance is actually paid, it will be recorded in the formal accounts, and the same value can be imputed to informal care for which the allowance is not paid. To estimate the full social costs of informal care, the analyst merely has to fill in the gaps left by existing financial assistance. Public support for care is assumed to be an accurate indicator of social valuations. Using current public valuations in cost–benefit analyses goes somewhat against the rationale of economic appraisal, as the economist is supposedly advising the government on how best to organize its caring policies, given that its current valuations are unreliable. To insert these valuations into the economist's calculations may contaminate the appraisal with inaccurate data from the very arrangements the economist is trying to appraise. If current valuations were wholly reliable, then formal economic appraisal would be redundant and the judgement of political decision makers could stand on its own. Economic appraisal, if it is to fulfil its purpose, cannot afford to borrow too many social valuations from current public decision making.

Informal care may impose other costs besides the opportunity costs of time spent caring, notably financial, future and accommodation costs (Netten, 1993). Financial costs arise from expenditure on the goods and services associated with informal care that would not otherwise be purchased: examples are extra spending on heating, food and travel. Carers may also incur capital costs if they adapt properties to permit satisfactory care of the severely disabled. Future costs are the long-term costs resulting from the present commitments of informal carers: lost training opportunities, impaired job mobility, and disrupted pension contributions are included in this category. Accommodation costs derive from the changes of residence that occur when informal caring relationships are established. Old people who move in with their offspring are releasing property for other people but also occupying space in the home of the informal carers. The net accommodation cost depends on the comparative social values of the property being released and occupied; it could be positive or negative according to which value predominates.

These various other costs are unlikely to outweigh the opportunity cost of time, but they demonstrate that a full evaluation of informal care should go beyond the analysis of time use.

Attempts to evaluate informal care are subject to all the usual problems confronting cost–benefit analyses. Three problems are worth highlighting. The first is the use of market prices to obtain the social values of lost working or leisure time. Market prices coincide with social valuations only under perfect competition. Any imperfections or market failures, such as monopoly power, increasing returns to scale, externalities or imperfect information, cause social valuations to differ from market prices and require the cost–benefit analyst to calculate adjusted shadow prices. Almost all markets have imperfections, and social valuations should be adjusted accordingly. Such adjustments are troublesome, and so economic appraisals often use unadjusted market prices as the source of their valuations. Despite the theoretical objections to this method, cost–benefit analysts may feel that the market price is superior to any crude calculations of shadow prices. The continued reliance on unadjusted market prices illustrates the approximate character of formal economic appraisals.

The second problem lies in isolating the informal service being valued. Even if market prices and social valuations are roughly equal, it is still awkward to translate market pricing into social values of specific informal services. Most consumption decisions relate only obliquely to the items the cost–benefit analyst wants to evaluate. In valuing the loss of leisure time, for example, decisions between modes of transport are seldom based on time savings alone. Commuters paying more for faster journeys are normally paying for greater comfort as well, and the relative valuations of the time saved and increased comfort are by no means obvious. Similarly, variations in the nature and quality of the service obscure comparisons of equivalent private and public services. Informal care is a personalized undertaking, frequently tailored to particular individuals or households and with no close equivalents in formal services or anywhere else. Each household makes its own arrangements which differ in key respects from arrangements elsewhere. As a result, the correspondence between typical informal arrangements and observable market prices of equivalent services will be elusive.

The third problem is the influence of the income distribution on market prices. All market pricing, efficient or not, reflects the ability to pay, and the preferences of the rich have a bigger influence on pricing than those of the poor. Using market prices as social valuations creates a bias in economic appraisals towards the more prosperous sections of society. Cost–benefit analysts can, in theory, introduce social welfare weightings to offset the effects of income differences, but most studies adopt a simpler approach that avoids explicit social welfare valuations (Sugden and Williams, 1978, Chapter 7). Unless one is prepared to disaggregate the population into income groups, identify the separate impact of policy changes on each, and then specify the relevant social welfare weightings, cost–benefit analysis will be tacitly approving the existing patterns of income and wealth. The unsavoury choice is between a manageable method that shuns equity considerations and a less manageable one that allows for them. Economists sometimes sidestep this choice by claiming that economic appraisal, as a positive technique, can be kept apart from normative matters; social welfare weightings, in this view, have no place in economic analysis. One cannot erase equity considerations from cost–benefit analysis, however, and there is always an implicit set of social welfare weightings based on the current income distribution.

Informal care is too amorphous and intangible to be easily susceptible to economic appraisal, and the economic literature has neglected it largely because of the difficulties encountered. Even so, a more efficient and equitable planning of care should treat informal activities on the same basis as formal ones. Assigning real economic costs to informal care is an advance on treating it as a free good and at least recognizes that unpaid domiciliary care places a burden on informal carers, while relieving everyone else of the responsibility for looking after old people. A laissez-faire approach to informal care would be inequitable and carry no guarantee of efficiency except by the distorted criteria allotting zero costs to informal activities. A more integrated care framework, coupled with public support for informal carers, can spread the costs of care more evenly among the population, increase the quantity and quality of informal care, and improve efficiency. Economic evaluation will never produce a perfectly planned, wholly efficient balance of care, but it can discourage policy makers from ignoring non-monetary costs. Rough indications of the real costs of informal care can be a valuable input into the debates about caring policies. The main contribution of economic appraisal is not as a complete, self-contained planning device, but as an aid to better informed policy discussion.

POLICY ISSUES

Population ageing makes it harder to coordinate formal and informal care. Some informal care is provided within a single generation by spouses, but old people living alone usually receive care from younger relatives, chiefly daughters and daughters-in-law (Nissel and Bonnerjea,

1982; Parker, 1990, Chapter 2; Arber and Ginn, 1990, 1991, Chapter 8). As the caring relationship is intergenerational, an ageing population reduces the potential supply of younger informal carers for each old person. The long-run trend in fertility has been downwards in virtually all developed countries, and as the average family size decreases then so does the pool of younger family members from which informal carers might be drawn (Eversley, 1982; Wicks, 1989). Younger family members have become more mobile than previously, and they are less likely to live near their elderly relatives. The willingness of people to provide informal care has held steady, but the falling size and increasing dispersion of younger generations will be a problem for future governments hoping to rely on informal care. Arguments that a switch from formal to informal care will solve the problems of population ageing overlook the fact that this 'solution' is itself restricted by population ageing. Policies to stimulate informal care will have to outweigh the negative influence of demographic change before they produce a rise in the availability of care.

A higher dependency ratio affects informal activities as well as formal ones, and in some cases the effect on informal activities will be greater. The informal economy has no clear division between the employed and unemployed. Any reserve of underutilized informal labour is much less visible than its equivalent in the formal sector, and one cannot tell whether people have an unfulfilled desire to undertake informal activities. Many informal carers, having chosen not to partake in the formal economy, possess no strong urge for full-scale economic activity, formal or informal. When informal carers are constrained, they are generally doing too much work rather than too little: offered a choice, they would prefer a decrease in their activity to an increase. It seems improbable that the economically inactive population have an unfulfilled wish to become informal carers and that population ageing gives them the chance to fulfil that wish.

When formal care is unavailable, informal carers may feel themselves obliged to fill the gap, but this is an act dictated by external circumstances. There is no pre-existing excess supply of informal carers waiting for someone to look after. The low supply of care from male relatives could perhaps be interpreted as an untapped source of informal activity. Most males, however, have chosen not to become involved in informal care, and they will be reluctant to participate in caring unless it is made compulsory or induced by financial or other incentives. Neither of these alternatives has much appeal. Some commentators (for example, Lagergren et al., 1984) have proposed making unpaid social care compulsory as a form of community service, but this is authoritarian and risks losing the distinctive qualities of voluntary informal relationships. Paying benefits to informal carers would be a more promising approach and might be desirable on other grounds (such as equity), but the payments required to compensate the most reluctant carers will be too high for this to be considered an attractive financial option. Informal care does not proffer an easy escape from demographic problems; the constraint on the availability of informal care is tighter than that on the availability of formal labour. To rely on the informal economy, which has no excess supply of carers, to resolve the 'dependency crisis' in the formal economy, which has an excess supply of labour, is inconsistent. Population ageing will create as many difficulties for the provision of informal care as for the rest of the economy.

A comprehensive assessment of the effects of population ageing should treat formal and informal care even-handedly. Economic analysts should acknowledge the real costs of informal care and then raise the same questions that arise with pensions and health care: what are the implications of population ageing for the real costs of caring in both the formal and informal economies? In the light of these implications, how should governments adjust the methods of care and the public resources devoted to caring? The policy issues are a particular instance, restricted to caring, of the augmented transfer problem described in Chapter 2. A full quantitative version of this policy problem, embodying economic evaluation of informal care, is unfeasible at present. Nor will it be feasible in the near future. Yet the general principle of evaluating informal activities is important for a topic such as caring. A total neglect of informal care, common in much policy discussion, means that the implicit weighting on informal care undervalues its true benefits and costs by several orders of magnitude. Any positive weighting, even if it is still an underestimate, would be an improvement on this situation. Detailed formal planning may be impossible, but it should be possible to reform caring policies in the right direction and give a more realistic valuation to the costs of informal care.

The best framework for equalizing the treatment of formal and informal care is to encourage greater sharing of care between the state and families. As soon as an informal carer receives real or financial support from the state, the formal/informal division has been weakened. Informal care becomes a matter of public interest, and the prospects for a more consistent approach to caring are enhanced. Historically, governments have stayed aloof from community care and concentrated their efforts on residential care and pension policies (Means and Smith, 1994, Chapter 2). This has been due partly to the belief that formal domiciliary caring services or public policies to assist informal carers would damage the foundations of community care by dissuading female relatives from performing their traditional caring roles. Assistance to informal carers was left strictly to voluntary, non-state organizations (Means, 1986). Recently, however, governments have become more sympathetic to public involvement in informal care and a transfer of care from the residential and hospital sectors to the domiciliary sector. The earlier arguments about the influence of formal services are no longer so widely accepted. Public support for informal care can increase the willingness of family members to provide care and permit them to sustain their caring activities; an extension of informal care can do away with unnecessary residential care and reduce total public spending on the care of the elderly. Where public involvement was once seen as displacing informal care and wasting public resources, it is now seen as supporting informal care and reducing public expenditure; a few authors have even criticized it as reinforcing (rather than undermining) female caring roles (Finch, 1984; Dalley, 1988). Public policies, if suitably designed, should be able to avoid destabilizing informal care or strengthening unequal gender roles. Wholesale opposition to public involvement on either of these grounds is unduly pessimistic.

Arguments for community care and a sharing of responsibilities between families and the state have become widespread in policy debates. The crucial issue is the precise form this sharing takes. Some versions of community care are little more than exercises in cutting public spending; others, put forward by social policy professionals, envisage an expansion in the activities of formal carers within households. The ideal system would be planned to accommodate population ageing and achieve efficiency and equity but still maintain a role for informal care provided voluntarily. Planning of care at the highest level can facilitate the overall assessment of aggregate resource requirements. With clear guidelines for public support of informal care, the public authorities are compelled to monitor the extent, nature and distribution of informal care. They are in a stronger position to evaluate the real economic consequences of population ageing than they would be if they allowed informal care to develop randomly and unrecorded. The greater visibility of informal care should ensure that it features fully in decision making and is not treated merely as a free good. Formal public involvement in community care should increase the government's ability to offer a coordinated response to population ageing and dissuade it from ignoring the real economic effects on informal carers. Planning has the further advantage that it can bring about more consistent provision among individuals and social groups.

Informal arrangements are notoriously random, depending on old people's readiness to seek assistance, the availability of willing relatives or neighbours, and the presence of appropriate voluntary organizations. If it is left solely to private initiative to request and provide informal services, the allocation of care will be biased towards those who are more vocal in staking their claims or more fortunate in their social surroundings. Proper monitoring of the needs of the elderly population can provide the information required to attain a more equitable allocation of care, and public planning can offset the arbitrariness of informal arrangements. Public involvement in community care is also the means by which a government can react to demographic changes. A planned element is a necessary (though not a sufficient) condition for making a smooth, well-informed response to population ageing.

Against the advantages of planned community care has to be set the risk of a top-down approach giving too little attention to the views of old people. According to some commentators, community care policies should empower the users of care and avoid a strictly centralized approach. User empowerment can take several different and often conflicting forms. Means and Smith (1994) distinguish three main approaches: two are based on exit and voice, following the terminology of Hirschman (1970), and the third on rights. An exit-based approach gives the users a choice between alternative sources of care and lets them exit from any alternative if they so wish. The users do not directly influence care, but they have a veto over any particular method on offer. A voice-based approach gives the users a say in the design and implementation of care. The aim is to avoid a paternalistic stance and increase users' participation in a democratic process of choosing and formulating their own care. A rights-based approach admits that, although user participation would be desirable, for many users it is not a viable option. To ensure a more equitable distribution of care, minimum standards can be guaranteed by giving users a legally enforceable right to a certain level of services. In policy discussion, the exit-based approaches are usually aligned with arguments for market reform and privatization, while the voice-based and rights-based approaches are aligned with arguments for more decentralized and equitable public services. A pure market model would rest upon commercial caring services and have negligible public intervention. A pure participation model would let the users specify their own public services within a publicly funded and provided scheme. The common desire to decentralize conceals a tension between the New Right arguments for markets and the New Left arguments for participation and democracy. Practical measures to introduce decentralized care have generally been a hybrid of these approaches.

The most prominent method of introducing decentralized care has been through case (or care) management. Case managers are social policy professionals who act as agents for the users of care and assist them in formulating the best package of care within the limits of current public funding. As a neutral intermediary between users and providers, the case manager should not be involved in providing care. Users have more influence than in a centralized system, but the precise extent of their involvement varies with the details of the scheme. Experiments conducted in the UK in the 1980s have suggested that the case management approach can achieve some of its objectives (Challis and Davies, 1986; Challis et al., 1988; Challis et al., 1993). When given adequate public support, domiciliary care has been able to deal effectively with high levels of disability and delay entry into residential institutions. Keeping old people in their own homes can preserve their independence and, for a given minimum standard of care, will normally be less costly than the residential alternatives. Case management can accommodate alternative relations between case managers, providers of care and users of care (Cambridge, 1992; Wistow et al., 1994). It has frequently been allied to the notion of quasi-markets based on a purchaser–provider split, with the purchasers (case managers) being allocated a public budget and spending it on what they regard as the best package of care for their clients (the users of care). This version of case management, proposed by the Griffiths Report (1988), has recently been implemented in the UK (Department of Health, 1989). The quasi-market structure aims to stimulate competition among providers of care and thereby attain greater cost-effectiveness. Whether the reforms accomplish this remains to be seen. At present there are doubts about the feasibility of a quasi-market in care; the case management structure corresponds only approximately to the quasi-market model (Hoyes and Means, 1993). General agreement over the desirability of case management hides a large disparity in the forms it can take. Further moves in this direction are likely, but it remains uncertain how decentralized care will evolve.

Case management is often represented as creating a mixed economy of care, with responsibilities shared between the state, voluntary organizations and private individuals. This can be misleading, because a de facto mixed economy of care has always existed through the large proportion of care provided informally. The important change is that the sharing of responsibility is now taking place within a more formal framework of case management, whereas previously it occurred spontaneously as informal care filled the gaps left by formal provision. Oddly enough, what appears to be a shift towards decentralization is bringing more comprehensive planning at the higher, macro levels. Under the old arrangements, centralized formal care contrasted sharply with decentralized informal care; the conduct of formal care at the micro level was closely planned, but the balance of care at the macro level was mostly unplanned. Case management affords a more conscious, planned coordination of the formal and informal care sectors. Planning is no longer confined to the internal organization of formal services, but broadens out to cover the external relationships between formal and informal care.

Broadly based planning of care will influence the relation between the formal and informal sectors, producing a partial formalization of what were previously unmonitored, unrecorded caring activities. This can be beneficial if it promotes greater efficiency and equity, but it can also have adverse effects on the nature of informal care. No longer spontaneous, informal care is weighed against formal care in a conscious planning decision that treats all forms of care even-handedly. Difficulties may arise when case management or other approaches to planning involve not just an imputed monetary value of informal care but an actual payment to informal carers. Payments can be made indirectly to new carers as an inducement for them to volunteer, to existing carers as a cash benefit, or to the recipients of care, who can then decide how the money should be spent.

Whenever carers receive a payment or benefit, their caring activities are becoming commodified and converging on a market transaction. If informal carers receive the full market rate for their caring time, then their activity should no longer be classified as informal and the formal/informal distinction will break down. Usually, however, payments to informal carers are at a level well below the equivalent market wage, which creates a distinct, lower-level, semi-formal labour market. Care payments may yield an unsatisfactory compromise that commodifies domiciliary care without giving it the same status as formal economic activities. Payments made through the recipients of care may set up market relationships where none existed before and turn informal carers into poorly paid domestic servants; measures aimed at user empowerment could have the unfortunate consequence of giving users too much market power over carers. Furthermore, an expansion of care payments could formalize current gender inequalities (as most low-paid carers will be female) and discourage women from entering conventional, better-paid employment (Ungerson, 1995). These potential disadvantages of care payments have to be evaluated alongside the advantages of offering proper compensation to informal carers, increasing the supply of care, and preventing excessive institutionalization of old people. A full-scale planning framework must carefully appraise formal care relative to informal and try to ensure evenness of treatment. Otherwise it could reinforce existing inequalities and inconsistencies instead of removing them.

Care continuously coordinated at the macro level should, at least in principle, adjust smoothly as the population ages. Formal guidelines for the management of care, combined with systematic monitoring of the elderly population, permit more accurate assessments of the resources to be allocated to care. Case management, as it becomes more common, can underpin a general planning of care and reduce the asymmetry between the formal and informal sectors. Care planned at the highest level simplifies the broad political decisions about public expenditure and renders visible the extent of public support for care. The chief impediment to planning will remain the lack of reliable information on the benefits and costs of informal care. This preserves an asymmetry between the formal and informal sectors, even when they have been brought together within a single framework. Introducing case management cannot on its own ensure a harmonious, equitable interaction between the formal and informal sectors, but it does offer an institutional structure for assessing the balance of care, which is a prerequisite for the consistent planning of care in response to population ageing.

9. Conclusion

Population ageing raises questions that extend into almost all areas of economics. It has macroeconomic implications for the economy as a whole, alongside microeconomic implications for the individual. It affects both public-sector and private-sector activities and goes beyond the confines of the formal economy to have important consequences for informal economic activity. A subject so broad and intricate cannot be expected to generate neat policy conclusions applicable in every country experiencing population ageing. Practical responses to ageing will require specific policy measures, tailored to particular institutional circumstances, covering issues such as employment, pensions and health care. Truly general propositions about the economic consequences of ageing are thin on the ground. Throughout the preceding chapters, however, several themes have recurred: the unimportance of demographic constraints, the influence of technical change, the institutional character of the 'ageing crisis', and the case for managed flexibility. By way of a general conclusion, it is appropriate to summarize these themes and reiterate their significance.

THE UNIMPORTANCE OF DEMOGRAPHIC CONSTRAINTS

Much popular and academic discussion of population ageing is couched in simple terms. Dependency ratios are rising, there are too few producers relative to workers, and the growing dependency burden will harm the economy's productivity and force painful retrenchment. The population is divided into the old, who consume without producing, and the young, who produce for themselves and the old as well. The old thereby depend on the young for all their consumption of goods and services. Any fall in the proportion of young to old will necessitate difficult adjustments of private consumption and public services and could cause an economic crisis unless the government introduces measures to curtail the resources demanded by the elderly.

This basic, often implicit model has an intuitive allure: a dichotomy between old and young accentuates the seemingly obvious effects of ageing on the economy. The model has serious deficiencies, though. Not all old people are dependants and not all young people are producers. To equate age with dependency and youth with productiveness suggests that old age has an immediate negative impact on productivity. In reality, the link between age and work is due largely to formal retirement policies rather than the physical effects of ageing; many retired people are quite capable of working. Arbitrary accounting procedures have excluded the informal economic activity of the old from the national economic accounts. Old age has been portrayed as a physical constraint on a person's productiveness, and the gradual physical decline from biological ageing has been strengthened into an unconditional loss of economic independence on reaching a certain threshold age. The young/old dichotomy has little to do with the physical attributes of old people, and is better seen as socially constructed. Biological ageing does not impose an immediate constraint on the economic activity of the individual, and most people have retired long before significant physical deterioration sets in.

Similar considerations apply at the aggregate level. Even if one accepts the young/old dichotomy, population ageing is unlikely to create an aggregate shortage of producers. Unemployment, a persistent feature of capitalist economies, reaches levels comparable to the size of the retired population. The economic status of the unemployed resembles that of the retired elderly, and any problems with the dependent elderly are already being encountered with the unemployed. Why should we single out population ageing as causing a special crisis of dependency, when we tolerate dependency as part of the normal functioning of the economy? The tacit assumption seems to be that, in the long run, capitalist economies tend towards full employment, leaving old age as the prime cause of dependency. This is a contentious issue in economics, but many economists, neoclassical and non-neoclassical, doubt whether continuous or even temporary full employment will ever be attained. Under these circumstances, the depiction of population ageing as a unique, external cause of dependency seems misplaced. Economic dependency has many causes, most of which have a strong social and institutional aspect. Both unemployment and retirement are socially created, and they are not reducible to the behaviour or physical characteristics of unemployed and retired individuals. Treating population ageing as if it tightens a binding demographic constraint on the economy is an oversimplification that denies the social determination of dependency.

TECHNICAL CHANGE AND
INCREASING FLEXIBILITY

Population ageing is a long-run process occurring over the same time spans as economic growth and major shifts in technology. Discussions of ageing have to allow for the implications of technical change and cannot safely assume that all other things remain equal. A key trend that should persist into the long-run future is the rise in labour productivity. As agriculture, manufacturing and services have increased their outputs per worker, the number of employees required to produce a given output has shrunk to a fraction of its former value; employment levels can be maintained only if total output rises sufficiently to offset the productivity gains. The total output of developed countries has indeed expanded rapidly in recent years, but not rapidly enough to yield full employment. Jobs have become scarcer and more unevenly distributed, so that sections of the working population face near-permanent unemployment. There are too few jobs for the available workers, in other words, a glut of producers. The contrast with the arguments over population ageing, which point to a supposed shortage of producers, is striking. Technical change and population ageing are elements in the same process of long-run structural change, a process generally dominated by the rise in productivity. As a result, the availability of work, not the availability of workers, may always be the main constraint on output.

The other key long-term trend is the growing flexibility and decentralization of production. Information technology, according to the post-Fordist view, encourages smaller scale, more diversified production with a less hierarchical employment pattern, shorter-term contractual arrangements, and more frequent movement between jobs. When extended to social policy, post-Fordism is expected to break down the centralized Fordist welfare state, which had formal retirement at its core, and bring more diversified and largely privatized arrangements. In the post-Fordist era, age will have diminishing importance in classifying the population: a new postmodern flexibility is replacing the old, centralized practices reliant on a fixed retirement age. People will still retire from employment, but at various ages and by various paths, some of which may permit a gradual withdrawal from work. As retirement becomes less age-based, other influences on retirement will come forth. Again, technical change serves to curtail the role of population ageing.

Recent economic changes may not truly represent a technologically driven transition from Fordism to post-Fordism; one could interpret events differently, for example, by giving greater weight to political and social factors. But whatever the causality behind the changes, the increasing diversity, fluidity and complexity of present-day societies should reduce the chances of intergenerational conflict. Long-standing social identities and hierarchies (such as those founded on religion, class, family, gender and race) are gradually being weakened, and so the ground for new social identities founded on age is hardly fertile. If age-consciousness did not emerge in the period of formal age-based retirement, then it seems unlikely to emerge in the new period of flexibility and diversity. At most, age-based interest groups can only be one among many other calls on a person's allegiance. Concern over intergenerational conflict seems out of step with social and economic developments lessening the prospect of a simple polar division between conflicting social groups. The main practical problems of population ageing take a much less intense form, centred on the old age-related Fordist accounting principles that never did stimulate much intergenerational conflict.

THE INSTITUTIONAL CHARACTER OF THE 'AGEING CRISIS'

Population ageing does not tighten real constraints on production, but it may nevertheless require adjustments to economic and social policies. When policies adhere to fixed accounting rules based on age, a change in the age distribution will necessitate readjustments of policy if the rules are to stay in place. The chief example of this is the balancing of public budgets. In the national income accounts, the retired elderly are non-contributors to public revenues but recipients of public pensions, income maintenance and social services financed largely (though not entirely) by working-age taxpayers. The accounts express in monetary form the idea that workers must produce real goods and services for the retired elderly. Discussion of the dependency burdens imposed on workers is actually referring, despite the language of work and dependency, to the financial burdens imposed on taxpayers.

Public accounts are a social artefact. If they are set up so as to contrast younger contributors with elderly claimants, then this is a product of public decision making as much as the characteristics of old people. Public budgets are sufficiently complex to embrace many dichotomies of contributors versus claimants: the young/old dichotomy is only one of them. A government can draw attention to population ageing if it keeps separate accounts for expenditures related to the retired elderly or if it follows generational accounting practices. This has rarely been done, and accounts are more often disaggregated by the types of expenditure than by the ages of the beneficiaries. Many public activities are unrelated to the age composition of the population, and public spending is subject to many influences other than age. In assessing overall public expenditure trends, demographic change should not be isolated but given its due place among the other influences on spending. Some academics, through the 'intergenerational conflict' paradigm, have asserted the special signifi- cance of age. Taken to an extreme, this paradigm would become one of the major abstractions in economics, perhaps even challenging the more usual disaggregations by individuals or social classes. To construct eco- nomics in these terms would grossly exaggerate the importance of ageing for the real economy.

Population ageing as a policy problem depends on the level of economic activity: the financial burdens on taxpayers are highest in times of recession and lowest in times of boom. Interest in ageing has been countercyclical, peaking during recessions when public budgets are most stretched. Ironically, the concern over ageing is greatest when labour supply most out- strips labour demand and the demographic constraint on the economy is at its slackest. Chronic unemployment raises the average tax rates required to support the dependent population of retired and unemployed; expansion- ary economic policies could reduce the financial burdens. If governments pursue a deflationary economic strategy, they have chosen to increase the incidence of financial dependency among the population. They may publicly regret unemployment, but see it as an admissible means of attain- ing other policy objectives. The failure to reach full employment raises the variability of the tax burden as well as its size. Compared with the more cyclical public expenditures, such as unemployment benefits, spending on the elderly is a fairly stable component of the total financial burden on taxpayers. Population ageing does not cause the periodic rises in govern- ment budget deficits, but it still receives blame for high public expenditures and can easily be held responsible for budgetary difficulties that have little connection with demographic change.

Alarmism about population ageing is at least partly ideological in character. Rising numbers of old people give an apparently objective case for lower public expenditure. Those hoping to dismember the welfare state can seize upon population ageing as an external circumstance beyond anyone's control that requires cuts in pensions and social services. People who would otherwise be reluctant to contemplate reduced social expenditures might be willing to accept the logic of rising dependency ratios and go along with a diminished welfare state. The 'ageing crisis' can be a rhetorical device to promote tax cuts, reduced public services, and privatization; interest in population ageing revived during the 1980s at a time when the political climate had swung towards laissez-faire policies and curbs on public spending. The ideological uses of population ageing create a narrowed-down, dramatized account of its economic importance, dwelling on its implications for tax rates and public finance and neglecting its implications for the rest of the economy. This hampers a proper understanding of population ageing, but it does illustrate the full extent to which the ageing problem has been socially constructed. The institutional context shapes both the real effect of ageing on the economy and the perception of ageing in policy debate.

MANAGED FLEXIBILITY

When a policy problem is institutionally specific, there are two alternative methods to adopt. The first treats existing institutions as given and considers the best way of proceeding under this restriction. Discussion is confined to minor policy adjustments without broaching the larger topic of institutional reform; the spirit is pragmatic and the time horizon is usually short. The other alternative acknowledges that institutions can be changed. A means of alleviating the policy problem may be to reform the institutions that brought on the problem in the first place. This raises the generality of the discussion and almost certainly creates an overlap with other policy issues. Analysis is more difficult because of the long time horizon but more penetrating if it succeeds. Both alternatives can be found in economics, the first in discussions of short-run economic policy, the second in discussions of long-run economic growth and technical change. Population ageing uncomfortably straddles the two alternatives. Narrow concerns over pensions and tax rates motivate much interest in ageing; discussion of these matters tends to be quantitative and pragmatic. The short-run perspective is at odds with the long-run nature of demographic change. Over the period in which population can change significantly, technology and institutions too can change: this is often taken to be a definition of the long run.

Treating existing institutions as given constricts the role of general theory. If current accounting practices stay unchanged, then policy analysis can be based on well-defined public budget constraints. The effects of population ageing are reduced to the quantitative investigation of public budgets, subject to extraneous assumptions about other external events that may affect public spending. Items such as unemployment may complicate the analysis, but they can be handled (or sidestepped) by assuming they are constant or follow a known trend. In the common distinction between projections and forecasts, a purely budgetary approach amounts to projections derived without a formal economic model, as against forecasts derived from a model. Whether this counts as economic analysis is disputable, but projections suffice for many purposes. If the aim is first to produce numerical estimates of future tax payments, a formal economic model is unlikely to improve greatly on projections or educated guesses about the relevant variables. General theorizing has little to offer this kind of piecemeal, practical stance.

Matters are different when discussion is broadened out to allow for changes in social institutions. As soon as institutions and technology can vary, demographic changes become only one among many other long-run influences on the economy. Population ageing may be trivial relative to the other factors that vary over a long-run time horizon, and a simple ceteris paribus approach risks overstating the importance of demographic change. Long-run analysis is exceedingly difficult, requiring a comprehensive account of how the economy will grow and evolve. Several long-run trends reduce the expected adverse effects of population ageing on the economy. This is true of the growth in labour productivity, which raises the capacity of the working population to support the inactive elderly, and the diminished significance of formal retirement, which weakens the link between age and economic inactivity. The impact of ageing will be dampened if flexible arrangements replace rigid, age-based employment practices and accounting procedures. Trends towards flexibility can be viewed with cautious optimism as reducing some of the economic problems created by population ageing. It should be remembered, however, that flexibility has so far appeared only in a limited form, chiefly as a decline in retirement at the statutory age and a rise in the various types of early exit from employment. Workers have seldom been able to choose the timing or nature of their retirement, and early exit has often brought an abrupt, involuntary cessation of work quite similar to formal retirement. If flexibility means nothing more than job insecurity and higher unemployment, then it will do little to improve the welfare of the elderly or offset the pejorative implications of old age; it is counterproductive if it merely denotes a deregulated free-for-all permitting commercial interests to dominate the less powerful. True flexibility in employment, retirement and social services will require genuine choices in which old people themselves play a part.

When flexibility is combined with planning, the outcome is what can be termed managed flexibility. Bottom-up choices made by or on behalf of individuals are integrated into a top-down structure determined centrally by the public authorities. Managed flexibility has been a common theme of recent policy discussion concerning the elderly and has appeared repeatedly in the preceding chapters. One example is flexible retirement procedures, whereby people can influence their own path between work and retirement. Another is case management in social care, whereby case managers (perhaps with the participation of the person being cared for) can decide the appropriate balance of care for each old person from the alternative sources available. The common principle behind these schemes is the marrying of genuine but limited choices with an overall planning framework. Choice has its own value and fits in with wider trends towards greater complexity and diversity in society; a planning framework ensures consistency between individuals or social groups and provides the means of responding to population ageing. Policies aimed at managed flexibility are hoping to increase choice without losing the value of coordinated public intervention. The greater flexibility and diversity chime with post-Fordism, but occur within a publicly managed framework that can be regarded as a refinement (or even extension) of the Fordist welfare state. Managed flexibility would be less of a break with earlier practices than would a wholesale deregulation and privatization of welfare; it could retain and develop the valuable features of the old welfare state, such as public coordination of care, while dropping the less attractive features, such as the strict classification of people by age. Future developments could well take the managed flexibility route, although harsher, deregulated forms of flexibility are a possible alternative.

One thing can be stated with reasonable confidence: institutional changes can solve some of the problems associated with ageing. To the extent that the 'ageing crisis' has been socially assembled, it can be socially disassembled. The institutionalized age restrictions imposed by formal retirement policies, employment practices and educational arrangements have added to the perception of ageing as a problem. If these restrictions could be lifted, then many of the institutions on which economic discussion of ageing rests would disappear or be transformed beyond recognition. Giving old people more choice over their work and retirement would diversify their activities and stifle the effects of population ageing on retirement. Ageing is seen as a problem for public policies largely because of the way they have been tied to age. Weakening this tie would diminish the institutionalized aspects of ageing and focus attention on its unavoidable biological aspects. When responding to ageing, a society should ideally be reforming its institutions in order to deal with the physical effects of old age and not the socially induced effects of earlier social and economic policies. There can never be a pure biological ageing separate from human society, but a removal of institutional age barriers can swing the balance towards the physical effects of old age and give a clearer view of the true economic consequences of population ageing.

This leaves a final paradox. A thoroughgoing approach to the economics of ageing must address the social construction of old age and go far beyond the usual boundaries of neoclassical economics, let alone the tiny branch of neoclassical economics concerned with ageing. It demands political economy rather than economics, that is to say, it spills over into politics and the other social sciences. Ageing, in fact, is even broader than what we normally understand by political economy and defies adequate treatment by a single discipline. To discuss ageing one has to touch upon the most persistent and tortuous problems of social analysis: the relations between nature and culture, genetics and environment, the individual and society, agency and structure, and static and historical methods. The daunting complexity of ageing has negative and positive sides. On the negative side, life for the social analyst becomes extremely difficult. Neat, formalized abstractions, so prevalent in neoclassical economics, can make little headway in depicting the effects of ageing. Messy, pluralistic, inter-disciplinary work is better suited to the character of ageing: while it yields no simple solution to policy problems, it can capture the depth and richness of the subject. On the positive side, the complexity of ageing counters the prevailing air of pessimism. Alarmism about population ageing is founded on simplified, rigid modelling that divides populations discretely into young and old, giving a spurious quantitative exactness to the burdens imposed by the elderly. The alarmist arguments are uncon-vincing when one takes into account the complexity of ageing. Fears of future crises have as much to do with current institutional arrangements as with the characteristics of old people. If the social institutions surrounding old age could be made more diversified and less restrictive, so as better to match the diversity of the elderly population, then there would be little reason to worry about population ageing. Current arrangements are far from immutable. The complexity of ageing gives scope for institutional innovations and grounds for optimism that the developed countries can adapt successfully to more aged populations.

Bibliography

Aaron, H.J. (1966), 'The social insurance paradox', *Canadian Journal of Economics and Political Science*, **32**, 371–4.

Aaron, H.J. (1982), *Economic Effects of Social Security*, Washington DC: The Brookings Institution.

Aaron, H.J., Bosworth, B.P. and Burtless, G. (1989), *Can America Afford to Grow Old?*, Washington DC: The Brookings Institution.

Abrams, M. (1978), *Beyond Three-score and Ten: A First Report on a Survey of the Elderly*, Mitcham, Surrey: Age Concern.

Abrams, M. (1980), *Beyond Three-score and Ten: A Second Report on a Survey of the Elderly*, Mitcham, Surrey: Age Concern.

Aglietta, M. (1979), *A Theory of Capitalist Regulation*, London: New Left Books.

Anderson, M. (1971), 'Family, Household and the Industrial Revolution' in Anderson, M. (ed.), *The Family*, Harmondsworth: Penguin.

Ando, A. and Modigliani, F. (1963), 'The "life-cycle" hypothesis of saving: aggregate implications and tests', *American Economic Review*, **53**, 55–84.

Arber, S. and Ginn, J. (1990), 'The meaning of informal care: gender and the contribution of elderly people', *Ageing and Society*, **10**, 429–54.

Arber, S. and Ginn, J. (1991), *Gender and Later Life: A Sociological Analysis of Resources and Constraints*, London: Sage.

Arber, S. and Ginn, J. (1995), 'Gender differences in the relationship between paid employment and informal care', *Work, Employment and Society*, **9**, 445–71.

Arestis, P. (1992), *The Post-Keynesian Approach to Economics: An Alternative Analysis of Economic Theory and Policy*, Cheltenham: Edward Elgar.

Arestis, P. (1996), 'Post-Keynesian economics: towards coherence', *Cambridge Journal of Economics*, **20**, 111–35.

Asimakopoulos, A. (1989), 'Financing social security – who pays?', *Journal of Post Keynesian Economics*, **11**, 655–60.

Atkinson, A.B. and Sutherland, H. (1993), 'Two Nations in Early Retirement? The Case of Britain' in Atkinson, A.B. and Rein, M. (eds), *Work, Age and Social Security*, London: Macmillan.

Auerbach, A.J., Gokhale, J. and Kotlikoff, L.J. (1991), 'Generational Accounts: A Meaningful Alternative to Deficit Accounting' in Bradford, D. (ed.), *Tax Policy and the Economy*, Vol.5, Cambridge, MA: MIT Press.

Auerbach, A.J., Gokhale, J. and Kotlikoff, L.J. (1994), 'Generational accounting: a meaningful way to evaluate fiscal policy', *Journal of Economic Perspectives*, **8**, 73–94.

Auerbach, A.J. and Kotlikoff, L.J. (1987), *Dynamic Fiscal Policy*, Cambridge: Cambridge University Press.

Auerbach, A.J., Kotlikoff, L.J., Hagemann, R. and Nicoletti, G. (1989), 'The economic dynamics of an ageing population: the case of four OECD countries', *OECD Economic Studies*, **12**, 111–47.

Barr, N. (1979), 'Myths my grandpa taught me', *Three Banks Review*, **124**, 27–55.

Barr, N. (1993), *The Economics of the Welfare State*, 2nd edn, London: Weidenfeld and Nicolson.

Barro, R.J. (1974), 'Are government bonds net wealth?', *Journal of Political Economy*, **84**, 1095–117.

Bebbington, A.C. (1988), 'The expectation of life without disability in England and Wales', *Social Science and Medicine*, **27**, 321–6.

Becker, G. S. (1964), *Human Capital*, New York: Columbia University Press.

Becker, G.S. (1971), *The Economics of Discrimination*, 2nd edn, Chicago: University of Chicago Press.

Becker, G.S. (1976), *The Economic Approach to Human Behavior*, Chicago: University of Chicago Press.

Becker, G.S. (1991), *A Treatise on the Family,* Enlarged edn, Cambridge, MA: Harvard University Press.

Becker, G.S. (1993), 'Nobel lecture: the economic way of looking at behavior', *Journal of Political Economy*, **101**, 385–409.

Bell, J.M. and Mendus, S. (eds) (1988), *Philosophy and Medical Welfare*, Cambridge: Cambridge University Press.

Berger, M.C. (1985), 'The effect of cohort size on earnings growth: a re-examination of the evidence', *Journal of Political Economy*, **93**, 561-73.

Berlin, I. (1969), 'Two Concepts of Liberty' in Berlin, I., *Four Essays on Liberty*, Oxford: Oxford University Press.

Bernheim, B.D. (1987), 'Dissaving after Retirement: Testing the Pure Life-cycle Hypothesis' in Bodie, Z., Shoven, J. and Wise, D.A. (eds), *Issues in Pension Economics*, Chicago: University of Chicago Press.

Bernheim, B.D. (1991), 'How strong are bequest motives? Evidence based on estimates of the demand for life insurance and annuities', *Journal of Political Economy*, **99**, 899–927.

Beveridge, W. (1942), *Social Insurance and Allied Services*, Command 6404, London: HMSO.

Binney, E.A. and Estes, C.L. (1988), 'The retreat of the state and its transfer of responsibility: the intergenerational war', *International Journal of Health Services*, **18**, 83–96.

Birdsall, N. (1988), 'Economic Approaches to Population Growth' in Chenery, H.B. and Srinivasan, T.N. (eds), *Handbook of Development Economics*, Vol. 1, Amsterdam: North Holland.

Blanchet, D. (1993), 'Does an Ageing Labour Force Call For Large Adjustments in Training or Wage Policies?' in Johnson, P. and Zimmermann, K.F. (eds), *Labour Markets in an Ageing Europe*, Cambridge: Cambridge University Press.

Blanchet, D. and Kessler, D. (1991), 'Optimal pension funding with demographic instability and endogenous returns on investment', *Journal of Population Economics*, **4**, 137–54.

Blankart, C.B. (1993), 'Income taxation, consumption taxation, intergenerational transfers, and government behavior', *Public Finance/Finances Publiques*, **48** (Supplement), 7–15.

Blinder, A.S., Gordon, R.H. and Wise, D.E. (1983), 'Social Security, Bequests and the Life-cycle Theory of Saving: Cross-sectional Tests' in Modigliani, F. and Hemming, R.C.L. (eds), *The Determinants of National Saving and Wealth*, New York: St Martin's Press.

Bloom, D.E., Freeman, R.B. and Korenman, S.D. (1987), 'The labour market consequences of generational crowding', *European Journal of Population*, **3**, 131–76.

Boadway, R.W., Marchand, M. and Pestieau, P. (1991), 'Pay-as-you-go social security in a changing environment', *Journal of Population Economics*, **4**, 257–80.

Boadway, R.W. and Wildasin, D.E. (1989), 'A median voter model of social security', *International Economic Review*, **30**, 307–28.

Boaz, R.R. and Mueller, C.F. (1992), 'Paid work and unpaid help by caregivers of the disabled and frail elderly', *Medical Care*, **30**, 149–58.

Bodie, Z., Marcus, A.J. and Merton, R.C. (1988), 'Defined Benefit versus Defined Contribution Pension Plans: What are the Real Trade-offs?' in Bodie, Z., Shoven, J.B. and Wise, D.A. (eds), *Pensions in the US Economy*, Chicago: University of Chicago Press.

Bond, J. (1976), 'Dependency and the Elderly: Problems of Conceptualisation and Measurement' in Munnichs, J.M.A. and van den Heuval, W.J.A. (eds), *Dependency and Interdependence in Old Age*, The Hague: Martinus Nijhoff.

Bond, J., Briggs, R. and Coleman, P. (1993), 'The Study of Ageing' in Bond, J., Coleman, P. and Peace, S.M. (eds), *Ageing in Society: An Introduction to Social Gerontology*, 2nd edn, London: Sage.

Booth, T. (1985), *Home Truths: Old People's Homes and the Outcome of Care*, Aldershot: Gower.

Börsch-Supan, A. (1991), 'Aging population: problems and policy options in the US and Germany', *Economic Policy*, **6**, 103–39.

Börsch-Supan, A. (1992), 'Saving and consumption patterns of the elderly: the German case', *Journal of Population Economics*, **5**, 289–303.

Börsch-Supan, A. and Stahl, K. (1991), 'Life-cycle savings and consumption constraints: theory, empirical evidence, and fiscal implications', *Journal of Population Economics*, **4**, 233–55.

Bös, D. and von Weizsäcker, R.K. (1989), 'Economic consequences of an ageing population', *European Economic Review*, **33**, 345–54.

Boserup, E. (1965), *The Conditions of Economic Growth*, London: Allen and Unwin.

Boskin, M. (1977), 'Social security and the retirement decision', *Economic Inquiry*, **15**, 1–25.

Breyer, F. (1994), 'The political economy of intergenerational redistribution', *European Journal of Political Economy*, **10**, 61–84.

Brody, E.M. (1981), '"Women in the middle" and family help to older people', *The Gerontologist*, **21**, 471–80.

Brody, J.A. (1985), 'Prospects for an ageing population', *Nature*, **315**, 463–6.

Bromley, D., Isaacs, A. and Bytheway, B. (1982), 'Review symposium: ageing and the rectangular curve', *Ageing and Society*, **2**, 283–392.

Broome, J. (1985), 'The economic value of life', *Economica*, **52**, 281–94.

Broome, J. (1993), 'Qualys', *Journal of Public Economics*, **50**, 149–67.

Browning, E.K. (1975), 'Why the social insurance budget is too large in a democracy', *Economic Inquiry*, **13**, 373–88.

Buchanan, J.M. and Tullock, G. (1962), *The Calculus of Consent*, Ann Arbor: University of Michigan Press.

Burtless, G. and Moffitt, R.A. (1984), 'The Effect of Social Security Benefits on the Labor Supply of the Aged' in Aaron, H.J. and Burtless, G. (eds), *Retirement and Economic Behavior*, Washington DC: Brookings Institution.

Burtless, G. and Moffitt, R.A. (1985), 'The joint choice of retirement age and postretirement hours of work', *Journal of Labor Economics*, **3**, 209–36.

Busse, E.W. (1985), 'Normal Aging: The Duke Longitudinal Studies' in Bergener, M., Ermini, M. and Staheline, H.B. (eds), *Thresholds in Aging*, New York: Academic Press.

Butler, A., Oldman, C. and Greve, J. (1983), *Sheltered Housing for the Elderly*, London: Allen and Unwin.

Bytheway, B. and Johnson, J. (1990), 'On defining ageism', *Critical Social Policy*, **10**, 27–39.

Callinicos, A.T. (1989), *Against Postmodernism: A Marxist Critique*, Cambridge: Polity Press.

Cambridge, P. (1992), 'Case management in community services: organisational responses', *British Journal of Social Work*, **22**, 495–517.

Campbell, C.D. and Campbell, R.G. (1976), 'Conflicting views on the effect of old age and survivors insurance on retirement', *Economic Inquiry*, **14**, 369–88.

Carstairs, V. (1981), 'Our Elders' in Shegog, R.F.A. (ed.), *The Impending Crisis of Old Age: A Challenge to Ingenuity*, Oxford: Oxford University Press.

Casey, B. and Laczko, F. (1989), 'Early retired or long-term unemployed? The changing situation of non-working men from 1979 to 1986', *Work, Employment and Society*, **3**, 509–26.

Cavan, R.S., Burgess, E.W., Havighurst, R.J. and Goldhamer, H. (1949), *Personal Adjustment in Old Age*, Chicago: Science Research Associates.

Challis, D., Chessum, R., Chesterman, J., Luckett, R. and Woods, R. (1988), 'Community care for the frail elderly: an urban experiment', *British Journal of Social Work*, **18** (Supplement), 13–42.

Challis, D., Chesterman, J., Darton, R. and Traske, K. (1993), 'Case Management in the Care of the Aged: The Provision of Care in Different Settings' in Bornat, J., Pereira, C., Pilgrim, D. and Williams, F. (eds), *Community Care: A Reader*, London: Macmillan.

Challis, D. and Davies, B. (1986), *Case Management in Community Care*, Aldershot: Gower.

Chang, C.F. and White-Means, S.I. (1995), 'Labour supply of informal caregivers', *International Review of Applied Economics*, **9**, 192–205.

Charness, N. (ed.) (1985), *Ageing and Human Performance*, Chichester: John Wiley.

Cipolla, C.M. (1978), *The Economic History of World Population*, Harmondsworth: Penguin.

Clark, R.L. and Spengler, J.J. (1980), *The Economics of Individual and Population Aging*, Cambridge: Cambridge University Press.

Coale, A.J. and Hoover, E.M. (1958), *Population Growth and Economic Development in Low-income Countries*, Princeton, NJ: Princeton University Press.

Cochrane, S.H. (1975), 'A review of some microeconomic models of fertility', *Population Studies*, **29**, 373–90.

Cohen, G. and Faulkner, D. (1984), 'Memory in old age: "good in parts"', *New Scientist*, **11**, 49–51.

Coleman, P. (1993), 'Psychological Ageing' in Bond, J., Coleman, P. and Peace, S.M. (eds), *Ageing in Society: An Introduction to Social Gerontology*, 2nd edn, London: Sage.

Coriat, B. and Petit, P. (1991), 'Deindustrialisation and Tertiarisation: Towards a New Economic Regime' in Amin, A. and Dietrich, M. (eds), *Towards a New Europe? Structural Change in the European Economy*, Aldershot: Edward Elgar.

Costello, N., Michie, J. and Milne, S. (1989), *Beyond the Casino Economy: Planning for the 1990s*, London: Verso.

Cowgill, D.O. (1974), 'The aging of populations and societies', *Annals of the American Academy of Political and Social Science*, **415**, 1–18.

Cowgill, D.O. and Holmes, L.D. (eds) (1972), *Aging and Modernisation*, New York: Appleton.

Creedy, J. (1992), 'Financing Pensions in an Ageing Population' in Creedy, J., *Income, Inequality and the Life Cycle*, Aldershot: Edward Elgar.

Creedy, J. and Disney, R. (1989a), 'Can we afford to grow older? Population ageing and social security', *European Economic Review*, **33**, 367–76.

Creedy, J. and Disney, R. (1989b), 'The New Pension Scheme in Britain' in Dilnot, A. and Walker, I. (eds), *The Economics of Social Security*, Oxford: Oxford University Press.

Creedy, J. and Disney, R. (1992), 'Financing state pensions in alternative pay-as-you-go schemes', *Bulletin of Economic Research*, **44**, 39–53.

Creedy, J. and Morgan, M.H. (1992), 'Pension and tax structures in an ageing population', *Journal of Economic Studies*, **19**, 50–65.

Cumming, E. (1963), 'Further thoughts on the theory of disengagement', *International Social Sciences Journal*, **15**, 377–93.

Cumming, E. and Henry, W. (1961), *Growing Old: The Process of Disengagement*, New York: Basic Books.

Cutler, D.M., Poterba, J.M., Sheiner, L.M. and Summers, L.H. (1990), 'An aging society: opportunity or challenge?', *Brookings Papers on Economic Activity*, **1**, 1–73.

Dahrendorf, R. (1959), *Class and Class Conflict in Industrial Society*, London: Routledge and Kegan Paul.

Dalley, G. (1988), *Ideologies of Caring: Rethinking Community and Collectivism*, London: Macmillan.

Dalley, G. (1991), 'Beliefs and behaviour: professionals and the policy process', *Journal of Ageing Studies*, **5**, 163–80.

Daniels, N. (1988), *Am I My Parents' Keeper? An Essay on Justice Between the Young and the Old*, New York: Oxford University Press.

Daniels, N. (1989), 'Justice and Transfers between Generations' in Johnson, P., Conrad, C. and Thomson, D. (eds), *Workers Versus Pensioners*, Manchester: Manchester University Press.

Dant, T. (1988), 'Dependency and old age: theoretical accounts and practical understandings', *Ageing and Society*, **8**, 171–88.

Danziger, S., van der Gaag, J., Smolensky, E. and Taussig, M.K. (1982), 'The life-cycle hypothesis and the consumption behavior of the elderly', *Journal of Post Keynesian Economics*, **5**, 208–27.

Davidson, P. (1994), *Post Keynesian Macroeconomic Theory*, Cheltenham: Edward Elgar.

Davies, D.R. and Sparrow, P.R. (1985), 'Age and Work Behaviour' in Charness, N. (ed.), *Ageing and Human Performance*, Chichester: John Wiley.

De Beauvoir, S. (1977), *Old Age*, Harmondsworth: Penguin.

De Uriarte, B. (1990), 'On the free will of rational agents in neoclassical economics', *Journal of Post Keynesian Economics*, **12**, 751–61.

Delsen, L. (1990), 'Part-time early retirement in Europe', *Geneva Papers on Risk and Insurance*, **15**, 139–57.

Delsen, L. and Reday-Mulvey, G. (1996), *Gradual Retirement in the OECD Countries*, Aldershot: Dartmouth.

Denton, F.T. and Spencer, B.G. (1975), 'Health care costs when the population changes', *Canadian Journal of Economics*, **8**, 130–35.

Department of Health (1989), *Caring For People: Community Care in the Next Decade and Beyond*, Command 849, London: HMSO.

Dex, S. and Phillipson, C. (1986), 'Social Policy and the Older Worker' in Phillipson, C. and Walker, A. (eds), *Ageing and Social Policy: A Critical Assessment*, Aldershot: Gower.

DHSS (Department of Health and Social Security) (1984), *Population, Pension Costs and Pensioners' Income*, Command 993, London: HMSO.

Diamond, P.A. (1977), 'A framework for social security analysis', *Journal of Public Economics*, **8**, 275–98.

Diamond, P.A. and Hausman, J.A. (1984), 'Individual retirement and savings behaviour', *Journal of Public Economics*, **23**, 81–114.

Dilnot, A., Disney, R., Johnson, P. and Whitehouse, E. (1994), *Pensions Policy in the UK: An Economic Analysis*, London: Institute for Fiscal Studies.

Disney, R. (1995), 'Occupational pension schemes: prospects and reforms in the UK', *Fiscal Studies*, **16**, 19–39.

Disney, R. (1996), 'Ageing and saving', *Fiscal Studies*, **17**, 83–101.

Doeringer, P.B. and Piore, M.J. (1971), *Internal Labor Markets and Manpower Analysis*, Lexington: Heath.

Donaldson, L. (1991), *Fertility Transition: The Social Dynamics of Population Change*, Oxford: Basil Blackwell.

Downs, A. (1957), *An Economic Theory of Democracy*, New York: Harper and Row.

Drissen, E. and van Winden, F. (1991), 'Social security in a general equilibrium model with endogenous government behavior', *Journal of Population Economics*, **4**, 89–110.

Drury, E. (1994), 'Age discrimination against older workers in the European Union', *Geneva Papers on Risk and Insurance*, **19**, 496–502.

Easterlin, R.A. (1968), *Population, Labor Force and Long Swings in Economic Growth: The American Experience*, New York: NBER.

Easterlin, R.A. (1980), *Birth and Fortune: The Impact of Numbers on Personal Welfare*, London: Grant McIntyre.

Easterlin, R.A. (1987), 'The new age structure of poverty in America: permanent or transient?', *Population and Development Review*, **13**, 195–208.

Easterlin, R.A., Macdonald, C. and Macunovich, D.J. (1990), 'How have American baby boomers fared? Earnings and economic well-being of young adults, 1964–1987', *Journal of Population Economics*, **3**, 277–90.

Edwards, R. (1979), *Contested Terrain: The Transformation of the Workplace*, London: Heinemann.

Eichner, A.S. (ed.) (1979), *A Guide to Post-Keynesian Economics*, London: Macmillan.

Eilenstine, D.L. and Cunningham, J.P. (1972), 'Projected consumption demands for a stationary population', *Population Studies*, **26**, 223–31.

Erikson, E.H. (1965), *Childhood and Society*, Harmondsworth: Penguin.

Ermisch, J.F. (1981), 'Paying the piper: demographic change and pension contributions', *Policy Studies*, **1**, 213–20.

Ermisch, J.F. (1983), *The Political Economy of Demographic Change: Causes and Implications of Population Trends in Great Britain*, London: Heinemann.

Ermisch, J.F. (1988), 'Fortunes of birth: the impact of generation size on the relative earnings of young men', *Scottish Journal of Political Economy*, **35**, 266–82.

Ermisch, J.F. (1989), 'Intergenerational transfers in industrialised countries: effects of age distribution and economic institutions', *Journal of Population Economics*, **1**, 269–84.

Ermisch, J.F. (1990), *Fewer Babies, Longer Lives: Policy Implications of Current Demographic Trends*, York: Joseph Rowntree Foundation.

Espenshade, T.J. (1978), 'How a trend towards a stationary population affects consumer demand', *Population Studies*, **32**, 147–58.

Esposito, L. (1978), 'Effect of social security on savings: review of studies using US time-series data', *Social Security Bulletin*, **41**, 9–17.

Estes, C.L., Swan, J.H. and Gerard, L.E. (1982), 'Dominant and competing paradigms in gerontology: towards a political economy of old age', *Ageing and Society*, **2**, 151–64.

Ettner, S.L. (1996), 'The opportunity costs of elder care', *Journal of Human Resources*, **31**, 189–205.

Eversley, D.E.C. (1982), 'The Demography of Retirement – Prospects to the Year 2030' in Fogarty, M.P. (ed.), *Retirement Policy: The Next Fifty Years*, London: Heinemann.

Fair, R.C. and Dominguez, K.M. (1991), 'Effects of the changing US age distribution on macroeconomic equations', *American Economic Review,* **81**, 1276–94.

Falkingham, J. (1989), 'Dependency and ageing in Britain: a re-examination of the evidence', *Journal of Social Policy*, **18**, 211–33.

Falkingham, J. and Gordon, C. (1990), 'Fifty Years On: The Income and Household Composition of the Elderly in London and Britain' in Bytheway, B. and Johnson, J. (eds), *Welfare and the Ageing Experience*, London: Avebury.

Featherstone, M. and Hepworth, M. (1993), 'Images of Ageing' in Bond, J., Coleman, P. and Peace, S.M. (eds), *Ageing in Society: An Introduction to Social Gerontology*, 2nd edn, London: Sage.

Feldstein, M.S. (1974), 'Social security, induced retirement and aggregate capital accumulation', *Journal of Political Economy*, **82**, 905–26.

Feldstein, M.S. (1976), 'Social security and saving: the extended life-cycle theory', *American Economic Review*, **66**, 77–86.

Feldstein, M.S. (1977), 'Social Security and Private Savings: International Evidence in an Extended Life-cycle Model' in Feldstein, M.S. and Inman, R. (eds), *The Economics of Public Services*, London: Macmillan.

Fennell, G., Phillipson, C. and Evers, H. (1988), *The Sociology of Old Age*, Milton Keynes: Open University Press.

Finch, J. (1984), 'Community care: developing non-sexist alternatives', *Critical Social Policy*, **3**, 6–18.

Finch, J. (1989), *Family Obligations and Social Change*, Cambridge: Polity Press.

Fischer, D.H. (1978), *Growing Old in America*, New York: Oxford University Press.

Fogarty, M. (1975), *40 to 60: How We Waste the Middle Aged*, London: Centre for Studies in Social Policy/Bedford Square Press.

Fogarty, M. (1990), *The Role of Personal and Occupational Pensions in Retirement*, Resource Paper EE4, London: Age Concern.

Fox, J. (ed.) (1989), *Health Inequalities in European Countries,* Aldershot: Gower.

Freeman, R.B. (1979), 'The effect of demographic factors on age-earnings profiles', *Journal of Human Resources*, **14**, 289–318.

Freer, C.B. (1985), 'Geriatric screening: a reappraisal of preventive strategies in the care of the elderly', *Journal of the Royal College of General Practitioners*, **35**, 288–90.

Freer, C.B. and Williams, I. (1988), 'The Role of the General Practitioner and the Primary Health Care Team' in Wells, N.E.J. and Freer, C.B. (eds), *The Ageing Population: Burden or Challenge?*, London: Macmillan.

Friedman, M. (1953), 'The Methodology of Positive Economics' in Friedman, M., *Essays in Positive Economics*, Chicago: University of Chicago Press.
Fries, J.F. (1980), 'Aging, natural death and the compression of morbidity', *New England Journal of Medicine*, **303**, 130–35.
Fries, J.F. (1983), 'The compression of morbidity', *Milbank Memorial Fund Quarterly*, **61**, 397–419.
Fries, J.F. (1989), 'The compression of morbidity: near or far?', *Milbank Memorial Fund Quarterly*, **67**, 208–32.
Fries, J.F. and Crapo, L.M. (1981), *Vitality and Aging: Implications of the Rectangular Curve*, San Francisco, CA: W.H. Freeman.
Fries, J.F. and the Health Project Consortium (1993), 'Reducing health care costs by reducing the need and demand for medical services', *New England Journal of Medicine*, **329**, 321–25.
Fuchs, V.R. (1982), 'Self-employment and labor force participation of older males', *Journal of Human Resources*, **17**, 339–59.
Fuchs, V.R. (1984), '"Though much is taken"': reflections on aging, health and medical care', *Milbank Memorial Fund Quarterly*, **62**, 143–66.
Gale, W.G. and Scholz, J.K. (1994), 'Intergenerational transfers and the accumulation of wealth', *Journal of Economic Perspectives*, **8**, 145–60.
Gershuny, J. (1983), *Social Innovation and the Division of Labour*, Oxford: Oxford University Press.
Ghez, G.R. and Becker, G.S. (1975), *The Allocation of Time and Goods over the Life Cycle*, New York: NBER.
Giarini, O. (1990), 'Introduction: the opportunities of the four pillars strategy', *Geneva Papers on Risk and Insurance*, **15**, 95–9.
Gibbs, I. (1991), 'Income, capital and the cost of care in old age', *Ageing and Society*, **11**, 373–97.
Gillion, C. (1991), 'Ageing populations: spreading the costs', *Journal of European Social Policy*, **1**, 107–28.
Ginn, J. (1993), 'Grey power: age-based organisations' response to structured inequalities', *Critical Social Policy*, **13**, 23–47.
Ginsburg, N. (1979), *Class, Capital and Social Policy*, London: Macmillan.
Goldberg, E. M. and Connelly, N. (1982), *The Effectiveness of Social Care for the Elderly: An Overview of Recent and Current Evaluative Research*, London: Heinemann.
Goldschmidt-Clermont, L. (1990), 'Economic measurement of non-market household activities: is it useful and feasible?', *International Labour Review*, **129**, 279–99.
Goldschmidt-Clermont, L. (1992), 'Measuring Households' Non-monetary Production' in Ekins, P. and Max-Neef, M. (eds), *Real-life Economics: Understanding Wealth Creation*, London: Routledge.

Gordon, R. and Blinder, A.S. (1980), 'Market wages, reservation wages and retirement decisions', *Journal of Public Economics*, **14**, 277–308.

Gorz, A. (1989), *Critique of Economic Reason*, London: Verso.

Gough, I. (1979), *The Political Economy of the Welfare State*, London: Macmillan.

Graebner, W. (1980), *A History of Retirement: The Meaning and Function of an American Institution, 1885–1978*, New Haven, CONN.: Yale University Press.

Griffiths Report (1988), *Community Care: An Agenda for Action*, London: HMSO.

Gruenberg, E.M. (1977), 'The failures of success', *Milbank Memorial Fund Quarterly*, **55**, 3–24.

Grundy, E. (1984), 'Mortality and morbidity among the old', *British Medical Journal*, **288**, 663–4.

Grundy, E. (1991), 'Age Related Change in Later Life' in Murphy, M. and Hobcraft, J. (eds), *Population Research in Britain*, London: Population Investigation Committee.

Guillemard, A-M. (1989), 'The Trend Towards Early Labour Force Withdrawal and the Reorganisation of the Life Course: A Cross-national Analysis' in Johnson, P., Conrad, C. and Thomson, D. (eds), *Workers Versus Pensioners*, Manchester: Manchester University Press.

Guillemard, A-M., Taylor, P.E. and Walker, A. (1996), 'Managing an ageing workforce in Britain and France', *Geneva Papers on Risk and Insurance*, **21**, 478–501.

Guillemard, A-M. and van Gunsteren, H. (1991), 'Pathways and their Prospects: A Comparative Interpretation of the Meaning of Early Exit' in Kohli, M., Rein, M., Guillemard, A-M. and van Gunsteren, H. (eds), *Time for Retirement*, Cambridge: Cambridge University Press.

Hadley, R. and Hatch, S. (1981), *Social Welfare and the Failure of the State: Centralised Social Services and the Participatory Alternatives*, London: Allen and Unwin.

Hagemann, R.P. and Nicoletti, G. (1989), 'Population ageing: economic effects and some policy implications for financing public pensions', *OECD Economic Studies*, **12**, 51–96.

Hall, M.R.P. (1988), 'Geriatric Medicine Today' in Wells, N. E. J. and Freer, C. B. (eds), *The Ageing Population: Burden or Challenge?*, London: Macmillan.

Hamouda, O. and Harcourt, G.C. (1988), 'Post-Keynesianism: from criticism to coherence?', *Bulletin of Economic Research*, **40**, 1–33.

Hansen, A.H. (1939), 'Economic progress and declining population growth', *American Economic Review*, **29**, 1–15.

Hansson, I. and Stuart, C. (1989), 'Social security as trade among living generations', *American Economic Review*, **79**, 1182–95.

Hargreaves Heap, S. (1989), *Rationality in Economics*, Oxford: Basil Blackwell.

Harris, A.I. (1971), *Handicapped and Impaired in Great Britain*, London: HMSO.

Harrod, R.F. (1939), 'Modern population trends', *Manchester School of Economic and Social Studies*, **10**, 1–20.

Hausman, J.A. and Wise, D.A. (1985), 'Social Security, Health Status and Retirement' in Wise, D. A. (ed.), *Pensions, Labor and Individual Choice*, Chicago: University of Chicago Press.

Haveman, R. (1994), 'Should generational accounts replace public budgets and deficits?', *Journal of Economic Perspectives*, **8**, 95–111.

Havighurst, R.J. (1954), 'Flexibility and the social roles of the retired', *American Journal of Sociology*, **59**, 309–11.

Havighurst, R.J. and Albrecht, R. (1953), *Older People*, London: Longmans, Green.

Hayek, F.A. (1989), *The Fatal Conceit: The Errors of Socialism*, Chicago: University of Chicago Press.

Heller, P.S., Hemming, R.C.L. and Kohnert, P.W. (1986), *Aging and Social Expenditure in the Major Industrial Countries, 1980–2025*, IMF Occasional Paper 47, Washington DC: IMF.

Hemming, R.C.L. (1978), 'State pensions and personal savings', *Scottish Journal of Political Economy*, **25**, 135–47.

Hemming, R.C.L. and Kay, J.A. (1982), 'The costs of the State Earnings Related Pension Scheme', *Economic Journal*, **92**, 300–319.

Hendricks, J. and Hendricks, C.D. (1977), *Aging in Mass Society: Myths and Realities*, Cambridge, MA: Winthrop.

Hendricks, J. and McAllister, C.F. (1983), 'An alternative perspective on retirement: a dual economic approach', *Ageing and Society*, **3**, 279–99.

Heron, A. and Chown, S.M. (1967), *Age and Function*, London: Churchill.

Higgins, J. (1989), 'Defining community care: realities and myths', *Social Policy and Administration*, **23**, 3–16.

Hills, J. (1992), *Does Britain have a 'Welfare Generation'? An Empirical Analysis of Intergenerational Equity*, LSE Welfare State Programme, Discussion Paper WSP/76.

Hills, J. (1995), 'The Welfare State and Redistribution Between Generations' in Falkingham, J. and Hills, J. (eds), *The Dynamics of Welfare: The Welfare State and the Life Cycle*, Hemel Hempstead: Prentice Hall/Harvester Wheatsheaf.

Hirschman, A.O. (1970), *Exit, Voice and Loyalty*, Cambridge, MA: Harvard University Press.

Hirshleifer, J. (1985), 'The expanding domain of economics', *American Economic Review*, **75**, 53–68.

Hockey, J. and James, A. (1993), *Growing Up and Growing Old: Ageing and Dependency in the Life Course*, London: Sage.

Hodgson, G.M. (1982), 'Theoretical and policy implications of variable productivity', *Cambridge Journal of Economics*, **6**, 213–26.

Hodgson, G.M. (1984), *The Democratic Economy*, Harmondsworth: Penguin.

Hodgson, G.M. (1986), 'Behind methodological individualism', *Cambridge Journal of Economics*, **10**, 211–24.

Hoggett, P. (1991), 'The new public sector management', *Policy and Politics*, **19**, 243–56.

Hopkin, W.A.B. (1953), 'The economics of an ageing population', *Lloyds Bank Review*, **27**, 25–36.

Hoyes, L. and Means, R. (1993), 'Quasi-Markets and the Reform of Community Care' in Le Grand, J. and Bartlett, W. (eds), *Quasi-Markets and Social Policy*, London: Macmillan.

Hudson, B. (1987), 'Collaboration in social welfare: a framework for analysis', *Policy and Politics*, **15**, 175–82.

Hugman, R. (1994), *Ageing and the Care of Older People in Europe*, London: Macmillan.

Hunt, A. (1978), *The Elderly at Home: A Study of People Aged 65 and Over Living in the Community in England in 1976*, London: OPCS.

Hurd, M.D. (1987), 'Savings of the elderly and desired bequests', *American Economic Review*, **77**, 298–312.

Hurd, M.D. (1989), 'Mortality risk and bequests', *Econometrica*, **57**, 779–813.

Hurd, M.D. (1990), 'Research on the elderly: economic status, retirement, and consumption and saving', *Journal of Economic Literature*, **38**, 565–637.

Hurd, M.D. and Boskin, M.J. (1984), 'The effect of social security on retirement in the early 1970s', *Quarterly Journal of Economics*, **99**, 767–90.

Ippolito, R.A. (1991), 'Encouraging long-term tenure: wage tilt or pensions?', *Industrial and Labor Relations Review*, **44**, 520–35.

Jackson, W.A. (1989), 'Utilitarian pension and retirement policies under population ageing', *Journal of Population Economics*, **2**, 73–8.

Jackson, W.A. (1991a), 'Dependence and Population Ageing' in Hutton, J., Hutton, S., Pinch, T. and Shiell, A. (eds), *Dependency to Enterprise*, London: Routledge.

Jackson, W.A. (1991b), 'On the treatment of population ageing in economic theory', *Ageing and Society*, **11**, 59–68.

Jackson, W.A. (1992a), 'The employment distribution and the creation of financial dependence', *Journal of Post Keynesian Economics*, **14**, 267–80.

Jackson, W.A. (1992b), 'Population ageing and intergenerational conflict: a post-Keynesian view', *Journal of Economic Studies*, **19**, 26–37.

Jackson, W.A. (1993), 'Culture, society and economic theory', *Review of Political Economy*, **5**, 453–69.

Jackson, W.A. (1994), 'The economics of ageing and the political economy of old age', *International Review of Applied Economics*, **8**, 31–45.

Jackson, W.A. (1995), 'Population growth: a comparison of evolutionary views', *International Journal of Social Economics*, **22** (6), 3–16.

Jacobs, K., Kohli, M. and Rein, M. (1991), 'The Evolution of Early Exit: A Comparative Analysis of Labor Force Participation Patterns' in Kohli, M., Rein, M., Guillemard, A-M. and van Gunsteren, H. (eds), *Time for Retirement*, Cambridge: Cambridge University Press.

Jessop, B. (1994), 'Post-Fordism and the State' in Amin, A. (ed.), *Post-Fordism: A Reader*, Oxford: Basil Blackwell.

Johnson, M.L. (1982), 'The Implications of Greater Activity in Later Life' in Fogarty, M.P. (ed.), *Retirement Policy: The Next Fifty Years*, London: Heinemann.

Johnson, M.L. (1993), 'Dependency and Interdependency' in Bond, J., Coleman, P. and Peace, S.M. (eds), *Ageing in Society: An Introduction to Social Gerontology*, 2nd edn, London: Sage.

Johnson, M.L. (1995), 'Interdependency and the generational compact', *Ageing and Society*, **15**, 243–65.

Johnson, P. (1985), *The Economics of Old Age in Britain: A Long-run View 1881–1981*, CEPR Discussion Paper No. 47, London: CEPR.

Johnson, P. (1989), 'The Structured Dependency of the Elderly: A Critical Note' in Jefferys, M. (ed.), *Growing Old in the Twentieth Century*, London: Routledge.

Johnson, P., Conrad, C. and Thomson, D. (eds) (1989), *Workers Versus Pensioners: Intergenerational Justice in an Ageing World*, Manchester: Manchester University Press.

Johnson, P. and Falkingham, J. (1988), 'Intergenerational transfers and public expenditure on the elderly in modern Britain', *Ageing and Society*, **8**, 129–46.

Johnson, P. and Falkingham, J. (1992), *Ageing and Economic Welfare*, London: Sage.

Kalecki, M. (1943), 'Political aspects of full employment', *Political Quarterly*, **14**, 322–31.

Kelley, A.C. (1988), 'Economic consequences of population changes in the Third World', *Journal of Economic Literature*, **26**, 1685–728.

Kessler, D. (1988), 'The four pillars of retirement', *Geneva Papers on Risk and Insurance*, **13**, 342–9.

Kessler, D. (1989), 'But why is there Social Security?' in Johnson, P.,

Conrad, C. and Thomson, D. (eds), *Workers Versus Pensioners*, Manchester: Manchester University Press.

Kessler, D. (1990), 'Solutions to the coming crisis in social security: save today or work tomorrow?', *Geneva Papers on Risk and Insurance*, **15**, 122–38.

Kessler, D. (1996), 'Preventing conflicts between generations: for an active management of the allocation of resources between generations', *Geneva Papers on Risk and Insurance*, **21**, 435–68.

Keynes, J. M. (1933), 'Thomas Robert Malthus' in Keynes, J.M., *Essays in Biography*, London: Macmillan.

Keynes, J.M. (1936), *The General Theory of Employment, Interest and Money*, London: Macmillan.

Keynes, J.M. (1937), 'Some Economic Consequences of a Declining Population' in Keynes, J.M., *Collected Writings*, Volume XIV, London: Macmillan.

King, M. and Dicks-Mireaux, L. (1982), 'Asset-holding and the life cycle', *Economic Journal*, **92**, 247–67.

Klevmarken, N.A. (1993), 'On Ageing and Earnings' in Johnson, P. and Zimmermann, K.F. (eds), *Labour Markets in an Ageing Europe*, Cambridge: Cambridge University Press.

Knapp, M. (1980), 'Planning for balance of care of the elderly: a comment', *Scottish Journal of Political Economy*, **27**, 288–94.

Knapp, M. (1984), *The Economics of Social Care*, London: Macmillan.

Kohli, M., Rein, M., Guillemard, A-M. and van Gunsteren, H. (eds) (1991), *Time for Retirement: Comparative Studies of Early Exit from the Labor Force*, Cambridge: Cambridge University Press.

Kotlikoff, L.J. (1988), 'Intergenerational transfers and savings', *Journal of Economic Perspectives*, **2**, 41–58.

Kotlikoff, L.J. (1992), *Generational Accounting: Knowing Who Pays, and When, For What We Spend*, New York: Free Press.

Kuznets, S.S. (1930), *Secular Movements in Production and Prices: Their Nature and Bearing upon Capital Fluctuations*, Boston: Houghton Mifflin.

Kuznets, S.S. (1958), 'Long swings in the growth of population and in related economic variables', *Proceedings of the American Philosophical Society*, **102**, 25–52.

Kuznets, S.S. (1974), 'Population and Economic Growth' in Kuznets, S.S., *Population, Capital and Growth*, London: Heinemann.

Laczko, F., Dale, A., Arber, S. and Gilbert, N. (1988), 'Early retirement in a period of high unemployment', *Journal of Social Policy*, **17**, 313–34.

Laczko, F. and Phillipson, C. (1991), *Changing Work and Retirement:Social Policy and the Older Worker*, Milton Keynes: Open University Press.

Lagergren, M., Lundh, L., Orkan, M. and Sanne, C. (1984), *Time to Care:*

A Report Prepared for the Swedish Secretariat for Futures Studies, Oxford: Pergamon Press.

Lapp, J.S. (1985), 'Mandatory retirement as a clause in an employment insurance contract', *Economic Inquiry*, **23**, 69–71.

Laslett, P. (1971), *The World We Have Lost*, Cambridge: Cambridge University Press.

Laslett, P. (1977), *Family Life and Illicit Love in Earlier Generations: Essays in Historical Sociology*, Cambridge: Cambridge University Press.

Laslett, P. (1989), *A Fresh Map of Life: The Emergence of the Third Age*, London: Weidenfeld and Nicolson.

Law, C.M. and Warnes, A.M. (1976), 'The changing geography of the elderly in England and Wales', *Transactions of the Institute of British Geographers*, New Series **1**, 453–71.

Lazear, E.P. (1979), 'Why is there mandatory retirement?', *Journal of Political Economy*, **87**, 1261–84.

Lazear, E.P. (1981), 'Aging, earnings profiles, productivity and hours restrictions', *American Economic Review*, **71**, 606–20.

Lazear, E.P. (1990), 'Pensions and deferred benefits as strategic compensation', *Industrial Relations*, **29**, 263–80.

Le Grand, J. (1982), *The Strategy of Equality*, London: George Allen and Unwin.

Le Grand, J. (1991), 'Quasi-markets and social policy', *Economic Journal*, **101**, 1256–67.

Le Grand, J. and Bartlett, W. (eds) (1993), *Quasi-Markets and Social Policy*, London: Macmillan.

Lee, R.D. and Lapkoff, S.F. (1988), 'Intergenerational flows of time and goods: consequences of slowing population growth', *Journal of Political Economy*, **96**, 618–51.

Leibenstein, H. (1974), 'An interpretation of the economic theory of fertility', *Journal of Economic Literature*, **12**, 457–79.

Leimer, R.D. and Lesnoy, S.D. (1982), 'Social security and private saving: new time-series evidence', *Journal of Political Economy*, **90**, 606–42.

Lemon, B.W., Bengtson, V.L. and Petersen, J.A. (1972), 'An exploration of the activity theory of ageing: activity types and life satisfaction among in-movers to a retirement community', *Journal of Gerontology*, **27**, 511–23.

Lipietz, A. (1992), *Towards a New Economic Order: Postfordism, Ecology and Democracy*, Cambridge: Polity Press.

Livi-Bacci, M. (1992), *A Concise History of World Population*, Oxford: Basil Blackwell.

Loasby, B.J. (1976), *Choice, Complexity and Ignorance: An Enquiry into Economic Theory and the Practice of Decision Making*, Cambridge: Cambridge University Press.

Longman, P. (1987), *Born to Pay: The New Politics of Aging in America*, Boston, MA: Houghton Mifflin.

Loomes, G. and McKenzie, L. (1990), 'The Scope and Limitations of QALY Measures' in Baldwin, S., Godfrey, C. and Propper, C. (eds), *Quality of Life: Perspectives and Policy*, London: Routledge.

Lösch, A. (1937), 'Population cycles as a cause of business cycles', *Quarterly Journal of Economics*, **51**, 649–62.

Lotka, A.J. (1907), 'Relation between birth rates and death rates', *Science*, **26**, 21–2.

Lydall, H. (1955), 'The life-cycle in income, saving and asset ownership', *Econometrica*, **23**, 131–50.

Malthus, T.R. (1970), *An Essay on the Principle of Population*, Harmondsworth: Penguin.

Mankiw, N.G. and Weil, D.N. (1989), 'The baby boom, the baby bust and the housing market', *Regional Science and Urban Economics*, **19**, 235–58.

Manton, K.G. (1982), 'Changing concepts of morbidity and mortality in the elderly population', *Milbank Memorial Fund Quarterly*, **60**, 183–244.

Marmor, T., Smeeding, T. and Green, V. (eds) (1994), *Economic Security and Intergenerational Justice*, Washington DC: Urban Institute Press.

Marmot, M.G. and McDowall, M.E. (1986), 'Mortality decline and widening social inequalities', *Lancet*, **2**, 274–6.

Marshall, V.W. (1980), *Last Chapters: A Sociology of Aging and Dying*, Monterey: Brooks/Cole.

Marshall, V.W. (ed.) (1986), *Later Life*, London: Sage.

Marshall, V.W. (1996), 'The State of Theory in Aging and the Social Sciences' in Binstock, R.H. and George, L.K. (eds), *Handbook of Aging and the Social Sciences*, 4th edn, San Diego, CA: Academic Press.

Martin, G.M. and Ogawa, N. (1988), 'The Effect of Cohort Size on Relative Wages in Japan' in Lee, R.D., Arthur, W.B. and Rodgers, G. (eds), *Economics of Changing Age Distributions in Developed Countries*, Oxford: Oxford University Press.

Masson, P.R. and Tryon, R.W. (1990), 'Macroeconomic effects of projected population ageing in industrial countries', *IMF Staff Papers*, **37**, 453–85.

Maynard, A.K. (1988), 'Economic Resources and Ageing' in Wells, N.E.J. and Freer, C.B. (eds), *The Ageing Population: Burden or Challenge?*, London: Macmillan.

McKeown, T. (1976), *The Modern Rise of Population*, London: Edward Arnold.

McKeown, T. and Record, R.G. (1962), 'Reasons for the decline of mortality in England and Wales during the nineteenth century', *Population Studies*, **16**, 94–122.

McLoughlin, J. (1991), *The Demographic Revolution*, London: Faber and Faber.

McPherson, B.D. (1983), *Aging as a Social Process: An Introduction to Individual and Population Aging*, Toronto: Butterworths.

Means, R. (1986), 'The Development of Social Services for Elderly People: Historical Perspectives' in Phillipson, C. and Walker, A. (eds), *Ageing and Social Policy: A Critical Assessment*, Aldershot: Gower.

Means, R. and Smith, R. (1994), *Community Care: Policy and Practice*, London: Macmillan

Meek, R.L. (1953), *Marx and Engels on Malthus*, London: Lawrence and Wishart.

Meijdam, L. and Verbon, H.A.A. (1996), 'Aging and political decision making on public pensions', *Journal of Population Economics*, **9**, 141–58.

Menchik, P.L. and David, M. (1983), 'Income distribution, lifetime savings and bequests', *American Economic Review*, **73**, 672–90.

Mendus, S. (1991), 'Human Nature and the Culture of Enterprise' in Hutton, J., Hutton, S., Pinch, T. and Shiell, A. (eds), *Dependency to Enterprise*, London: Routledge.

Midwinter, E. (1989), 'Workers versus pensioners?', *Social Policy and Administration*, **23**, 205–10.

Mincer, J. (1974), *Schooling, Experience and Earnings*, New York: NBER.

Minkler, M. (1986), '"Generational equity" and the new victim blaming: an emerging public policy issue', *International Journal of Health Services*, **16**, 539–51.

Minkler, M. and Robertson, A. (1991), 'The ideology of age/race wars: deconstructing a social problem', *Ageing and Society*, **11**, 1–23.

Minns, R. (1996), 'The political economy of pensions', *New Political Economy*, **1**, 375–91.

Mirer, T.W. (1979), 'The wealth–age relation among the aged', *American Economic Review*, **69**, 435–43.

Mirer, T.W. (1980), 'The dissaving behavior of the retired aged', *Southern Economic Journal*, **46**, 1197–205.

Mishra, R. (1981), *Society and Social Policy: Theories and Practice of Welfare*, 2nd edn, London: Macmillan.

Mitchell, O.S. and Fields, G.S. (1982), 'The Effect of Pensions and Earnings on Retirement: A Review Essay' in Ehrenberg, R.G. (ed.), *Research in Labor Economics*, Vol. 5, Greenwich: JAI Press.

Mitchell, O.S. and Fields, G.S. (1984), *Retirement, Pensions and Social Security*, Cambridge, MA: MIT Press.

Modigliani, F. (1975), 'The Life-cycle Hypothesis of Saving Twenty Years Later' in Parkin, M. and Nobay, A. R. (eds), *Contemporary Issues in Economics*, Manchester: Manchester University Press.

Modigliani, F. and Brumberg, R. (1954), 'Utility Analysis and the Consumption Function: An Interpretation of Cross-section Data' in

Kurihara, K. (ed.), *Post Keynesian Economics*, Brunswick, NJ: Rutgers University Press.

Mooney, G.A. (1978), 'Planning for balance of care of the elderly', *Scottish Journal of Political Economy*, **25**, 149–64.

Munnell, A. (1974), *The Effect of Social Security on Personal Savings*, Cambridge, MA: Ballinger.

Munnichs, J.M.A. (1976), 'Dependency, Interdependency and Autonomy: An Introduction' in Munnichs, J.M.A. and van den Heuval, W.J.A. (eds), *Dependency and Interdependency in Old Age*, The Hague: Martinus Nijhoff.

Munnichs, J.M.A., Mussen, P., Olbrich, E. and Coleman, P.G. (1985), *Life Span and Change in a Gerontological Perspective*, Orlando, CA: Academic Press.

Murphy, K., Plant, M. and Welch, F. (1988), 'Cohort Size and Earnings in the United States' in Lee, R.D., Arthur, W.B. and Rodgers, G. (eds), *Economics of Changing Age Distributions in Developed Countries*, Oxford: Oxford University Press.

Musgrove, P. (1982), *US Household Consumption, Income, and Demographic Changes: 1975–2025*, Washington DC: Resources for the Future.

Muurinen, J-M. (1986), 'The economics of informal care: labor market effects in the national hospice study', *Medical Care*, **24**, 1007–16.

Myles, J. (1989), *Old Age in the Welfare State: The Political Economy of Public Pensions*, Lawrence, KS: University Press of Kansas.

Myles, J. (1990), 'States, Labor Markets and Life Cycles' in Friedland, R. and Robertson, S. (eds), *Beyond the Marketplace: Rethinking Economy and Society*, New York: Aldine de Gruyter.

National Economic Development Office (1989), *Defusing the Demographic Time Bomb*, London: NEDO.

Netten, A. (1993), 'Costing Informal Care' in Netten, A. and Beecham, J. (eds), *Costing Community Care: Theory and Practice*, Aldershot: Ashgate.

Ng, Y-K. (1983), *Welfare Economics: Introduction and Development of Basic Concepts*, London: Macmillan.

Nissel, M. and Bonnerjea, L. (1982), *Family Care of the Handicapped Elderly: Who Pays?*, London: Policy Studies Institute.

O'Connor, J. (1973), *The Fiscal Crisis of the State*, New York: St Martin's Press.

OECD (1988a), *Ageing Populations: The Social Policy Implications*, Paris: OECD.

OECD (1988b), *Reforming Public Pensions*, Paris: OECD.

OECD (1995), 'Effects of ageing populations on government budgets', *OECD Economic Outlook*, **57**, 33–42.

Olshansky, S.J. and Ault, A.B. (1986), 'The fourth stage of the epidemiological transition: the age of delayed degenerative diseases', *Milbank Memorial Fund Quarterly*, **64**, 355–8.

Olshansky, S.J., Carnes, B.A. and Cassel, C. (1990), 'In search of Methuselah: estimating the upper limits to human longevity', *Science*, **250**, 634–40.

Omran, A.R. (1971), 'The epidemiological transition: a theory of the epidemiology of population change', *Milbank Memorial Fund Quarterly*, **49**, 509–38.

Paish, F. and Peacock, A.T. (1954), 'The economics of dependence 1952–1982', *Economica*, **21**, 279–99.

Parker, G. (1990), *With Due Care and Attention: A Review of Research on Informal Care*, London: Family Policy Studies Centre.

Parker, S. (1982), *Work and Retirement*, London: George Allen and Unwin.

Pearson, M., Smith, S. and White, S. (1989), 'Demographic influences on public spending', *Fiscal Studies*, **10**, 48–65.

Peters, W. (1991), 'Public pensions in transition: an optimal policy path', *Journal of Population Economics*, **4**, 155–75.

Phillips Committee (1954), *Report of the Committee on the Economic and Financial Problems of the Provision for Old Age*, Command 993, London: HMSO.

Phillipson, C. (1982), *Capitalism and the Construction of Old Age*, London: Macmillan.

Phillipson, C. (1991), 'Intergenerational relations: conflict or consensus in the twentieth century?', *Policy and Politics*, **19**, 27–36.

Phillipson, C. (1996), 'Intergenerational Conflict and the Welfare State' in Walker, A. (ed.), *The New Generational Contract: Intergenerational Relations, Old Age and Welfare*, London: UCL Press.

Piachaud, D. (1986), 'Disability, retirement and unemployment of older men', *Journal of Social Policy*, **15**, 145–62.

Pierson, C. (1991), *Beyond the Welfare State? The New Political Economy of Welfare*, Cambridge: Polity Press.

Piore, M. and Sabel, C.F. (1984), *The Second Industrial Divide: Possibilities for Prosperity*, New York: Basic Books.

Preston, S.H. (1984), 'Children and the elderly: divergent paths for America's dependants', *Demography*, **21**, 435–57.

Preston, S.H. (1988), 'Age-structural Influences on Public Transfers to Dependants' in Riley, M.W. (ed.), *Social Structures and Human Lives: Social Change and the Life Course*, Volume 1, Newbury Park, CA: Sage.

Quadagno, J. (1989), 'Generational equity and the politics of the welfare state', *Politics and Society*, **17**, 353–76.

Qureshi, H. and Walker, A. (1986), 'Caring for Elderly People: The Family and the State' in Phillipson, C. and Walker, A. (eds), *Ageing and Social Policy: A Critical Assessment*, Aldershot: Gower.

Rainwater, L. and Rein, M. (1993), 'The Economic Well-being of Older Men in Six Countries' in Atkinson, A.B. and Rein, M. (eds), *Work, Age and Social Security*, London: Macmillan.

Reday-Mulvey, G. (1990), 'Work and retirement: future prospects for the baby-boom generation', *Geneva Papers on Risk and Insurance*, **15**, 100–113.

Reddaway, W.B. (1939), *The Economics of a Declining Population*, London: George Allen and Unwin.

Rein, M. and Jacobs, K. (1993), 'Ageing and Employment Trends: A Comparative Analysis for OECD Countries' in Johnson, P. and Zimmermann, K.F. (eds), *Labour Markets in an Ageing Europe*, Cambridge: Cambridge University Press.

Rex, J. (1961), *Key Problems in Sociological Theory*, London: Routledge and Kegan Paul.

Riegel, K.F. (1973), 'Dialectical operations: the final period of cognitive development', *Human Development*, **16**, 346–70.

Riley, M.W. and Foner, A. (1968), *Aging and Society, Volume 1: An Inventory of Research Findings*, New York: Russell Sage Foundation.

Rosen, S. (1977), 'Social Security and the Economy' in Boskin, M. (ed.), *The Crisis in Social Security*, San Francisco, CA: Institute for Contemporary Studies.

Rosenmayr, L. (1981), 'Objective and subjective perspectives of life span research', *Ageing and Society*, **1**, 29–49.

Royal Commission on Population (1949), *Report*, London: HMSO.

Russell, L.B. (1981), 'An aging population and the use of medical care', *Medical Care*, **19**, 633–43.

Rustin, M. (1989), 'The Trouble with "New Times"' in Hall, S. and Jacques, M. (eds), *New Times: The Changing Face of Politics in the 1990s,* London: Lawrence and Wishart.

Samuelson, P.A. (1958), 'An exact consumption-loan model of interest with or without the social contrivance of money', *Journal of Political Economy*, **66**, 467–82.

Samuelson, P.A. (1975), 'Optimum social security in a life-cycle growth model', *International Economic Review*, **16**, 539–44.

Sanford, J.R.A. (1975), 'Tolerance of debility in elderly dependants by supporters at home: its significance for hospital practice', *British Medical Journal*, **3**, 471–3.

Sauvy, A. (1948), 'Social and economic consequences of the ageing of Western European populations', *Population Studies*, **2**, 115–24.

Sawyer, M.C. (1985), *The Economics of Michal Kalecki*, London: Macmillan.

Schaie, K.W. (1978), 'Towards a stage theory of adult cognitive development', *Journal of Ageing and Human Development*, **8**, 129–38.

Schmähl, W. (1989), 'Labour Force Participation and Social Pension Systems' in Johnson, P., Conrad, C. and Thomson, D. (eds), *Workers Versus Pensioners*, Manchester: Manchester University Press.

Schmähl, W. (1990), 'Demographic change and social security: some elements of a complex relationship', *Journal of Population Economics*, **3**, 159–77.

Schmidt, C.M. (1993), 'Ageing and Unemployment' in Johnson, P. and Zimmermann, K.F. (eds), *Labour Markets in an Ageing Europe*, Cambridge: Cambridge University Press.

Schneider, E.L. and Brody, J.A. (1983), 'Ageing, natural death and the compression of morbidity: another view', *New England Journal of Medicine*, **309**, 854–6.

Schuller, T. and Walker, A. (1990), *The Time of Our Life: Education, Employment and Retirement in the Third Age*, London: Institute for Public Policy Research.

Schultz, T.W. (1961), 'Investment in human capital', *American Economic Review*, **51**, 1–17.

Schulz, J.H. (1996), 'Economic Security Policies' in Binstock, R.H. and George, L.K. (eds), *Handbook of Aging and the Social Sciences*, 4th edn, San Diego: Academic Press.

Sen, A.K. (1983), 'Poor, relatively speaking', *Oxford Economic Papers*, **35**, 153–69.

Shanas, E. (1979), 'Social myth as hypothesis: the case of family relationships of old people', *Gerontology*, **19**, 3–9.

Shanas, E., Townsend, P., Wedderburn, D., Henning, F., Milhof, P. and Stehouwer, J. (1968), *Old People in Three Industrialised Societies*, London: Routledge and Kegan Paul.

Shegog, R.F.A. (ed.) (1981), *The Impending Crisis of Old Age: A Challenge to Ingenuity*, Oxford: Oxford University Press.

Shimowada, I. (1992), 'Aging and the four pillars in Japan', *Geneva Papers on Risk and Insurance*, **17**, 40–80.

Sidell, M. (1995), *Health in Old Age: Myth, Mystery and Management*, Buckingham: Open University Press.

Simon, H.A. (1957), *Models of Man: Social and Rational*, New York: Wiley.

Simon, J.L. (1977), *The Economics of Population Growth*, Princeton, NJ: Princeton University Press.

Simon, J.L. (1981), *The Ultimate Resource*, Princeton, NJ: Princeton University Press.

Sixsmith, A. (1986), 'Independence and Home in Later Life' in

Phillipson, C., Bernard, M. and Strang, P. (eds), *Dependency and Interdependency in Old Age*, London: Croom Helm.

Smeeding, T.M. (1993), 'Cross-national Patterns of Retirement and Poverty among Men and Women in the mid-1980s: Full Stop or Gradual Withdrawal?' in Atkinson, A.B. and Rein, M. (eds), *Work, Age and Social Security*, London: Macmillan.

Smith, A. (1982), 'Intergenerational transfers as social insurance', *Journal of Public Economics*, **19**, 97–106.

Smith, K. and Wright, K.G. (1994), 'Informal care and economic appraisal: a discussion of possible methodological approaches', *Health Economics*, **3**, 137–48.

Smith, R. (1984) 'The structured dependency of the elderly: some sceptical historical thoughts', *Ageing and Society*, **4**, 409–28.

Solomou, S. (1988), *Phases of Economic Growth, 1850-1973: Kondratieff Waves and Kuznets Swings*, Cambridge: Cambridge University Press.

Stone, R. and Short, P. (1990), 'The competing demands of employment and informal caregiving to disabled elders', *Medical Care*, **28**, 513–26.

Sugden, R. and Williams, A.H. (1978), *The Principles of Practical Cost-benefit Analysis,* Oxford: Oxford University Press.

Tawney, R.H. (1964), *Equality*, London: George Allen and Unwin.

Taylor, P.E. and Walker, A. (1994), 'The ageing workforce: employers' attitudes towards older people', *Work, Employment and Society*, **8**, 569–91.

Taylor, P.E. and Walker, A. (1996), 'Intergenerational Relations in the Labour Market: The Attitudes of Employers and Older Workers' in Walker, A. (ed.), *The New Generational Contract: Intergenerational Relations, Old Age and Welfare*, London: UCL Press.

Taylor, R.C. (1988), 'The Elderly as Members of Society: An Examination of Social Differences in an Elderly Population' in Wells, N.E.J. and Freer, C.B.(eds), *The Ageing Population: Burden or Challenge?*, London: Macmillan.

Taylor, R.C. and Ford, G. (1983), 'Inequalities in old age: an examination of age, sex and class differences in a sample of community elderly', *Ageing and Society*, **3**, 183–208.

Taylor, R.C., Ford, G. and Barber, J.H. (1983), *The Elderly at Risk: A Critical Review of Problems and Progress in Screening and Case-finding*, Mitcham, Surrey: Age Concern.

Teague, P. (1990), 'The political economy of the regulation school and the flexible specialisation scenario', *Journal of Economic Studies*, **17**, 32–54.

Thane, P.M. (1990), 'The debate on the declining birth-rate in Britain: the "menace" of an ageing population, 1920s–1950s', *Continuity and Change*, **5**, 283–305.

Thomae, H. (ed.) (1976), *Patterns of Aging: Findings from the Bonn Longitudinal Study of Aging*, Basle: Karger.

Thomson, D. (1989), 'The Welfare State and Generational Conflict: Winners and Losers' in Johnson, P., Conrad, C. and Thomson, D. (eds), *Workers Versus Pensioners*, Manchester: Manchester University Press.

Thomson, D. (1991), *Selfish Generations: The Ageing of New Zealand's Welfare State*, Wellington: Bridget Williams.

Thomson, D. (1992), 'Generations, Justice, and the Future of Collective Action' in Laslett, P. and Fishkin, J. (eds), *Justice Between Age Groups and Generations*, New Haven: Yale University Press.

Titmuss, R.M. (1970), *The Gift Relationship*, London: Allen and Unwin.

Townsend, P. (1979), *Poverty in the United Kingdom*, Harmondsworth: Penguin.

Townsend, P. (1981), 'The structured dependency of the elderly: a creation of social policy in the twentieth century', *Ageing and Society*, 1, 5–28.

Townsend, P. (1985), 'A sociological approach to the measurement of poverty', *Oxford Economic Papers*, 37, 669–76.

Townsend, P. (1986), 'Ageism and Social Policy' in Phillipson, C. and Walker, A. (eds), *Ageing and Social Policy: A Critical Assessment*, Aldershot: Gower.

Townsend, P. and Wedderburn, D. (1965), *The Aged in the Welfare State*, London: Bell.

Ungerson, C. (1995), 'Gender, cash and informal care: European perspectives and dilemmas', *Journal of Social Policy*, 24, 31–52.

Van Praag, B. (1988), 'The notion of population economics', *Journal of Population Economics*, 1, 3–16.

Veall, M.R. (1986), 'Public pensions as optimal social contracts', *Journal of Public Economics*, 31, 237–51.

Venti, S.F. and Wise, D.A. (1989), 'Aging, Moving and Housing Wealth' in Wise, D.A. (ed.), *The Economics of Aging*, Chicago: University of Chicago Press.

Verbon, H.A.A. (1993), 'Public pensions: the role of public choice and expectations', *Journal of Population Economics*, 6, 123–35.

Verbrugge, L.M. (1984), 'Longer life but worsening health? Trends in health and mortality of middle-aged and older persons', *Milbank Memorial Fund Quarterly*, 62, 473–519.

Verhoeven, M.J.M. and Verbon, H.A.A. (1991), 'Expectations on pension schemes under non-stationary conditions', *Economics Letters*, 36, 99–103.

Victor, C. and Evandrou, M. (1987), 'Does Social Class Matter in Later Life?' in di Gregorio, S. (ed.), *Social Gerontology: New Directions*, London: Croom Helm.

Vincent, J. (1996), 'Who's afraid of an ageing population? Nationalism, the free market, and the construction of old age as an issue', *Critical Social*

Policy, **16**, 3–26.

Walker, A. (1980), 'The social creation of poverty and dependency in old age', *Journal of Social Policy*, **9**, 49–75.

Walker, A. (1981), 'Towards a political economy of old age', *Ageing and Society*, **1**, 73–94.

Walker, A. (1982a), 'Dependency and old age', *Social Policy and Administration*, **16**, 115–35.

Walker, A. (1982b), 'The Meaning and Social Division of Community Care' in Walker, A. (ed.), *Community Care: The Family, The State and Social Policy*, Oxford: Basil Blackwell.

Walker, A. (1986), 'Pensions and the Production of Poverty in Old Age' in Phillipson, C. and Walker, A. (eds), *Ageing and Social Policy: A Critical Assessment*, Aldershot: Gower.

Walker, A. (1990), 'The economic "burden" of ageing and the prospect of intergenerational conflict', *Ageing and Society*, **10**, 377–96.

Walker, A. (1993a), 'Community Care Policy: From Consensus to Conflict' in Bornat, J., Pereira, C., Pilgrim, D. and Williams, F. (eds), *Community Care: A Reader*, London: Macmillan.

Walker, A. (1993b), 'Poverty and Inequality in Old Age' in Bond, J., Coleman, P. and Peace, S.M. (eds), *Ageing in Society: An Introduction to Social Gerontology*, 2nd edn, London: Sage.

Walker, A. (1996), 'Intergenerational Relations and the Provision of Welfare' in Walker, A. (ed.), *The New Generational Contract: Intergenerational Relations, Old Age and Welfare*, London: UCL Press.

Wall, R. (1984), 'Residential isolation of the elderly: a comparison over time', *Ageing and Society*, **4**, 483–503.

Wall, R. (1989), 'The Living Arrangements of the Elderly in Europe in the 1980s' in Bytheway, B. (ed.), *Becoming and Being Old*, London: Sage.

Wall, R. (1992), 'Relationships Between the Generations in British Families Past and Present' in Marsh, C. and Arber, S. (eds), *Families and Households: Divisions and Change*, London: Macmillan.

Wall, R. (1996), 'Intergenerational Relationships Past and Present' in Walker, A. (ed.), *The New Generational Contract: Intergenerational Relations, Old Age and Welfare*, London: UCL Press.

Warnes, A.M. (1983), 'Migration in late working age and early retirement', *Socio-economic Planning Science*, **17**, 291–302.

Warnes, A.M. and Law, C.M. (1984), 'The elderly population of Great Britain: locational trends and policy implications', *Transactions of the Institute of British Geographers*, New Series, **9**, 37–59.

Warr, P. (1994), 'Research into work performance of older employees', *Geneva Papers on Risk and Insurance*, **19**, 472–80.

Webb, A. (1991), 'Coordination: a problem in public-sector management',

232 *The political economy of population ageing*

Policy and Politics, **19**, 29–42.

Weil, D.N. (1994), 'The saving of the elderly in micro and macro data', *Quarterly Journal of Economics*, **109**, 55–81.

Weiss, Y. (1972), 'On the optimal pattern of labour supply', *Economic Journal*, **82**, 1293–315.

Welch, F. (1979), 'Effects of cohort size on earnings: the baby boom babies' financial bust', *Journal of Political Economy*, **87**, 565–97.

Welford, A.T. (1958), *Ageing and Human Skill*, London: Oxford University Press.

Welford, A.T. (1976), 'Thirty years of psychological research on age and work', *Journal of Occupational Psychology*, **49**, 129–38.

Wenger, G.C. (1986), 'What Do Dependency Measures Measure? Challenging Assumptions' in Phillipson, C., Bernard, M. and Strang, P. (eds), *Dependency and Interdependency in Old Age*, London: Croom Helm.

Wheeler, R. (1982), 'Staying put: a new development in policy?', *Ageing and Society*, **2**, 299–329.

Wheeler, R. (1986), 'Housing Policy and Elderly People' in Phillipson, C. and Walker, A. (eds), *Ageing and Social Policy: A Critical Assessment*, Aldershot: Gower.

Wheelock, J. (1992), 'The Household in the Total Economy' in Ekins, P. and Max-Neef, M. (eds), *Real-life Economics: Understanding Wealth Creation*, London: Routledge.

Wicks, M. (1989), 'Community care: the challenge for social policy', *Generations*, **9**, 31–46.

Wilkinson, R.G. (ed.) (1986), *Class and Health: Research and Longitudinal Data*, London: Tavistock.

Wilkinson, R.G. (1992), 'Income distribution and life expectancy', *British Medical Journal*, **304**, 165–8.

Williams, A.H. (1985), 'Public Policy Aspects of the Economics of Ageing' in Greenaway, D. and Shaw, G.K. (eds), *Public Choice, Public Finance and Public Policy*, Oxford: Basil Blackwell.

Willis, R.J. (1973), 'A new approach to the economic theory of fertility behavior', *Journal of Political Economy*, **81** (supplement), 14–64.

Wilson, G. (1991), 'Models of ageing and their relation to policy formation and service provision', *Policy and Politics*, **19**, 37–47.

Wilson, G. (1993), 'The challenge of an ageing electorate: changes in the formation of social policy in Europe?', *Journal of European Social Policy*, **3**, 91–105.

Wiseman, A.C. (1989), 'Projected long-term demographic trends and aggregate personal saving in the United States', *Journal of Post Keynesian Economics*, **11**, 497–508.

Wistow, G., Knapp, M., Hardy, B. and Allen, C. (1994), *Social Care in a*

Mixed Economy, Buckingham: Open University Press.

Wolf, D.A. and Soldo, B.J. (1994), 'Married women's allocation of time to employment and parental care', *Journal of Human Resources*, **29**, 1259–76.

World Bank (1994), *Averting the Old Age Crisis: Policies to Protect the Old and Promote Growth*, Washington DC: Oxford University Press.

Wray, L.R. (1991), 'Can the social security trust fund contribute to savings?', *Journal of Post Keynesian Economics*, **13**, 155–70.

Wright, K.G. (1987a), *The Economics of Informal Care of the Elderly*, University of York: CHE Discussion Paper 23.

Wright, K.G. (1987b), *Cost Effectiveness in Community Care*, University of York: CHE Discussion Paper 33.

Wright, K.G. (1988), 'The Elderly Today: An Economic Audit' in Wells, N.E.J. and Freer, C.B. (eds), *The Ageing Population: Burden or Challenge?*, London: Macmillan.

Wright, K.G., Cairns, J.A. and Snell, M.C. (1981), *Costing Care: The Costs of Alternative Patterns of Care for the Elderly*, Sheffield: Sheffield University Joint Unit for Social Services Research.

Wright, R.E. (1991), 'Cohort size and earnings in Great Britain', *Journal of Population Economics*, **4**, 295–305.

Zimmermann, K.F. (1991), 'Ageing and the labor market: age structure, cohort size and unemployment', *Journal of Population Economics*, **4**, 177–200.

Index

Aaron, H.J. 55, 125, 129, 136
Abrams, M. 72
accounting systems 17, 25, 29, 38–9,
        42, 183–90, 198–206
acquiescent functionalism 73, 80
activity theory 71–2
age composition:
    of labour force 100–107
    of populations 1, 2, 4, 5, 8, 9–10,
        11–12, 91,
    of UK 8, 15, 16
age discrimination 17, 42, 98–9, 101,
        106–7, 110–11, 118, 144–5, 167
age distribution 8–9, 51, 56, 163–4
age groups *see* birth cohorts
    older age groups
    younger age groups
age–earnings profiles 100–102, 103,
        104, 106, 108, 143
    see also income levels
age-related dependency 23–7, 91, 152,
        164–72
    structured 18, 27, 77–82, 139
age-related diseases 97, 148–53, 154
    see also biological ageing
ageing *see* population ageing
the ageing crisis 14, 16, 67, 90, 91,
        201–3
aggregate demand 84, 89, 90–91
Aglietta, M. 83
Albrecht, R. 71
allocative efficiency:
    in health care 156, 157, 160
altruistic behaviour 66–7
    see also informal care
    intergenerational contract
America *see* United States
Anderson, M. 178
Ando, A. 49, 54
Arber, S. 184, 191
Arestis, P. 84

Asimakopoulos, A. 129
Atkinson, A.B. 113
Auerbach, A.J. 38, 62, 89
Ault, A.B. 149
average-age criterion 2–3

baby-boom generation 102, 103–4
banded retirement 144–5
Barber, J.H. 167
Barr, N. 126, 176
Barro, R.J. 55
Bartlett, W. 180
Bebbington, A.C. 153
Becker, G.S. 13, 44, 46, 47, 49, 59,
        100, 101
behaviour *see* rational behaviour
Bell, J.M. 157
Bengtson, V.L. 71
bequest model 55–6
    see also savings and investments
Berger, M.C. 103
Berlin, I. 20
Bernheim, B.D. 54, 55
Beveridge, W. 77, 135
Binney, E.A. 39, 42
biographical studies 73
biological ageing 19, 24, 50, 69, 70,
        72, 73, 92, 96–8, 199
    age-related diseases 97, 148–53, 154
Birdsall, N. 14
birth cohorts 39, 42, 54, 86–7, 102–3,
        112, 120
birth control 13
birth rates 2, 3, 8, 9, 15, 16
    see also fertility rates
    mortality rates
Blanchet, D. 66, 104
Blankart, C.B. 134
Blinder, A.S. 54, 60
Bloom, D.E. 103
Boadway, R.W. 66

Boaz, R.R. 169
Bodie, Z. 143
Bond, J. 96, 165
Bonnerjea, L. 190
Booth, T. 165
Börsch-Supan, A. 54, 55, 64
Bös, D. 65
Boserup, E. 13
Boskin, M. 60
Bosworth, B.P. 129, 136
Breyer, F. 66
Briggs, R. 96
Brody, J.A. 153, 179
Bromley, D. 153
Broome, J. 157
Browning, E.K. 65–6
Brumberg, R. 49, 54
Buchanan, J.M. 65
budget deficits 128, 136
budget surpluses 128–9, 136
Burtless, G. 60, 129, 136
business/trade cycle 86
Busse, E.W. 72
Butler, A. 170
Bytheway, B. 153

Cairns, J.A. 19, 160, 161, 162, 185
Callinicos, A.T. 83
Cambridge, P. 195
Campbell, C.D. 60
Campbell, R.G. 60
capital 57, 62, 63, 82–4, 85–6, 87, 129, 136
capitalism 74, 75, 76, 79, 80, 83–4, 87–8, 89, 90–91, 199
care *see* formal care
    health care
    informal care
carers 166, 168–9, 170
    female 166, 178–9, 184, 190, 196
    male 191
    see also informal care
Carnes, B.A. 150
Carstairs, V. 150
case finding 167
case management 194–6, 197, 204–5
    see also health care
Casey, B. 113
Cassel, C. 150
Cavan, R.S. 71

centralized dependency 82
Challis, D. 195
Chang, C.F. 169
Charness, N. 99
children 4, 6, 55–6, 57
    see also younger age groups
choice behaviour 113, 204–5
    see also decision making
    retirement decisions
Chown, S.M. 98
chronologized practices 119, 120
Cipolla, C.M. 10
Clark, R.L. 14, 60, 85
Coale, A.J. 13, 56
Coale–Hoover model 13, 56–7
Cochrane, S.H. 13
Cohen, G. 97
Coleman, P. 96, 97
collectivism 45
communism 74
community care *see* domiciliary care
    informal care
competitive economies 102–4, 174–5, 177, 180
competitive equilibrium 46–7
conflict theory 74–5, 76
Connelly, N. 165
Conrad, C. 37
consumption patterns 49, 52, 64
Coriat, B. 83
Costello, N. 83
Cowgill, D.O. 76
Crapo, L.M. 150
Creedy, J. 134, 135, 136
cultural values 79, 92, 111
culture of dependency 20, 81
Cumming, E. 72
Cunningham, J.P. 64
curative medicine 151, 153, 154–5, 167
    see also health care
Cutler, D.M. 64

Dahrendorf, R. 74
Dalley, G. 171, 193
Daniels, N. 39
Dant, T. 81
Danziger, S. 54
David, M. 54
Davidson, P. 84

Davies, B. 195
Davies, D.R. 109
de Beauvoir, S. 80
de Uriarte, B. 45
death:
  age at 150–51, 153
  causes of 149, 150, 151
  see also mortality rates
decentralized dependency 82
dechronologization 119–20
decision making 22, 25, 50, 51–2, 62,
    67–8, 97
  on care provision 166, 171–2,
    179–90
  choice behaviour 113, 204–5
  on retirement 59–60, 113–17, 134,
    139–42
  see also policy issues
defined benefit principle 143
defined contribution principle 143
  see also pension payments
degenerative diseases 149–50
  see also age-related diseases
Delsen, L. 117, 142
demand *see* aggregate demand
demographic change 61–2, 64, 74–5,
    84–6, 150, 204
  health care and 158, 163
  pensions and 126
  unemployment and 88–9
demographic determinism 24, 88–9
demographic transition model 11–12
demographics 1, 2–9, 10–16, 74,
    198–9
  population economics 47–8, 74–5,
    84–9
Denton, F.T. 150
Department of Health (UK) 164, 195
Department of Health and Social
    Security (DHSS) (UK) 136
dependency 16, 18–43
  age-related 23–7, 91, 154, 164–72
  avoidance of 164–72, 181
  centralized 82
  consequences of 22–3, 27–43
  cost of 164–5
  culture of 20, 81
  decentralized 82
  definition 18–21, 22, 81, 199
  distribution of 27, 127–8

economic 2, 6, 8, 18, 19, 20–21, 22,
    25–42, 201–3
  economic disincentives 33–6, 125,
    131–2
  increases in 27–43
  interdependency 21–2
  intergenerational conflict 36–42, 65,
    80, 103–4, 127–8, 201, 202
  measurement of 23–7
  negative aspects 21–2, 43
  physical 18, 19–20, 21, 22, 24–5,
    164–72
  political 18, 20, 22, 24–5
  significance of 21–3
  structured 18, 27, 77–82, 139
  transfer problems 29–33
dependency levels 160, 161, 162, 164,
    168, 184, 185
dependency ratios 6–8, 18–19, 23–4,
    26–7, 129, 134, 191, 198–9
developing countries *see* Third World
    countries
Dex, S. 98
Diamond, P.A. 51, 54
Dicks-Mireaux, L. 54
diet *see* nutrition
Dilnot, A. 123
disability benefits 113, 116
  see also social security benefits
disabled people *see* physical incapacity
discrimination *see* age discrimination
    indirect discrimination
disengagement theory 71, 72–3
disequilibrium arguments 69–70, 83–9
  see also market-clearing equilibria
disincentives *see* economic
    disincentives
    political disincentives
Disney, R. 55, 134, 135, 136, 143
doctors 156
  see also health care
Doeringer, P.B. 102
domestic sector 175, 176
  see also informal economic activity
domiciliary care 77, 79, 159, 160–64,
    165, 169, 179, 182–3, 193
  see also health care
    informal care
Dominguez, K.M. 64
Donaldson, L. 13

Downs, A. 65
Drissen, E. 67
Drury, E. 110
dynamic labour supply 59

early exit/retirement 59, 60, 77, 82–3,
        99, 106–7, 110, 112–17, 137–41,
        143–4
earnings *see* wages
Easterlin, R.A. 13, 42, 87, 102–4
economic activity 1–2, 6, 8, 19–21, 25,
        81, 173
    formal 174–5
    informal 25, 26, 29, 32–3, 40,
        173–8, 191, 193, 199
        see also informal care
        unemployment
economic conditions 15, 56, 85, 88–9,
        120
    mortality rates and 149
    pension payments and 124–5
    population ageing and 10–12, 61,
        78–9, 99
    population decline and 85–6
    population growth and 13–14, 15,
        84–5, 87
    population youthening and 56–7
economic cycles 86–7
economic dependency 2, 6, 8, 18, 19,
        20–21, 22, 25–43, 201–3
        see also unemployment
economic disincentives 33–6, 125,
        131–2
economic and fiscal policies 1, 37–9,
        63–4, 183–90, 201–3
economic problems:
    of population ageing 1–2, 6, 14–16,
        23
economic theory 198–206
    disequilibrium 69–70, 83–9
    empirical alternatives 89, 90
    general equilibrium 61–4, 88–9
    ideology and 90–92
    market-clearing equilibria 44, 46–7,
        61, 69–70, 83
    modernization theory 76–7, 80–81,
        92, 178, 179
    neoclassical 16, 44–68, 69, 80, 83,
        84, 88, 89, 92, 93, 102, 176
    non-neoclassical 69–94

public economics 176–7
    structural 70–83, 83
economics of politics approach 65
education *see* training and education
Edwards, R. 102
efficiency criteria 134
    see also technical efficiency
Eichner, A.S. 84
Eilenstine, D.L. 64
employer attitudes 95–100, 107,
        110–11, 114, 117–18, 119–20
employment policies 110, 111
    see also economic activity
empowerment 194
Engels, F. 74, 75
epidemiological transition theory
        149–50
equilibrium *see* general equilibrium
        theory, market-clearing
        equilibria
Erikson, E.H. 98
Ermisch, J.F. 41, 103, 112, 136, 158
Espenshade, T.J. 64
Esposito, L. 56
Estes, C.L. 39, 42, 77
ethnomethodology 73
Ettner, S.L. 184
Evandrou, M. 168
Evers, H. 71
Eversley, D.E.C. 191
exit-based empowerment 194
experience *see* learning process

Fair, R.C. 64
Falkingham, J. 24, 26, 150, 168, 178
family groups 37, 178, 181
    conflict in 182
    older people in 76, 80, 178–9
    one-person households 178, 179
        see also informal care
family size 13, 178, 191
Faulkner, D. 97
Featherstone, M. 80
Feldstein, M.S. 56
female education 13
female workers 15, 37, 112
    retirement age 136, 144
    unpaid work 25, 26
females:

as care providers 166, 178–9, 184, 190, 196
  see also males
Fennell, G. 71
fertility rates 1, 5–6, 9–10, 11–12, 13, 16, 47, 48, 75, 86, 125, 191
  see also birth rates
  mortality rates
Fields, G.S. 60
financial independence 26
Finch, J. 179, 193
first-best outcomes 35, 61
fiscal policies *see* economic and fiscal policies
Fischer, D.H. 76
flexible pensions 142–3, 204
flexible retirement 139–42, 145–7, 200, 204
flexible specialization 83
Fogarty, M. 144, 145
Foner, A. 98
Ford, G. 167, 168
Fordist economics 82–3, 92, 118–20, 146
  post-Fordism 82–3, 118–20, 146, 180, 200–201, 205
Fordist life cycle 119
formal care 20, 34, 36–7, 179, 180, 181–3
  balance of care 159–64, 179–90
  case management 194–6, 197, 204–5
  cost of 34, 36–7, 148, 164–5
  institutionalization of 20, 76, 77, 78–9, 171, 201–3
  planning of 183–97
  types of 164–72
    see also informal care
    social services
formal economies 174–5, 177
Fox, J. 149
France 114, 117
free riders 123–4
Freeman, R.B. 103
Freer, C.B. 167
Friedman, M. 50
Fries, J.F. 150, 167
Fuchs, V.R. 60, 150, 155
functionalist sociology 70–71, 73–4, 76

funded pension schemes 34, 36–7, 65–7, 121–8, 142–3

Gale, W.G. 55
general equilibrium theory 61–4, 88–9
generation size 9, 10, 102–4, 125
generational accounting 38–9, 42
generational planning 65–8, 159
generations:
  as collective entities 42
  definition 39
  overlapping generations model 61–2, 65, 66
Gerard, L.E. 77
geriatric hospitals 160
Germany 72, 114, 117
gerontology *see* social gerontology
Gershuny, J. 180
Ghez, G.R. 59
Giarini, O. 122
Gibbs, I. 170
Gillion, C. 135
Ginn, J. 42, 184, 191
Ginsburg, N. 79
Gokhale, J. 38
Goldberg, E.M. 165
Goldschmidt-Clermont, L. 177
Gordon, C. 178
Gordon, R.H. 54, 60
Gorz, A. 138
Gough, I. 79
government policies *see* policy issues
gradual retirement 59, 139–42
Graebner, W. 76
Great Britain *see* United Kingdom
Green, V. 39
Greve, J. 170
Griffiths Report (UK) 195
Gruenberg, E.M. 154
Grundy, E. 153, 178
Guillemard, A-M. 111, 113, 115, 116, 118–19

Hadley, R. 180
Hagemann, R.P. 129
Hall, M.R.P. 157
Hamouda, O. 84
Hansen, A.H. 85
Hansson, I. 66

Harcourt, G.C.   84
Hargreaves Heap, S.   45–6
Harris, A.I.   19
Harrod, R.F.   85
Hatch, S.   180
Hausman, J.A.   54, 60
Haveman, R.   39
Havighurst, R.J.   71
Hayek, F.A.   13
health:
    age-related diseases   97, 148–53, 154
    causes of death   149, 150, 151
    definition of   157, 159
    degenerative diseases   149–50
    improvements in   149–53, 154
    infectious diseases   149–50
    see also life expectancy
health care   8–9, 17, 24–5, 64, 148–59
    balance of care   159–64, 178–80
    case finding   167
    cost-effectiveness of   159–61
    curative medicine   151, 153, 154–5,
        167
    demand for   155–6
    doctors   156
    domiciliary   77, 79, 159, 160–64,
        165, 169, 179, 182–3, 193
    effects of   153–4
    hospital care   157, 159–64
    institutional   159–64, 165, 170, 171,
        179
    physical dependency and   19
    preventive measures   151–2
    private   155
    quality of   160, 162
    screening programmes   166–7
    social costs   161–2
    types of   148, 156, 157–8, 159–64
    for younger people   153–4
    see also formal care
        informal care
health care crisis   155
health care expenditure   148, 152,
    153–64
health care organization   148, 155,
    156–64
health care planning   154–9
health education   167
health standards   12–13, 149
Heller, P.S.   158

Hemming, R.C.L.   56, 136, 158
Hendricks, C.D.   96, 97
Hendricks, J.   77, 96, 97
Henry, W.   72
Hepworth, M.   80
Heron, A.   98
hierachical social structure   76, 80, 178
Higgins, J.   169
Hills, J.   41–2
Hirschman, A.O.   194
Hirshleifer, J.   44, 46
historical survey   10–11, 14, 15, 70–71
Hockey, J.   79
Hodgson, G.M.   45, 58, 177
Hoggett, P.   180
Holmes, L.D.   76
home improvements   170
Hoover, E.M.   13, 56
Hopkin, W.A.B.   77
hospital care   157, 159–64
    see also health care
household structure *see* family groups
housing   64, 166, 167, 169–70, 188
    importance of   169
    sheltered   170
Hoyes, L.   195
Hudson, B.   171
Hugman, R.   177
human capital theory   49, 100, 102,
    107, 108, 110
    see also life-cycle modelling
Hunt, A.   72
Hurd, M.D.   55, 60

ideology:
    of population ageing   90–92, 201–3
    see also Marxian theories
implicit contracts   123
impurity principle   177
income   168
    importance of   71
    national   88
    real   124, 129, 130, 131
income differences   78, 125, 145–6
income levels   8, 13, 20, 21, 66, 76,
    113–20, 127–8, 130
    age-earnings profiles   100–102, 103,
        104, 106, 108, 143
    low pay   24–5
    poverty   30, 77, 78, 131, 138, 139,
        166, 167–8

savings and investments 32, 34, 36, 49, 52–8, 122, 143–4, 168
unearned incomes 32
  see also pension schemes
  wages
income maintenance 122
income redistribution 51, 122–3, 127, 132
independence 22, 23, 78, 81–2
  importance of 166
  physical 164–72
  see also dependency
  income levels
index-linked pensions 124, 131
indirect discrimination 110–11
  see also age discrimination
individual saving *see* savings and investments
individualism 22–3, 35, 44–5, 46, 49, 51–2, 63, 65, 68, 69–70, 92
  see also rational behaviour
industrial gerontology 98–9
infant mortality 10
  see also mortality rates
infectious diseases 149, 150, 154
inflation 124
informal care 17, 24–5, 40, 159, 173–4, 176, 178–97
  assessment of 180–81
  balance of care 159–64, 179–80
  benefits of 169
  characteristics of 181, 184, 185, 193–4
  costs of 161–2, 168–9, 183–90
  domiciliary 77, 79, 159, 160–64, 165, 169, 179, 182–3, 193
  by females 166, 178–9, 184, 190, 196
  government reliance on 166, 168–9, 173–4, 182–3
  importance of 179
  involuntary 184, 185, 186–7
  by males 191
  monitoring of 180
  planning for 183–97
  quality of 181
  support for 166, 168–9, 183, 188, 191–3, 196
  time spent on 186–7

  see also formal care
  health care
informal economic activity 25, 26, 29, 32–3, 40, 173–8, 191, 199
  domestic 175, 176
  voluntary 175–6, 193
information technology *see* new technologies
institutional care 159–64, 165, 170, 171, 179
  see also health care
institutional structure 61, 70, 72, 90–91, 92
  see also structural arguments
institutionalization:
  of care 20, 76, 77, 78–9, 171, 201–3
instrumental rationality 45
intelligence 97–8
  see also learning process
intergenerational conflict 36–42, 65, 80, 103–4, 127–8, 201, 202
intergenerational contract 36–7, 40, 66–7, 123, 131–3
intergenerational transfers 41–2, 55
  see also pay-as-you-go pensions
internal labour markets 102, 104–8, 113, 114, 119
  see also labour supply
intertemporal planning 67
investment *see* capital
investments *see* savings and investments
Ippolito, R.A. 59, 102
Isaacs, A. 153

Jackson, W.A. 13, 25, 45, 50, 88, 134
Jacobs, K. 113, 117
James, A. 79
Japan 117–18
Jessop, B. 119
Job Release Scheme (UK) 106, 114
job-specific skills 96, 107–9, 110
Johnson, M.L. 178
Johnson, P. 21, 22, 24, 37, 80, 81, 150, 168

Kalecki, M. 88
Kay, J.A. 136
Kelley, A.C. 14, 57
Kessler, D. 37, 51, 66, 122, 136

Keynes, J.M.   57, 84, 85
Keynesian economics   15, 16, 36, 57,
    82, 84–6, 87–9, 119, 136, 138
  post-Keynesian   84
King, M.   54
Klevmarken, N.A.   103
Knapp, M.   160, 185
Kohli, M.   113, 117
Kohnert, P.W.   158
Kondratieff cycle   86
Korenman, S.D.   103
Kotlikoff, L.J.   38, 55, 62
Kuznets, S.S.   13, 87
Kuznets cycle   86–7

labour force participation   112–20
    see also retirement
labour supply   34, 35, 58–60, 63, 77–8,
    82–3, 87–8, 102,106, 113, 168–9
    see also internal labour markets
labour supply regulation   59, 120
Laczko, F.   82, 113, 143
Lagergren, M.   191
laissez-faire policies   40, 46, 51, 120,
    123, 136, 163–4, 202
Lapkoff, S.F.   41
Lapp, J.S.   59
Laslett, P.   71, 80, 178
later retirement   129–30, 133–4, 135,
    136, 139, 141, 146–7
Law, C.M.   8
Lazear, E.P.   59, 102
Le Grand, J.   155, 180
learning process   96
    see also training and education
learnt abilities   97
Lee, R.D.   41
legal structure   144–5
Leibenstein, H.   13
Leimer, R.D.   56
leisure time   58, 71, 134, 138, 184,
    186–7
Lemon, B.W.   71
Lesnoy, S.D.   56
life expectancy   64, 122–3, 148, 149,
    150, 178
life skills   96, 109, 111
life spans   150, 151, 152, 153–4
life-cycle dependency   18–19
life-cycle modelling   48–68

life cycles   38, 118, 119, 122–3, 159
    survival curves   150–52
life-history *see* biographical studies
lifetime employment   117–18
Lipietz, A.   83
Livi-Bacci, M.   11
living standards   12–13, 21, 30, 31, 76,
    78, 79, 99, 103, 127, 130, 131,
    132, 149, 168
Loasby, B.J.   45
Longman, P.   36
Loomes, G.   157
Lösch, A.   86
Lotka, A.J.   10
low-paid workers   24–5
    see also income levels
    wages
Lydall, H.   54

Macdonald, C.   103
Macunovich, D.J.   103
males:
  as informal carers   191
  retirement age   45, 136, 144
    see also females
Malthus, T.R.   74
Malthusian economics   13, 15, 47, 85
Malthusian population principle
    74–5, 85
managed flexibility *see* flexible
    pensions
    flexible retirement
Mankiw, N.G.   64
Manton, K.G.   153
manual work   107, 109, 168
Marchand, M.   66
Marcus, A.J.   143
the market   84, 85
  definition   46
market economies   20, 22, 164, 174–6,
    177, 180, 195
market power theory   101
market-clearing equilibria   44, 46–7,
    61, 69–70, 83
Marmor, T.   39, 149
Marmot, M.G.   149
Marshall, V.W.   69, 73
Martin, G.M.   103
Marxian theories   74–5, 77, 79, 88,
    90–91

Masson, P.R. 64
Maynard, A.K. 159
McAllister, C.F. 77
McDowall, M.E. 149
McKenzie, L. 157
McKeown, T. 13, 150
McLoughlin, J. 14
McPherson, B.D. 80, 97
Means, R. 179, 192, 193, 194, 195
means-tested pensions 134–5
median-voter framework 65–6
medical care *see* health care
medical research 157–8
Medicare scheme (US) 155
Meek, R.L. 74
Meijdam, L. 67
memory loss 97–8
Menchik, P. L. 54
Mendus, S. 22, 157
mental decline 96, 97
    see also biological ageing
mental dependency 18, 19
Merton, R.C. 143
Michie, J. 83
migration 8, 9
Mill, J.S. 15
Milne, S. 83
Mincer, J. 100
Minkler, M. 39
Minns, R. 122, 126
Mirer, T.W. 54
Mishra, R. 79
Mitchell, O.S. 60
modernization theory 76–7, 80–81,
    92, 178, 179
Modigliani, F. 49, 54
Moffitt, R.A. 60
Mooney, G.A. 157, 160, 162, 185
morale *see* status
morbidity rates 149
    compression of 151–2, 153
Morgan, M.H. 135
mortality rates 1, 2, 5, 9–10, 11–13,
    99, 125, 149, 150
    infant 10
    survival curves 150–52
    see also birth rates
    fertility rates
Mueller, C.F. 169
multigenerational families *see* family

groups
Munnell, A. 56
Munnichs, J.M.A. 21, 72
Murphy, K. 103
Musgrove, P. 64
Muurinen, J.M. 169
Myles, J. 76, 119

National Economic Development
    Office (UK) 14
neoclassical economics:
    alternatives to 69–94
    characteristics of 44–8, 69, 80, 83,
        84, 89, 92, 93, 176
    dependency and 22–3, 43
    general equilibrium theory 61–4,
        88–9
    labour supply and 58–60, 88
    life-cycle modelling 48–68
    market-clearing equilibria 44, 46–7,
        61, 69–70, 83
    population ageing and 16, 44–68,
        69–70, 102, 128–9, 136
    public-choice models 65–8, 134
    savings and 54–8
Netherlands 114, 117
Netten, A. 160, 185, 188
new technologies 17, 92, 99, 107, 108,
    112, 119, 120, 180, 200
Ng, Y-K. 35
Nicoletti, G. 129
Nissel, M. 190
normalized behaviour 45–6
Notestein, F. 11
nutrition 12–13, 149–50, 167

occupational pensions 113–14, 118,
    122, 125–6, 142–3
occupational psychology 98
O'Connor, J. 79
OECD 122, 126, 158
OECD countries 4–5, 6–7
    see also individual countries
Ogawa, N. 103
older age groups 1, 2, 4, 18
    capabilities 164–72
    definition 39, 173
    needs monitoring 193–4
    see also population ageing
Oldman, C. 170

Olshansky, S.J. 149, 150
Omran, A.R. 149
one-person households 178, 179
    see also family groups
overlapping generations model 61–2,
    65, 66

Paish, F. 28, 29, 32, 77
Parker, G. 191
Parker, S. 139
Parsons, T. 71
partial retirement 118
part-time work 112, 117, 118, 122,
    184
paternalism 20, 79
    see also welfare systems
pay-as-you-go pensions 17, 21, 121–2,
    123–37, 141, 142, 146–7
Peacock, A.T. 28, 29, 32, 77
Pearson, M. 158
pension budgets 125, 128–37
pension payments 122
    absolute value 130–32
    defined benefit 143
    defined contribution 143
    levels of 129, 130, 132–3, 136,
        145–6
    means-tested 134–5
    relative 130–32
pension policies 121–8, 142–7
pension reform 17, 39–40, 127,
    129–30, 133, 136, 143
pension schemes 17, 26, 32, 52, 59–60,
    63, 106–7, 121–43
    adjustment methods 135
    flexible 142–3, 204
    funded 34, 36–7, 65–7, 121–8,
        142–3
    index-linked 124, 131
    occupational 113–14, 118, 122,
        125–6, 142–3
    pay-as-you-go 17, 21, 121–2,
        123–37, 141, 142, 146–7
    public 56, 60, 65–7, 77, 78, 80, 82,
        118, 122, 135–6
    SERPS 135–6
    types of 121–8
    unfunded 56
    see also retirement

personal relationships *see* family
    groups
Pestieau, P. 66
Peters, W. 66
Petersen, J.A. 71
Petit, P. 83
Phillips Committee (UK) 15, 135
Phillipson, C. 42, 71, 77, 79, 82, 98,
    113
physical decline 72, 96–7
    see also biological ageing
physical dependency 18, 19–20, 21,
    22, 24–5, 164–72
physical incapacity 4, 17, 24, 25, 170
    mental dependency 18, 19
    in older age groups 4, 17, 78, 97, 99,
        116, 154
physical independence 164–72
Piachaud, D. 116
Pierson, C. 79
Piore, M.J. 83, 102
Plant, M. 103
policy issues 23, 30–33, 34–6, 51,
    71–2, 79, 89, 135
    economic and fiscal 1, 37–9, 63–4,
        183–90, 201–3
    employment 110, 111
    on informal care 166, 168–9, 183,
        188, 191–3, 196
    intergenerational conflict 36–42, 65,
        80, 103–4, 127–8, 201, 202
    pensions 121–8, 142–7
    public-choice 65–8, 134
    retirement 59, 72, 77–8, 80, 101,
        102, 106, 113, 134, 139, 142–7
    social 1, 22, 63–4, 79, 164–72,
        179–80, 190–97, 203–6
    training 109
political dependency 18, 20, 22, 24–5
political disincentives 37
political parties 65–6, 67
population ageing:
    analysis of 93–4
    causes 9–14, 153–4, 199
    consequences of 1–2, 16, 18, 64
    definition 1–2
    historical survey 10–11, 14, 15,
        70–71
    patterns of 73, 103

retirement policies 59, 72, 77–8, 80,
    101, 102, 106, 113, 134, 139,
    142–7
retraining *see* training and education
Rex, J. 74
Ricardo, D. 15, 74
Riegel, K.F. 98
rights-based empowerment 194
Riley, M.W. 98
Robertson, A. 39
role theory 71
Rosen, S. 56
Rosenmayr, L. 73
Royal Commission on Population
    (UK) 15
Russell, L.B. 150
Rustin, M. 83

Sabel, C.F. 83
Samuelson, P.A. 61, 125
Sauvy, A. 15
saving disincentives 35–6
    see also economic disincentives
savings and investments 32, 34, 36, 49,
    52–8, 122, 143–4, 168
Sawyer, M.C. 88
Schaie, K.W. 98
Schmähl, W. 135
Schmidt, C.M. 103
Schneider, E.L. 153
Scholz, J.K. 55
school-leaving age 2, 6
Schuller, T. 144
Schultz, T.W. 49
Schulz, J.H. 122
screening programmes 166–7
    see also health care
secondary labour markets 102, 108
    see also labour supply
second-best outcomes 35, 61
self-care *see* independence
self-esteem *see* status
Sen, A.K. 131
services *see* social services
    formal care
    informal care
Shanas, E. 72, 179
Shegog, R.F.A. 14
sheltered housing 170

Shimowada, I. 118
Short, P. 169
Sidell, M. 167
Simon, J.L. 13, 45
single households *see* one-person
    households
Sixsmith, A. 169
skills acquisition 96, 107-9, 110, 111
Smeeding, T.M. 39, 113
Smith, K. 184, 185
Smith, R. 80, 179, 192, 194
Smith, S. 158
Snell, M.C. 19, 160, 161, 162, 185
social conditions 14, 24, 27, 50, 149
social gerontology 73, 76
social policies 1, 22, 63–4, 79, 169,
    185, 190–97, 203–6
social security benefits 77, 78, 80, 106,
    113, 115–16, 168
social services 1, 8–9, 17, 60, 64, 148,
    164
    balance of care 159–64, 178–80
    decision making on 166, 171–2,
        179–80
        see also dependency
    formal care
    informal care
social structure 42, 70, 71, 73, 75–6,
    80, 88, 103, 178
    structured dependency 77–82
social theory 45, 69, 70–71, 72, 92
social welfare *see* welfare systems
socialism 74, 80
Soldo, B.J. 184
Solomou, S. 87
Sparrow, P.R. 109
special interest groups *see* pressure
    groups
Spencer, B.G. 150
spending patterns 52–4
Spengler, J.J. 14, 60, 85
Stahl, K. 55
standard of living *see* living standards
State Earnings Related Pension
    Scheme (SERPS) (UK) 135–6
status:
    of older people 65, 71, 76, 78, 81,
        106, 115, 178

statutory retirement age *see* retirement
   age
Stone, R. 169
structural arguments 70–83, 88
structured dependency 18, 27, 77–82,
   139
Stuart, C. 66
Sugden, R. 190
support ratios 6–7
   see also dependency ratios
survival curves 150–52
   see also mortality rates
Sutherland, H. 113
Swan, J.H. 77
Sweden 117
symbolic interactionism 73

tastes theory 101
Tawney, R. H. 22
tax disincentives 35, 36
   see also economic disincentives
tax systems 32, 33–4, 36, 37, 63–4, 80,
   202
  health care provision and 148
  pay-as-you-go pensions 17, 21,
    121–2, 123–37, 141, 142, 146–7
Taylor, P.E. 111
Taylor, R.C. 167, 168
Teague, P. 83
technical change *see* new technologies
technical efficiency:
  in health care 156–7, 160
Thane, P.M. 15
Third Age approach 71
Third World countries 5–6, 56–7
Thomae, H. 72
Thomson, D. 37, 40
threshold ages 2–3, 4, 18–19
Townsend, P. 73, 77, 78, 131, 166, 168
training and education 17, 49, 52, 58,
   71, 107–12
  funding of 112
training policies 109
training time 108
transfer possibilities 30–32
transfer problems:
  dependency generated 29–33
Tryon, R.W. 64
Tullock, G. 65

uncertainty 50
unemployment 15, 21, 25–6, 28–9, 75,
   77–8, 79, 82, 84, 87–9, 91, 99,
   102, 103, 106, 111–12, 115, 138,
   199
   see also economic dependency
    productivity levels
unemployment benefits *see* social
   security benefits
unfunded public pensions 56
Ungerson, C. 196
United Kingdom:
  age composition 8
  early retirement 106, 113, 117
  health care 164, 182–3, 195
  pension schemes 135–6
  population ageing 3–5, 72, 178
  unemployment 115
United States:
  Medicare scheme 155
  older people 54–5
  population ageing 32, 64, 72–3
  population growth 87
  retirement age 60, 117, 118, 144–5
  welfare system 36, 38, 136
unpaid work 25, 26, 29
   see also economic activity

value–added tax (VAT) 134
van Gunsteren, H. 119
van Praag, B. 47
van Winden, F. 67
Veall, M.R. 66
Venti, S.F. 54
Verbon, H.A.A. 66, 67
Verbrugge, L.M. 99
Verhoeven, M.J.M. 67
Victor, C. 168
Vincent, J. 39
voice-based empowerment 194
voluntary sector 175–6, 193
   see also informal care
   informal economic activity
von Weizsäcker, R.K. 65
voting power 67

wages 58, 74, 75, 88, 100–102, 111,
   124
  low pay 24–5

productivity and 100–107
  see also income levels
Walker, A. 18, 39, 40, 42, 77, 111, 139, 144, 168, 182
Wall, R. 178
Warnes, A.M. 8
Warr, P. 109
Webb, A. 171
Wedderburn, D. 78
Weil, D.N. 55, 64
Weiss, Y. 59
Welch, F. 103
the welfare generation 37–8, 42
welfare pluralism 180
welfare state 76, 79, 80, 82, 119, 120, 179, 202
welfare system reform 40
welfare systems 20, 23, 27, 32, 33, 41–2, 189–90
  intergenerational contract 36–7, 40, 66–7, 131–3
  paternalism 20, 79
  payment for 37–40
  privatization 40
  support for 37–8, 40–41
  in United States 36, 38
  see also social services
Welford, A.T. 98, 99, 109
Wenger, G.C. 19
Wheeler, R. 170
Wheelock, J. 174, 175
White, S. 158
White-Means, S.I. 169
Wicks, M. 191
Wilkinson, R.G. 97, 149
Williams, A.H. 28, 29, 30, 33, 190
Williams, I. 167
Willis, R.J. 13
Wilson, G. 42, 152
Wise, D.E. 54, 60

Wiseman, A.C. 54
Wistow, G. 195
Wolf, D.A. 184
women *see* females
work:
  attitudes to 137
  definition of 118
  value of 71
work experience 98, 99
work opportunities 108–9, 111–12, 137, 144–5, 146
work practices 82–3, 98, 112
working class 74, 75, 76, 79, 80
working conditions 58
working hours 35, 59, 137, 138–41
  part-time 112, 117, 118, 122, 184
working life 109, 110, 111–12, 117–18, 119–20
World Bank 14, 126
Wray, L.R. 129
Wright, K.G. 19, 160, 161, 162, 168, 184, 185, 187
Wright, R.E. 103

young workers 106, 107–9, 111, 112, 198–9
younger age groups 1, 5, 18, 76
  as carers 190–91
  children 4, 6, 55–6, 57
  health care 153–4
  housing for 169
  intergenerational conflict 36–42, 65, 80, 103–4, 127–8, 201, 202
  intergenerational contract 36–7, 40, 66–7, 131–3
  migration patterns 8
  savings and investments 52–3, 55
  screening programmes 167

Zimmermann, K.F. 103